# 21 December 2012: End of the World?

# 21 DECEMBER 2012 : END OF THE WORLD?

*Edited By*
**Dr. P. Pathak**
**Krishna Kumari**

PPH

PRASHANT PUBLISHING HOUSE
NEW DELHI-110 094

*First Published 2009*

*ISBN : 978-81-906344-9-6*

*Published by :*
**PRASHANT PUBLISHING HOUSE**
C-34, 28 Futa Road, Gali No. 3,
West Karawal Nagar, Delhi-110 094
Ph.: 011-22963970, Mob.: 9810396373

Printed in India

Published by Prashant Publishing House, Delhi-110 094,

# Contents

# PREFACE

One of the time periods of the Long Count of the Maya is the baktun, which last 144,000 days. In some texts of the Maya a new period of the Long Count is said to begin after 13 baktuns (exactly 1,872,000 days). Such a new period in the Long Count of the maya will probably begin on 21 December 2012, when the Long Count returns to 0.0.0.0.0, and some people expect to see special things in the sky or on Earth then that would not otherwise be expected. The interest for 21 December 2012 seems to have been spurred by publications by John Major Jenkins, who is of the opinion that the Maya designed their Long Count in order that the coming special data 0.0.0.0.0 corresponds to a southern solstice (when the winter begins in the northern hemisphere) when the Sun stands in the Milky Way in the sky. Mr. Jenkins reached this opinion based on extensive research of Maya texts and other traces. The basic arguments of many stories about 21 December 2012 are that on exactly 21 December 2012 there is a certain special astronomical conjunction that is so rare that it doesn't repeat for a long period of time (centuries, or even millennia) before or after that date. 21 December 2012 corresponds to the round date 0.0.0.0.0 in the Long Count of the Maya. The Maya had the knowledge to predict that special conjunction precisely and accurately to one day.

# 1

# Introduction

The Maya civilization is a Mesoamerican civilization, noted for the only known fully developed written language of the pre-Columbian Americas, as well as its spectacular art, monumental architecture, and sophisticated mathematical and astronomical systems. Initially established during the Preclassic period, many of these reached their apogee of development during the Classic period (c. 250 CE to 900 CE), and continued throughout the Postclassic period until the arrival of the Spanish. At its peak, it was one of the most densely populated and culturally dynamic societies in the world.

The Maya civilization shares many features with other Mesoamerican civilizations due to the high degree of interaction and cultural diffusion that characterized the region. Advances such as writing, epigraphy, and the calendar did not originate with the Maya; however, their civilization fully developed them. Maya influence can be detected as far as central Mexico, more than 1000 km (625 miles) from the Maya area. Many outside influences are found in Maya art and architecture, which are thought to result from trade and cultural exchange rather than direct external conquest. The Maya peoples never disappeared, neither at the time of the Classic period decline nor with the arrival of the Spanish *conquistadores* and the subsequent Spanish colonization of the Americas. Today, the Maya and their descendants form sizable populations throughout the Maya area and maintain a distinctive set of traditions and beliefs that are the result of the merger of pre-Columbian and post-Conquest ideologies (and structured by the almost total adoption of Roman

Catholicism). Many different Mayan languages continue to be spoken as primary languages today; the Rabinal Achí, a play written in the Achi' language, was declared a Masterpiece of the Oral and Intangible Heritage of Humanity by UNESCO in 2005.

## GEOGRAPHICAL POSITION

The geographic extent of the Maya civilization, known as the Maya area, extended throughout the southern Mexican states of Chiapas, Tabasco, and the Yucatan Peninsula states of Quintana Roo, Campeche and Yucatan. The Maya area also extended throughout the northern Central American region, including the present-day nations of Guatemala, Belize, El Salvador and western Honduras.

As the largest sub-region in Mesoamerica, it encompassed a vast and varied landscape, from the mountainous regions of the Sierra Madre to the semi-arid plains of northern Yucatan. Climate in the Maya region can vary tremendously, as the low-lying areas are particularly susceptible to the hurricanes and tropical storms that frequent the Caribbean.

The Maya area is generally divided into three loosely defined zones: the southern Maya highlands, the southern (or central) Maya lowlands, and the northern Maya lowlands. The southern Maya highlands include all of elevated terrain in Guatemala and the Chiapas highlands. The southern lowlands lie just north of the highlands, and incorporate the Peten of the Mexican states of Campeche and Quintana Roo and northern Guatemala, Belize and El Salvador. The northern lowlands cover the remainder of the Yucatan Peninsula, including the Puuc hills.

## HISTORY

### Preclassic

While the Maya area was initially inhabited around the 10th millennium BCE, the first clearly "Maya" settlements were established in approximately 1800 BCE in Soconusco region of the Pacific Coast. This point in time, known as the Early Preclassic, was characterized by sedentary communities and the introduction of pottery and fired clay figurines.

Archaeological evidence suggests the construction of ceremonial architecture in Maya area by approximately 1000 BCE. The earliest configurations of such architecture consist of simple burial mounds, which would be the precursors to the stepped pyramids subsequently erected in the Late Preclassic. Prominent Middle and Late Preclassic settlement zones are located in the southern Maya lowlands, specifically in the Mirador and Peten Basins. Important sites in the southern Maya lowlands include Nakbe, El Mirador, Cival, and San Bartolo. In the Guatemalan Highlands Kaminal Juyú emerges around 800 BCE. For many centuries it controlled the Jade and Obsidian sources for the Peten and Pacific Lowlands. The important early sites of Izapa, Takalik Abaj and Chocola at around 600 BCE were the main producers of Cacao. Mid-sized Maya communities also began to develop in the northern Maya lowlands during the Middle and Late Preclassic, though these lacked the size, scale, and influence of the large centers of the southern lowlands. Two important Preclassic northern sites include Komchen and Dzibilchaltun.

There is some disagreement about the boundaries which differentiate the physical and cultural extent of the early Maya and neighboring Preclassic Mesoamerican civilizations, such as the Olmec culture of the Tabasco lowlands and the Mixe-Zoque– and Zapotec–speaking peoples of Chiapas and southern Oaxaca, respectively. Many of the earliest significant inscriptions and buildings appeared in this overlapping zone, and evidence suggests that these cultures and the formative Maya influenced one another. Takalik Abaj, in the Pacific slopes of Guatemala, is the only site where Olmec and then Maya features have been found.

### Classic

The Classic period (c. 250 CE–900 CE) witnessed the peak of large-scale construction and urbanism, the recording of monumental inscriptions, and a period of significant intellectual and artistic development, particularly in the southern lowland regions. They developed an agriculturally intensive, city-centered empire consisting of numerous independent city-states. This includes the well-known cities of Tikal, Palenque, Copan and Calakmul, but also the lesser known Dos Pilas, Uaxactun, Altun

Ha, and Bonampak, among others. The Early Classic settlement distribution in the northern Maya lowlands is not as clearly known as the southern zone, but does include a number of population centers, such as Oxkintok, Chunchucmil, and the early occupation of Uxmal.

The most notable monuments are the stepped pyramids they built in their religious centers and the accompanying palaces of their rulers. The palace at Cancuen is the largest in the Maya area, though the site, interestingly, lacks pyramids. Other important archaeological remains include the carved stone slabs usually called *stelae* (the Maya called them *tetun*, or "tree-stones"), which depict rulers along with hieroglyphic texts describing their genealogy, military victories, and other accomplishments.

The Maya participated in long distance trade with many of the other Mesoamerican cultures, including Teotihuacan, the Zapotec and other groups in central and gulf-coast Mexico, as well as with more distant, non-Mesoamerican groups. For example the Tainos in the caribbean, also archaeologists found gold from Panama in the Sacred Cenote of Chichen Itza. Important trade goods included cacao, salt, sea shells, jade and obsidian.

### The Maya Collapse

For reasons that are still debated, the Maya centers of the southern lowlands went into decline during the 8th and 9th centuries and were abandoned shortly thereafter. This decline was coupled with a cessation of monumental inscriptions and large-scale architectural construction. Although there is no universally accepted theory to explain this "collapse," current theories fall into two categories: non-ecological and ecological.

Non-ecological theories of Maya decline are divided into several subcategories, such as overpopulation, foreign invasion, peasant revolt, and the collapse of key trade routes. Ecological hypotheses include environmental disaster, epidemic disease, and climate change. There is evidence that the Maya population exceeded carrying capacity of the environment including exhaustion of agricultural potential and overhunting of megafauna. Some scholars have recently theorized that an intense 200 year drought led to the collapse of Maya civilization. The drought theory originated from research performed by physical scientists studying lake beds, ancient pollen, and other data, not from the archaeological community.

### Postclassic Period

During the succeeding Postclassic period (from the 10th to the early 16th century), development in the northern centers persisted, characterized by an increasing diversity of external influences. The Maya cities of the northern lowlands in Yucatan continued to flourish for centuries more; some of the important sites in this era were Chichen Itza, Uxmal, Edzna, and Coba. After the decline of the ruling dynasties of Chichen and Uxmal, Mayapan ruled all of Yucatan until a revolt in 1450. (This city's name may be the source of the word "Maya", which had a more geographically restricted meaning in Yucatec and colonial Spanish and only grew to its current meaning in the 19th and 20th centuries). The area then degenerated into competing city-states until the Yucatan was conquered by the Spanish.

The Itza Maya, Ko'woj, and Yalain groups of Central Peten survived the "Classic Period Collapse" in small numbers and by 1250 reconstituted themselves to form competing city-states. The Itza maintained their capital at Tayasal (also known as Noh Peten), an archaeological site thought to underlay the modern city of Flores, Guatemala on Lake Peten Itza. It ruled over an area extending across the Peten Lakes region, encompassing the community of Eckixil on Lake Quexil. The Ko'woj had their capital at Zacpeten. Postclassic Maya states also continued to survive in the southern highlands. One of the Maya kingdoms in this area, the K'iche', is responsible for the best-known Maya work of historiography and mythology, the Popol Vuh. Other highland kingdoms included the Mam based at Huehuetenango, the Kaqchikels based at Iximche and the Chuj, based at San Mateo Ixtatan. The Poqomam possibly had their capital at Mixco Viejo.

### Colonial Period

Shortly after their first expeditions to the region, the Spanish initiated a number of attempts to subjugate the Maya and establish a colonial presence in the Maya territories of the Yucatan Peninsula and the Guatemalan highlands. This campaign, sometimes termed "The Spanish Conquest of Yucatan," would prove to be a lengthy and dangerous exercise for the *conquistadores* from the outset, and it would take some 170 years before the Spanish established substantive control over all Maya lands.

Unlike the Spanish campaigns against the Aztec and Inca Empires, there was no single Maya political center which once overthrown would hasten the end of collective resistance from the indigenous peoples. Instead, the conquistador forces needed to subdue the numerous independent Maya polities almost one by one, many of which kept up a fierce resistance. Most of the *conquistadores* were motivated by the prospects of the great wealth to be had from the seizure of precious metal resources such as gold or silver; however, the Maya lands themselves were poor in these resources. This would become another factor in forestalling Spanish designs of conquest, as they instead were initially attracted to the reports of great riches in central Mexico or Peru.

The last Maya states, the Itza polity of Tayasal and the Ko'woj city of Zacpeten, were continuously occupied and remained independent of the Spanish until late in the 17th century. They were finally subdued by the Spanish in 1697.

## POLITICAL STRUCTURES

A typical Classic Maya polity was a small hierarchical state (*ajawil, ajawlel,* or *ajawlil*) headed by a hereditary ruler known as an *ajaw* (later *k'uhul ajaw*). Such kingdoms were usually no more than a capital city with its neighborhood and several lesser towns, although there were greater kingdoms, which controlled larger territories and extended patronage over smaller polities.

Each kingdom had a name that did not necessarily correspond to any locality within its territory. Its identity was that of a political unit associated with a particular ruling dynasty. For instance, the archaeological site of Naranjo was the capital of the kingdom of Saal. The land (chan ch'e'n) of the kingdom and its capital were called Wakab'nal or Maxam and were part of a larger geographical entity known as Huk Tsuk. Interestingly, despite constant warfare and eventual shifts in regional power, most kingdoms never disappeared from the political landscape until the collapse of the whole system in the 9th century CE. In this respect, Classic Maya kingdoms are highly similar to late Post Classic polities encountered by the Spaniards in Yucatan and Central Mexico: some polities could be subordinated to hegemonic rulers through conquests or dynastic unions and yet even then they persisted as distinct entities.

Mayanists have been increasingly accepting a "court paradigm" of Classic Maya societies which puts the emphasis on the centrality of the royal household and especially the person of the king. This approach focuses on Maya monumental spaces as the embodiment of the diverse activities of the royal household. It considers the role of places and spaces (including dwellings of royalty and nobles, throne rooms, temples, halls and plazas for public ceremonies) in establishing power and social hierarchy, and also in projecting aesthetic and moral values to define the wider social realm.

Spanish sources invariably describe even the largest Maya settlements as dispersed collections of dwellings grouped around the temples and palaces of the ruling dynasty and lesser nobles. None of the Classic Maya cities shows evidence of economic specialization and commerce of the scale of Mexican Tenochtitlan. Instead, Maya cities could be seen as enormous royal households, the locales of the administrative and ritual activities of the royal court. They were the places where privileged nobles could approach the holy ruler, where aesthetic values of the high culture were formulated and disseminated, where aesthetic items were consumed. They were the self-proclaimed centers and the sources of social, moral, and cosmic order. The fall of a royal court as in the well-documented cases of Piedras Negras or Copan would cause the inevitable "death" of the associated settlement.

## ART

Many consider Maya art of their *Classic Era* (c. 250CE to 900 CE) to be the most sophisticated and beautiful of the ancient New World. The carvings and the reliefs made of stucco at Palenque and the statuary of Copan are especially fine, showing a grace and accurate observation of the human form that reminded early archaeologists of Classical civilizations of the Old World, hence the name bestowed on this era. We have only hints of the advanced painting of the classic Maya; mostly what have survived are funerary pottery and other Maya ceramics, and a building at Bonampak holds ancient murals that survived by serendipity. A beautiful turquoise blue color that has survived through the centuries due to its unique chemical characteristics is known as Maya Blue or Azul maya, and it is present in Bonampak, Tajín Cacaxtla, Jaina, and even in some Colonial Convents. The use of Maya Blue survived until the 16th century when the technique was lost. Some *Pre Classic* murals have been recently discovered at San Bartolo, and are by far the finest in style and iconography, regarded as the *Sistine Chapel* of the Maya. With the decipherment of the Maya script it was discovered that the Maya were one of the few civilizations where artists attached their name to their work.

## ARCHITECTURE

As unique and spectacular as Greek or Roman architecture, Maya architecture spans many thousands of years; yet, often the most dramatic and easily recognizable as Maya are the fantastic stepped pyramids from the Terminal Pre-classic period and beyond.

There are also cave sites that are important to the Maya. These cave sites include Jolja Cave, the cave site at Naj Tunich, the Candelaria Caves, and the Cave of the Witch. There are also cave-origin myths among the Maya. Some cave sites are still used by the modern Maya in the Chiapas highlands.

It has been suggested that, in conjunction to the Maya Long Count Calendar, every fifty-two years, or cycle, temples and pyramids were remodeled and rebuilt. It appears now that the rebuilding process was often instigated by a new ruler or for political matters, as opposed to matching the calendar cycle. However, the process of rebuilding on top of old structures is indeed a common one. Most notably, the North Acropolis at Tikal seems to be the sum total of 1,500 years of architectural modifications. In Tikal and Yaxha, there are the *Twin Pyramid* complexes (7 in Tikal and 1 in Yaxha, that commemorate the end of a *Baktún*

Through observation of the numerous consistent elements and stylistic distinctions, remnants of Maya architecture have become an important key to understanding the evolution of their ancient civilization.

## Urban Design

As Maya cities spread throughout the varied geography of Mesoamerica, site planning appears to have been minimal. Maya architecture tended to integrate a great degree of natural features, and their cities were built somewhat haphazardly as dictated by the topography of each independent location. For instance, some cities on the flat limestone plains of the northern Yucatan grew into great sprawling municipalities, while others built in the hills of Usumacinta utilized the natural loft of the topography to raise their towers and temples to impressive heights. However, some semblance of order, as required by any large city, still prevailed.

Classic Era Maya urban design could easily be described as the division of space by great monuments and causeways. Open public plazas were the gathering places for people and the focus of urban design, while interior space was entirely secondary. Only in the Late Post-Classic era did the great Maya cities develop into more fortress-like defensive structures that lacked, for the most part, the large and numerous plazas of the Classic.

At the onset of large-scale construction during the Classic Era, a predetermined axis was typically established in a cardinal direction. Depending on the location of natural resources such as fresh-water wells, or *cenotes*, the city grew by using *sacbeob* (causeways) to connect great plazas with the numerous platforms that created the sub-structure for nearly all Maya buildings. As more structures were added and existing structures re-built or remodeled, the great Maya cities seemed to take on an almost random identity that contrasted sharply with other great Mesoamerican cities such as Teotihuacan and its rigid grid-like construction.

At the heart of the Maya city were large plazas surrounded by the most important governmental and religious buildings, such as the royal acropolis, great pyramid temples and occasionally ball-courts. Though city layouts evolved as nature dictated, careful attention was placed on the directional orientation of temples and observatories so that they were constructed in accordance with Maya interpretation of the orbits of the heavenly bodies. Immediately outside of this ritual center were the structures of lesser nobles, smaller temples, and individual shrines; the less sacred and less important structures had a greater degree of privacy. Outside of the constantly evolving urban core were the less permanent and more modest homes of the common people.

### Building Materials

A surprising aspect of the great Maya structures is their lack of many advanced technologies seemingly necessary for such constructions. Lacking draft animals necessary for wheel-based modes of transportation, metal tools and even pulleys, Maya architecture required abundant manpower. Yet, beyond this enormous requirement, the remaining materials seem to have been readily available. All stone for Maya structures appears to have been taken from local quarries. They most often used limestone which remained pliable enough to be worked with stone tools while being quarried and only hardened once removed from its bed. In addition to the structural use of limestone, much of their mortar consisted of crushed, burnt and mixed limestone that mimicked the properties of cement and was used as widely for stucco finishing as it was for mortar. Later improvements in quarrying techniques reduced the necessity for this limestone-stucco as the stones began to fit quite perfectly, yet it remained a crucial element in some post and lintel roofs. In the case of the common Maya houses, wooden poles, adobe and thatch were the primary materials; however, instances of what appear to be common houses of limestone have been discovered as well. Also notable throughout Maya architecture is the corbel arch (also known as a "false arch"), whose limitations kept their structures generally weighty rather than airy.

### Notable Constructions

- Ceremonial platforms were commonly limestone platforms of typically less than four meters in height where public ceremonies and religious rites were performed. Constructed in the fashion of a typical foundation platform, these were often accented by carved figures, altars and perhaps *tzompantli*, a stake used to display the heads of victims or defeated Mesoamerican ballgame opponents.

- Palaces were large and often highly decorated, and usually sat close to the center of a city and housed the population's elite. Any exceedingly large royal palace, or one consisting of many chambers on different levels might be referred to as an acropolis. However, often these were one-story and consisted of many small chambers and typically at least one interior courtyard; these structures appear to take into account the needed functionality required of a residence, as well as the decoration required for their inhabitants stature.
- E-Groups are specific structural configurations present at a number of centers in the Maya area. These complexes are oriented and aligned according to specific astronomical events (primarily the sun's solstices and equinoxes) and are thought to have been observatories. These structures are usually accompanied by iconographic reliefs that tie astronomical observation into general Maya mythology. The structural complex is named for Group E at Uaxactun, the first documented in Mesoamerica.
- Pyramids and temples. Often the most important religious temples sat atop the towering Maya pyramids, presumably as the closest place to the heavens. While recent discoveries point toward the extensive use of pyramids as tombs, the temples themselves seem to rarely, if ever, contain burials. Residing atop the pyramids, some of over two-hundred feet, such as that at El Mirador, the temples were impressive and decorated structures themselves. Commonly topped with a roof comb, or superficial grandiose wall, these temples might have served as a type of propaganda. As they were often the only structure in a Maya city to exceed the height of the surrounding jungle, the roof combs atop the temples were often carved with representations of rulers that could be seen from vast distances.
- Observatories. The Maya were keen astronomers and had mapped out the phases of celestial objects, especially the

Moon and Venus. Many temples have doorways and other features aligning to celestial events. Round temples, often dedicated to Kukulcan, are perhaps those most often described as "observatories" by modern ruin tour-guides, but there is no evidence that they were so used exclusively, and temple pyramids of other shapes may well have been used for observation as well.

- Ball courts. As an integral aspect of the Mesoamerican lifestyle, the courts for their ritual ball-game were constructed throughout the Maya realm and often on a grand scale. Enclosed on two sides by stepped ramps that led to ceremonial platforms or small temples, the ball court itself was of a capital "I" shape and could be found in all but the smallest of Maya cities.

## WRITING AND LITERACY

The Maya writing system (often called *hieroglyphs* from a superficial resemblance to the Ancient Egyptian writing) was a combination of phonetic symbols and logograms. It is most often classified as a logographic or (more properly) a logosyllabic writing system, in which syllabic signs play a significant role.

It is the only writing system of the Pre-Columbian New World which is known to completely represent the spoken language of its community. In total, the script has more than a thousand different glyphs, although a few are variations of the same sign or meaning, and many appear only rarely or are confined to particular localities. At any one time, no more than around 500 glyphs were in use, some 200 of which (including variations) had a phonetic or syllabic interpretation.

The earliest inscriptions in an identifiably-Maya script date back to 200–300 BC. However, this is preceded by several other writing systems which had developed in Mesoamerica, most notably that of the Zapotecs, and (following the 2006 publication of research on the recently-discovered Cascajal Block), the Olmecs. There is a pre-Maya writing known as "Epi-Olmec script" (post Olmec) which some researchers believe may represent a transitional script between Olmec and Maya writing, but the relationships between these remain unclear and the matter is unsettled. On January 5, 2006, National Geographic published the findings of Maya writings that could be as old as 400 BCE, suggesting that the Maya writing system is nearly as old as the oldest Mesoamerican writing known at that time, Zapotec. In the succeeding centuries the Maya developed their script into a form which was far more complete and complex than any other that has yet been found in the Americas.

Since its inception, the Maya script was in use up to the arrival of the Europeans, peaking during the Maya Classical Period (c. 200 to 900). Although many Maya centers went into decline (or were completely abandoned) during or after this period, the skill and knowledge of Maya writing persisted amongst segments of the population, and the early Spanish conquistadors knew of individuals who could still read and write the script. Unfortunately, the Spanish displayed little interest in it, and as a result of the dire impacts the conquest had on Maya societies, the knowledge was subsequently lost, probably within only a few generations.

At a rough estimate, in excess of 10,000 individual texts have so far been recovered, mostly inscribed on stone monuments, lintels, stelae and ceramic pottery. The Maya also produced texts painted on a form of paper manufactured from processed tree-bark, in particular from several species of strangler fig trees such as *Ficus cotinifolia* and *Ficus padifolia*.

This paper, common throughout Mesoamerica and generally now known by its Nahuatl-language name *amatl*, was typically bound as a single continuous sheet that was folded into pages of equal width, concertina-style, to produce a codex (book) that could be written on both sides.

Shortly after the conquest, all of the codices which could be found were ordered to be burnt and destroyed by zealous Spanish priests, notably Bishop Diego de Landa. Only three reasonably intact examples of Maya codices are known to have survived through to the present day. These are now known as the Madrid, Dresden, and Paris codices. A few pages survive from a fourth, the Grolier codex, whose authenticity is sometimes disputed, but mostly is held to be genuine. Further archaeology conducted at

Maya sites often reveals other fragments, rectangular lumps of plaster and paint chips which formerly were codices; these tantalizing remains are, however, too severely damaged for any inscriptions to have survived, most of the organic material having decayed.

The decipherment and recovery of the now-lost knowledge of Maya writing has been a long and laborious process. Some elements were first deciphered in the late 19th and early 20th century, mostly the parts having to do with numbers, the Maya calendar, and astronomy. Major breakthroughs came starting in the 1950s to 1970s, and accelerated rapidly thereafter. By the end of the 20th century, scholars were able to read the majority of Maya texts to a large extent, and recent field work continues to further illuminate the content.

In reference to the few extant Maya writings, Michael D. Coe, a prominent linguist and epigrapher at Yale University stated:

> "[O]ur knowledge of ancient Maya thought must represent only a tiny fraction of the whole picture, for of the thousands of books in which the full extent of their learning and ritual was recorded, only four have survived to modern times (as though all that posterity knew of ourselves were to be based upon three prayer books and 'Pilgrim's Progress')." (Michael D. Coe, The Maya, London: Thames and Hudson, 4th ed., 1987, p. 161.)

Most surviving pre-Columbian Maya writing is from stelae and other stone inscriptions from Maya sites, many of which were already abandoned before the Spanish arrived. The inscriptions on the stelae mainly record the dynasties and wars of the sites' rulers. Also of note are the inscriptions that reveal information about the lives of ancient Maya women. Much of the remainder of Maya hieroglyphics has been found on funeral pottery, most of which describes the afterlife.

### Writing Tools

Although the archaeological record does not provide examples, Maya art shows that writing was done with brushes made with animal hair and quills. Codex-style writing was usually done in black ink with red highlights, giving rise to the Aztec name for the Maya territory as the "land of red and black".

### Scribes and Literacy

Scribes held a prominent position in Maya courts. Maya art often depicts rulers with trappings indicating they were scribes or at least able to write, such as having pen bundles in their headdresses. Additionally, many rulers have been found in conjunction with writing tools such as shell or clay inkpots.

Although the number of logograms and syllabic symbols required to fully write the language numbered in the hundreds, literacy was not necessarily widespread beyond the elite classes. Graffiti uncovered in various contexts, including on fired bricks, shows nonsensical attempts to imitate the writing system.

## MATHEMATICS

In common with the other Mesoamerican civilizations, the Maya used a base 20 (vigesimal) and base 5 numbering system (see Maya numerals). Also, the preclassic Maya and their neighbors independently developed the concept of *zero* by 36 BC. Inscriptions show them on occasion working with sums up to the hundreds of millions and dates so large it would take several lines just to represent it. They produced extremely accurate astronomical observations; their charts of the movements of the moon and planets are equal or superior to those of any other civilization working from naked eye observation.

In common with the other Mesoamerican civilizations, the Maya had measured the length of the solar year to a high degree of accuracy, far more accurate than that used in Europe as the basis of the Gregorian Calendar. They did not use this figure for the length of year in their calendar, however. The calendar they used was crude, being based on a year length of exactly 365 days, which means that the calendar falls out of step with the seasons by one day every four years. By comparison, the Julian calendar, used in Europe from Roman times until about the 16th Century, accumulated an error of only one day every 128 years. The modern Gregorian calendar is even more accurate, accumulating only a day's error in approximately 3257 years.

## ASTRONOMY

Uniquely, there is some evidence to suggest the Maya appear to be the only pre-telescopic civilization to demonstrate knowledge of the Orion Nebula as being fuzzy, i.e. not a stellar pin-point. The information which supports this theory comes from a folk tale that deals with the Orion constellation's area of the sky. Their traditional hearths include in their middle a smudge of glowing fire that corresponds with the Orion Nebula. This is a significant clue to support the idea that the Maya detected a diffuse area of the sky contrary to the pin points of stars before the telescope was invented. Many preclassic sites are oriented with the Pleiades and Eta Draconis, as seen in La Blanca, Ujuxte, Monte Alto, and Takalik Abaj.

The Maya were very interested in zenial passages, the time when the sun passes directly overhead. The latitude of most of their cities being below the Tropic of Cancer, these zenial passages would occur twice a year equidistant from the solstice. To represent this position of the sun overhead, the Maya had a god named Diving God.

The Dresden Codex contains the highest concentration of astronomical phenomena observations and calculations of any of the surviving texts (it appears that the data in this codex is primarily or exclusively of an astronomical nature). Examination and analysis of this codex reveals that Venus was the most important astronomical object to the Maya, even more important to them than the sun.

## RELIGION

Like the Aztec and Inca who came to power later, the Maya believed in a cyclical nature of time. The rituals and ceremonies were very closely associated with celestial/terrestrial cycles which they observed and inscribed as separate calendars. The Maya priest had the job of interpreting these cycles and giving a prophetic outlook on the future or past based on the number relations of all their calendars. They also had to determine if the "heavens" or celestial matters were appropriate for performing certain religious ceremonies.

The Maya practiced human sacrifice. In some Maya rituals people were killed by having their arms and legs held while a priest cut the person's chest open and tore out his heart as an offering. This is depicted on ancient objects such as pictorial texts, known as codices (singular: codex). It is believed that children were often offered as sacrificial victims because they were believed to be pure.

Much of the Maya religious tradition is still not understood by scholars, but it is known that the Maya, like most pre-modern societies, believed that the cosmos has three major planes, the underworld, the sky, and the earth.

The Maya underworld is reached through caves and ball courts. It was thought to be dominated by the aged Maya gods of death and putrefaction. The Sun and Itzamna, both aged gods, dominated the Maya idea of the sky. The night sky was considered a window showing all supernatural doings. The Maya configured constellations of gods and places, saw the unfolding of narratives in their seasonal movements, and believed that the intersection of all possible worlds was in the night sky.

Maya gods were not separate entities like Greek gods. The gods had affinities and aspects that caused them to merge with one another in ways that seem unbounded. There is a massive array of supernatural characters in the Maya religious tradition, only some of which recur with regularity. Good and evil traits are not permanent characteristics of Maya gods, nor is only "good" admirable. What is inappropriate during one season might come to pass in another since much of the Maya religious tradition is based on cycles and not permanence.

The life-cycle of maize lies at the heart of Maya belief. This philosophy is demonstrated on the Maya belief in the Maize God as a central religious figure. The Maya bodily ideal is also based on the form of the young Maize God, which is demonstrated in their artwork. The Maize God was also a model of courtly life for the Classical Maya.

It is sometimes believed that the multiple "gods" represented nothing more than a mathematical explanation of what they observed. Each god was literally just a number or an explanation of the effects observed by a combination of numbers from multiple calendars. Among the many types of Maya calendars which were maintained, the most important included a 260-day cycle, a 365-day cycle which approximated the solar year, a cycle which recorded lunation periods of the Moon, and a cycle which tracked the synodic period of Venus.

Philosophically, the Maya believed that knowing the past meant knowing the cyclical influences that create the present, and by knowing the influences of the present one can see the cyclical influences of the future.

Even in the 19th century, there was Maya influence in the local branch of Christianity followed in Chan Santa Cruz. Among the K'iche's in the western highlands of Guatemala these same nine months are replicated, until this very day, in the training of the *ajk'ij*, the keeper of the 260-day-calendar called *ch'olk'ij*.

## AGRICULTURE

The ancient Maya had diverse and sophisticated methods of food production. It was formerly believed that shifting cultivation (swidden) agriculture provided most of their food but it is now thought that permanent raised fields, terracing, forest gardens, managed fallows, and wild harvesting were also crucial to supporting the large populations of the Classic period in some areas.

Indeed, evidence of these different agricultural systems persist today: raised fields connected by canals can be seen on aerial photographs, contemporary rainforest species composition has significantly higher abundance of species of economic value to ancient Maya, and pollen records in lake sediments suggest that corn, manioc, sunflower seeds, cotton, and other crops have been cultivated in association with the deforestation in Mesoamerica since at least 2500 BC.

Contemporary Maya peoples still practice many of these traditional forms of agriculture, although they are dynamic systems and change with changing population pressures, cultures, economic systems, climate change, and the availability of synthetic fertilizers and pesticides.

## REDISCOVERY OF THE PRE-COLUMBIAN MAYA

False-color IKONOS image of a *bajo* (lowland area) in Guatemala. The forest covering sites of Maya ruins appears yellowish, as opposed to the red color of surrounding forest. The more sparsely vegetated *bajos* appear blue-green.

Spanish American Colonies were largely cut off from the outside world, and the ruins of the great ancient cities were little known except to locals. In 1839 United States traveler and writer John Lloyd Stephens, after hearing reports of lost ruins in the jungle, visited Copan, Palenque, and other sites with English architect and draftsman Frederick Catherwood. Their illustrated accounts of the ruins sparked strong interest in the region and the people, and they have once again regained their position as a vital link in Mesoamerican heritage.

However, in many locations, Maya ruins have been overgrown by the jungle, becoming dense enough to hide structures just a few meters away. To help find ruins, researchers have turned to satellite imagery. The best way to find them is to look at the visible and near-infrared spectra. Due to their limestone construction, the monuments affected the chemical makeup of the soil as they deteriorated. Some moisture-loving plants stayed away, while others were killed off or discolored. The effects of the limestone ruins are still apparent today to some satellite sensors.

Much of the contemporary rural population of the Yucatan Peninsula, Chiapas (both in Mexico), Guatemala and Belize is Maya by descent and primary language.

Maya Civilization, an ancient Native American culture that represented one of the most advanced civilizations in the western hemisphere before the arrival of Europeans. The people known as the Maya lived in the region that is now eastern and southern Mexico, Guatemala, Belize, El Salvador, and western Honduras. They thrived for more than 2,000 years. The Maya built massive stone pyramids, temples, and sculpture; developed a system of writing using hieroglyphs; and recorded their achievements in mathematics and astronomy. Archaeologists long believed that Maya culture reached its highest development from about AD 300 to 900, during what is known as the Classic period. Recent discoveries in northern Guatemala, however, have challenged that assumption. There, archaeologists have found highly developed cities, sophisticated art, and examples of Maya writing that date from as early as 600 years before the Classic period began.

After 900 the Maya mysteriously declined in the southern lowlands of Guatemala. They later revived in the north on the Yucatan Peninsula and continued to dominate the area until the Spanish conquest in the 16th century. Descendants of the Maya still form a large part of the population of the region. Although many have adopted Spanish ways, a significant number of modern Maya maintain traditional cultural practices.

## PRECLASSIC PERIOD

Many aspects of Maya civilization developed slowly through a long Preclassic period, from about 2000 BC to AD 300. By the beginning of that period, Mayan-speaking Native Americans were settled in three adjacent regions of eastern and southern Mexico and Central America: the dry, limestone country along the north coast of Mexico's Yucatan Peninsula; the inland tropical jungle in the Peten region of northern Guatemala; and an area of volcanic highlands and mountain peaks in southern Guatemala near the Pacific Ocean.

The earliest Maya were farmers who lived in small, scattered villages of pole and thatch houses. They cultivated their fields as a community, planting seeds in holes made with a pointed wood stick. Later in the Preclassic period, they adopted intensive farming techniques such as continuous cultivation involving crop rotation and fertilizers, household gardens, and terraces. In some areas, they built raised fields in seasonal swamps. Their main crops included maize (corn), beans, squash, avocados, chili peppers, pineapples, papayas, and cacao, which was made into a chocolate drink with water and hot chilies. The women ground corn on specially shaped grinding stones and mixed the ground meal with water to make a drink known as *atole* or to cook as tortillas (flat cakes) on flat pottery griddles. The Maya also drank *balche* made from fermented honey mixed with the bark of the balche tree. Rabbits, deer, and turkeys were hunted for making stews. Fishing also supplied part of their diet. Turkeys, ducks, and dogs were kept as domesticated animals.

When they were not hunting, fishing, or in the fields, Maya men made stone tools, clay figurines, jade carvings, ropes, baskets, and mats. The women made painted pottery vessels out of coiled strands of clay, and they wove ponchos, men's loincloths, and women's skirts, out of fibers made from cotton or from the leaves of the maguey plant. They also used the bark of the wild fig tree to make paper, which they used primarily for ceremonial purposes. Since the Maya had neither draft animals nor wheeled vehicles, they carried goods for trade over the narrow trails with *tumplines* (backpacks supported by a strap slung across the forehead or chest) or transported them in dugout canoes along the coasts and rivers.

The early Maya probably organized themselves into kin-based settlements headed by chiefs. The chiefs were hereditary rulers who commanded a following through their political skills and their ability to communicate with supernatural powers. Along with their families, they composed an elite segment of society, enjoying the privileges of high social rank. However, these elites did not yet constitute a social class of nobles as they would in the Classic period. A council of chiefs or elders governed a group of several settlements located near one another. The council combined both political and religious functions.

Like other ancient farming peoples, the early Maya worshiped agricultural gods, such as the rain god and, later, the corn god. Eventually they developed the belief that gods controlled events in each day, month, and year, and that they had to make offerings to win the gods' favor. Maya astronomers observed the movements of the sun, moon, and planets, made astronomical calculations, and devised almanacs (calendars combined with astronomical observations). The astronomers' observations were used to divine auspicious moments for many different kinds of activity, from farming to warfare.

The Maya did not remain an entirely agricultural people living in villages during the pre-Classic period. Rulers and nobles directed the commoners in building major settlements, such as Kaminaljuyú, in the southern highlands, and Tikal, in the central lowlands of the Peten jungle. Pyramid-shaped mounds of rubble topped with altars or thatched temples sat in the center of these settlements, and priests performed sacrifices to the gods on them. As the Preclassic period progressed, the Maya increasingly used stone in building. Both nobles and commoners lived in extended family compounds.

During the Preclassic period the basic patterns of ancient Maya life were established. However, the period was not simply a rehearsal for the Classic period but a time of spectacular achievements. For example, enormous pyramids were constructed at the site of El Mirador, in the lowlands of Guatemala. These pyramids are among the largest constructions in the ancient Maya world. By about 500 BC El Mirador was a major population center that served as the seat of a powerful chiefdom. Pyramids also were built on large plazas at Cival, a royal metropolis near Tikal in Guatemala. Cival probably had 10,000 inhabitants.

The highland and the lowland regions were in close contact at this time. Obsidian, a smooth volcanic rock used to make weapons and tools, from highland Guatemala has been found at El Mirador, and a sculptural style that originated in the Pacific lowland region of Chiapas and Guatemala was common in the southern highlands. Kaminaljuyú was the most powerful chiefdom of the highlands, and it probably controlled the flow of obsidian to the lowlands. Control of this important resource allowed Kaminaljuyú to dominate trade networks. Economic and political institutions during this period were more advanced in the southern highland area.

## CLASSIC PERIOD

Classic Maya civilization became more complex in about AD 300 as the population increased and centers in the highlands and the lowlands engaged in both cooperation and competition with each other. Trade and warfare were important stimuli to cultural growth and development. The greatest developments occurred in the Peten jungle and surrounding regions of the lowlands where major city-states, such as Tikal, Palenque, Piedras Negras, and Copan, arose and developed from AD 300 to 900.

Society became more complex, with distinct social classes developing. Families of nobles formed a hereditary ruling class that stood apart from the common Maya. At the top of society, a hereditary king ruled over each Maya city. Kings were similar to the earlier ruling chiefs except that they formed a distinct social class along with other nobles. Under the direction of their kings, who also performed as priests, the centers of the lowland Maya became densely populated jungle cities with vast stone and masonry temple and palace complexes. The core area of Tikal, for example, covered about 9 sq km (about 3 sq mi) and included about 2700 structures with an estimated population of 11,300. The total area of Tikal, including the core, peripheral, and rural areas, is estimated at 314 sq km (121 sq mi) with an estimated population of 92,000.

During the Classic period, warfare was conducted on a fairly limited, primarily ceremonial scale. Maya rulers, who were often depicted on *stelae* (carved stone monuments) carrying weapons, attempted to capture and sacrifice one another for ritual and political purposes. The rulers often destroyed parts of some cities, but the destruction was directed mostly at temples in the ceremonial precincts; it had little or no impact on the economy or population of a city as a whole. Some city-states did occasionally conquer others, but this was not a common occurrence until very late in the Classic period when lowland civilization had begun to disintegrate. Until that time, the most common pattern of Maya warfare seems to have consisted of raids employing rapid attacks and retreats by relatively small numbers of warriors, most of whom were probably nobles.

Lowland Maya centers were true cities with large resident populations of commoners who sustained the ruling elites through payments of tribute in goods and labor. They built temples, palaces, courtyards, water reservoirs, and causeways. Walls, floors, and other surfaces in a lowland Maya city were smoothly covered with red or cream-colored limestone stucco, which shone brilliantly in the tropical sun. Sculptors carved stelae, which recorded information about the rulers, their family and political histories, and often included exaggerated statements about their conquests of other city-states.

## Society and Economy

Classic Maya kings carried the title *k'ul ahau* (supreme and sacred ruler). In the latter part of the Classic period, kings were assisted in governing by a hereditary ruling council. The power of the king existed as both a political and religious authority in this period. In contrast, the king's religious power declined during the Postclassic period (AD 900 to 1521) because the institution of priesthood appeared.

Merchants were important to Maya society because of the significance of trade. Principal interior trade routes connected all the great Classic lowland centers and controlled the flow of goods such as salt, obsidian, jade, cacao, animal pelts, tropical bird feathers, and luxury ceramics. In the early Classic period Teotihuacan in central Mexico emerged as the greatest city in Mesoamerica, an area that included modern Mexico and most of Central America. The religious and political power of Teotihuacan radiated throughout Mesoamerica. One result of Teotihuacan's influence was a highly integrated network of trade in which the Maya participated.

Highland Maya from the southern region carried obsidian for tools and weapons; grinding stones; jade; green parrot and quetzal feathers; a tree resin called copal to burn as incense; and cochineal, a red dye made from dried insects. Those from the lowlands brought jaguar pelts, chert (flint), salt, cotton fibers and cloth, balche, wax, honey, dried fish, and smoked venison. People either bartered goods directly or exchanged them for cacao beans, which were used as a kind of currency. Wealth acquired from trade enabled the upper classes to live in luxury, although there was little improvement in the lives of the lower classes.

A Maya nobleman wore an embroidered cotton loincloth trimmed with feathers; a robe of cotton, jaguar skin, or feathers; sandals; and an elaborate feather headdress that was sometimes as large as himself. His head had been fashionably elongated by being pressed between boards when he was a few days old, and his eyes had purposely been crossed in childhood by having objects dangled before them. His nose was built up with putty to give it an admired beak shape, and his ears and teeth were inlaid with jade. A noblewoman wore a loose white cotton robe that was often embroidered. Her head was also elongated, and she filed her teeth to points.

Nobles lived in houses of cut stone with plastered walls that often bore brightly painted murals. In the living room nobles gave banquets of turkey, deer, duck, chocolate, and balche. The guests were expected to bring gifts and to give a banquet in return. A dead noble was buried in a stone vault with jade and pottery ornaments, and occasionally with human sacrifices, which were provided to serve him in the afterlife.

Most of the Maya people were village farmers who gave two-thirds of their produce and much of their labor to the upper classes. Commoner men wore plain cotton loincloths and simple tunics. Women wore woven cotton blouses and skirts or loose-fitting sack dresses with simple embroidered patterns. Women and girls wore their hair long and took care that it was always combed and arranged attractively. Different hairstyles signaled the marital status of women. Both men and women tattooed their bodies with elaborate designs.

At the bottom of Maya society were slaves who were convicted criminals, poor commoners who sold themselves into bondage, captives of war, or individuals acquired by trade. Slaves performed menial tasks for their owners and they were often sacrificed when their owners died so that they could continue to serve in the afterlife.

### Religion

The Maya cosmos comprised a wide range of diverse and varied supernatural beings or deities. The chief god, *Hunab Ku*, the creator of the world, was considered too far above men to figure in worship. He was more important in his manifestation as *Itzamna,* a sky deity considered lord of the heavens and lord of day and night who brought rain and patronized writing and medicine. He was worshiped especially by the priests, and he appears to have been the patron deity of the royal lineages. Closer to the common people were *Yum Kaax,* the maize deity, and the four *Chacs,* or rain gods, each associated with a cardinal direction and with its own special color. Women worshiped *Ix Chel,* a rainbow deity associated with healing, childbirth, and weaving. All the Maya revered *Ixtab*, goddess of suicide, and thought that suicides went to a special heaven. The Maya also recognized the gods who controlled each day, month, and year.

The Maya performed many rituals and ceremonies to communicate with their deities. At stated intervals, such as the Maya New Year in July, or in emergencies—such as famine, epidemics, or a great drought—the people gathered in ritual plazas to honor the gods. They hung feathered banners in doorways all about the plaza. Groups of men or women in elaborate feathered robes and headdresses, with bells on their hands and feet, danced in the plaza to the music of drums, whistles, rattles, flutes, and wood trumpets. Worshipers took ritual steam baths and drank intoxicating balche. Participants often ingested other hallucinogenic drugs, such as mushrooms, and they smoked a very strong form of tobacco with hallucinogenic effects. Young Maya nobles played a sacred ball game on specially constructed courts. Without using their hands, players tried to knock a rubber ball through one of the vertical stone rings built into the walls of the court. On special occasions players who lost the game would be sacrificed to the gods.

Many ceremonies focused on sacrifices to gain the favor of the gods. The sacrifices took place on the great stone pyramids that rose above the plazas, with stairs leading to a temple and altar on top. The temple, a resting place for the god, was deeply carved or painted with designs and figures and was topped with a carved vertical slab of stone called a roof comb. Some had distinctive corbeled arches, in which each stone extended beyond the one beneath it until the two sides of the arch were joined by a single keystone at the top. Before the altar, smoke rose from copal incense burning in pottery vessels.

Worshipers sometimes gave the gods simple offerings of corn, fruit, game, or blood, which a worshiper obtained by piercing his own lips, tongue, or genitals. For major favors they offered the gods human sacrifice, usually children, slaves, or prisoners of war. A victim was painted blue and then ceremonially killed on top of the pyramid, either by being shot full of arrows or by having his arms and legs held while a priest cut open his chest with a sacrificial flint knife and tore out his heart as an offering. Captured rulers were sometimes ritually sacrificed by decapitating them with an axe.

### Science and Writing

Although Maya builders possessed many practical skills, the most distinctive Maya achievements were in abstract mathematics and astronomy. One of their greatest intellectual achievements was a pair of interlocking calendars, which was used for such purposes as the scheduling of ceremonies. One calendar was based on the sun and contained 365 days. The second was a sacred 260-day almanac used for finding lucky and unlucky days. The designation of any day included the day name and number from both the solar calendar and the sacred almanac. The two calendars can be thought of as two geared wheels that meshed together at one point along the rim, with the glyphs for the days of the sun calendar on one wheel and the glyphs for the days of the sacred almanac on the other. With each new day the wheels were turned by one gear. The name for each day was formed by combining the name for the sun calendar day with the name for the sacred almanac day.

Maya astronomers could make difficult calculations, such as finding the day of the week of a particular calendar date many thousands of years in the past or in the future. They also used the concept of zero, an extremely advanced mathematical concept. Although they had neither decimals nor fractions, they made accurate astronomical measurements by dropping or adding days to their calendar. For example, during 1000 years of observing the revolution of the planet Venus, which is completed in 583.92 days, Maya astronomers calculated the time of the Venusian year as 584 days.

The Maya method of reckoning time involved counting forward from a hypothetical fixed point and expressing the date in time periods based on the number 20 and counted in intervals of 1, 20, 360, 7200, and 144,000 days. Such dates appear on carved stone monuments dating to as early as the late Preclassic period, and they are prevalent throughout the lowlands on monuments from the Classic period.

The Maya developed a complex system of hieroglyphic writing to record not only astronomical observations and calendrical calculations, but also historical and genealogical information. Many recent advances have occurred in the decipherment of the Mayan script.

These breakthroughs made it possible to conclude that Mayan hieroglyphs were a mixture of glyphs that represent complete words and glyphs that represent sounds, which were combined to form complete words. Scribes carved hieroglyphs on stone stelae, altars, wooden lintels, and roof beams, or painted them on ceramic vessels and in books made of bark paper. Discoveries reported early in 2006 indicate that the Maya were writing more than 2,300 years ago, at least 600 years earlier than previously thought.

## Collapse of Classic Civilization

From about AD 790 to 889, Classic Maya civilization in the lowlands collapsed. Construction of temples and palaces ceased, and monuments were no longer erected. The Maya abandoned the great lowland cities, and population levels declined drastically, especially in the southern and central lowlands. Scholars debate the causes of the collapse, but they are in general agreement that it was a gradual process of disintegration rather than a sudden dramatic event.

A number of factors were almost certainly involved, and the precise causes were different for each city-state in each region of the lowlands. Among the factors that have been suggested are natural disasters, disease, soil exhaustion and other agricultural problems, peasant revolts, internal warfare, and foreign invasions. Whatever factors led to the collapse, their net result was a weakening of lowland Maya social, economic, and political systems to the point where they could no longer support large populations. Another result was the loss of inestimable amounts of knowledge relating to Maya religion and ritual.

## POSTCLASSIC PERIOD

After the collapse in the central and southern lowlands, Maya civilization continued and even flourished in the northern lowlands of Yucatan and in the southern highlands of Guatemala. The decline of the older powers in the south led to unprecedented growth in the Yucatan Peninsula and the rise of a number of new cities in that region.

Among these were Uxmal, Sayil, and Labna, characterized by a distinctive architectural style known as *Puuc*, which features elaborate mosaic decoration.

In Postclassic times (AD 900 to 1521) the city-states of Yucatan were ruled by a hereditary *halach uinic* (also called *ahau*) who was also the highest religious authority.

The halach uinic had very broad powers. He formulated domestic and foreign policy and appointed *batabs* (lesser lords), who administered the surrounding towns and villages. Local councils made up of clan leaders aided the batabs. Other local Maya officials collected taxes and kept order. Postclassic merchants and professional craftworkers composed a kind of middle class.

A high priest, known as *ahaucan*, conducted major ceremonies and was in charge of the education of priests and nobles. He was assisted by a hierarchy of priests who took part in ceremonies, kept vigils in the temples, performed healing rituals, taught, and served as oracles for the gods. Although similar features and patterns existed in the Classic political structure, the institution of priesthood appears only in the Postclassic.

At the same time, during the 9th century, a new group of Maya, known as the Putun (or Chontal) Maya, began to arrive in Yucatan from their homeland in the Gulf Coast region of Mexico. The Putuns were warriors and traders without equal in the Maya area.

At first they were interested in trade along rivers and overland routes. Eventually they became seafaring people whose merchants plied coastal trade routes around the peninsula and beyond in canoes. These large oceangoing canoes traveled the coast transporting huge loads of heavy and bulky goods much more efficiently than was possible in earlier times. Italian-Spanish explorer Christopher Columbus encountered such a canoe off the Caribbean coast of Honduras on his fourth voyage to the Americas in 1502.

Ports of trade, such as Xicalanco (now in Tabasco, Mexico), served as international meeting places that attracted not only Maya but also traders from highland Mexico to the west and Central America to the south.

Wealthy Maya merchants organized expeditions that traveled great distances in fleets of canoes or over well-constructed stone roads and causeways. Along the routes they built warehouses for goods and rest houses for their carriers. The need to protect the trade networks led the Putuns to develop very aggressive military forces.

Ethnically Maya, the Putuns adopted many stylistic influences from central Mexico in their art and architecture. Especially common was the image of the feathered serpent representing the deity known as Quetzalcoatl in Mexico and as Kukulcan to the Maya. One very powerful Putun group, the Itza, founded their capital at Chichen Itza.

### Chichen Itza

The Itza brought their Mexicanized Maya culture to Chichen Itza in the northern part of the Yucatan Peninsula. During their rule, Mexican-influenced cultures produced certain changes in the traditional Maya way of life.

In the social structure military lords rose in power, and the institution of a formalized priesthood separated from political rulers. This change was echoed in religion, in which the feathered serpent-god Kukulcan dominated all others.

The use of human sacrifice in worship became increasingly important. There were also new forms of sacrifice; the Itza threw victims into a sacred *cenote,* or natural well, along with offerings of pottery, gold, jade, and other valuables. This cenote, in fact, determined the location of Chichen Itza and was responsible for the city's importance as a pilgrimage center.

Chichen Itza was a very large city with a central area covering about 5 sq km (2 sq mi). Its architecture shows the introduction of columns, wider rooms and doorways, and sloping zones around the base of the buildings. The core area includes numerous temples and ball courts, one of which is the largest known in Mesoamerica.

One distinctive structure of the city is a round temple that functioned as an observatory. Statues and motifs of Kukulcan appeared on buildings, staircases, roofs, columns, and doorway lintels.

Life-size stone figures supported the altars, and great reclining stone figures, called *Chacmools,* were sculpted. Warriors depicted in bas-relief columns lack the Classic Maya distortion of head and eyes.

Pottery became monochrome, or single-colored, instead of multicolored, as it had been in the Classic era, but it was often carved or incised with intricate designs. Gold, copper, turquoise, and onyx were used in jewelry. Painted books, called *codices,* were made of bark fiber or deerskin. Trade and commerce, especially maritime exchange, increased.

### Mayapan

In about 1221 Mayapan, which became the dominant state in the northern lowlands, conquered Chichen Itza. Mayapan was smaller than Chichen Itza but more densely settled. Among its 3500 buildings were houses for nobles and commoners, and it was surrounded by a fortified stone wall 8 km (5 mi) long to protect it against neighboring groups.

Structures were packed very tightly in the 4 sq km (1.5 sq mi) area of this walled city. Warlords and merchants continued to gain in importance, and the continual call to arms took up the time of the common people, who spent less and less time on their crafts. Architecture, pottery, and carvings of the period are crude in comparison to those of earlier periods. Finally, in about 1450, a competing lineage defeated the rulers of Mayapan, and the entire peninsula fell into civil war. The following 100 years of warfare left the Maya vulnerable to the invading Spaniards.

### Spanish Conquest

The first Spaniards to encounter the Maya were a party of shipwrecked sailors who landed in Yucatan in 1511. Next came the expedition of Francisco Fernandez de Córdoba in 1517. In 1527 Francisco de Montejo attempted to conquer Yucatan, and in 1546 his son succeeded. By 1524 Spanish explorer Pedro de Alvarado had conquered the southern highland area, which had also fallen into tribal warfare.

Spanish domination of the entire Maya region was achieved in 1697, when the small group of Maya in the central Peten area was conquered by Martin de Ursua, the Spanish governor of the Yucatan. Many Maya were killed or died of European diseases that the Spanish brought with them. The Spanish forced most of the remainder to labor on Spanish farms or in gold and silver mines.

The modern descendants of the Maya still live as peasant farmers throughout the Maya region. They speak a mixture of Mayan and Spanish. One group, the Lacandón people of Mexico, still retains some ties with the past. They make pilgrimages with copal-burning incense pots to worship the old gods among the ruins of ancient pyramids and temples.

**2**

# The Historical Conflict

The news arrives every day: accusations of menacing maneuvers by the Mexican army in Chiapas, proclamations and declarations from different groups and leaders, peace commissions that grow and die like wild flowers in the fields. Violence and killings. Injustice and oppression.

Articles are published. Commentaries are transmitted. Books are written. Social and political analysts, newspapermen and observers from every corner of the world look for the roots of the conflict among today's players: the PRI, Bishop Samuel Ruiz, the professional partisans and troublemakers who appear to be the promoters and organizers of the war.

But the truth lies elsewhere.

The truth is that the Mayan war began almost 500 years ago and has never stopped.

The indians in the Yucatan peninsula who speak *la maya;* Tzeltals, Tzotzils and Chamulas from Chiapas; Lacandons in their jungle; Cakchikels and Quiches from Guatemala; Kekchís from Belize; Chontals, Choles, Tojolabals, Mams, Motozintlecs and Itzaes in the Peten - all of them are the descendants of the ancient Maya, whose long lost cities, civilization, Mathematics, calendar and Astronomy amaze us even today.

Yes, they are the same masked rebels that often appear in the news arriving from Chiapas.

Today, the Maya live in the same land that belonged to their ancestors, from Campeche and Yucatan to Honduras, and they keep being the same old headache to the white people who came to take their homeland in the first quarter of the 16th Century. The Maya nation today counts more than six million souls, making them the most numerous indian people in the Americas, north of Perú.

The ethnic mosaic they conform to is still full of the inextinguishable flame of their glorious past, showing live colors in spite of the centuries of harsh rule and exploitation.

Impoverished and forgotten peasants of the sierra; discriminated indians in the "white" cities of Chiapas (in which they are the majority), fabrics and tapestries, brilliant embroideries, exotic cuisinies full of the products from the jungle and of the condiments guarded with zeal for many years; partisans and heroes; murderers and murdered. And yes, a Nobel prize among them.

The Mayan land has never been really at peace since the white people arrived. Just take a look to any historical timeline to see that peace for them, has been but a brief rest between war periods, revolts, insurrections and riots.

Who are these seditious Maya that have never pledged to integrate to our so called civilization?

About 1,750 years ago, ancient Maya reached what we call their Classical Period. They raised buildings and constructions in the middle of the jungle that today amaze us. They fed their people with a stable system of food production, based on the cultivation of the *maize* (specially adverse conditions of their habitat notwithstanding), from the Yucatan to what is today known as Honduras.

With primitive instruments they devised a calendar system more precise than the Julian calendar used by the Romans, even more precise than the corrected Gregorian calendar (the Gregorian correction took place in the XVI Century, many years after the last great ceremonial center of the Maya was abandoned). Their numeric system, based on the number 20 (they surely counted using fingers and toes), which included the notion of positional value, handled concepts that no other culture, except the Hindu, managed to find.

The Maya discovered the vital concept of zero at least 300 years before the Hindu did so.

If we judge the achievements of the Maya culture, taking into account the limitations they suffered, there is no doubt that they qualify high among the advanced civilizations of the world. The environment in which they lived did not favor the development of complex technologies and cultivation systems. Accordingly, that environment was not capable of sustaining a sizable urban concentration, and that same scarce population did not encourage the development of political institutions, nor the formation of a consolidated state. Other ancient civilizations favored material accomplishments, political organization and imperial ideals, but the Maya worked much more on the intellectual and aesthetic fields.

As Betty Bell comments in her *Critical Examination of the Maya Culture,*

> "So we might say that the cultural interests of the Maya yielded towards the intellectual achievement, at least in part because their physical and evolutive circumstances denied them the political and technological advancements that were more important to other societies."

Their achievements in the fields of art and aesthetics; in the architecture of their cities; in the precision and complexity of their calendar; in their writing system; in their exact astronomical observations, and in their advanced Mathematics, set the Maya culture apart from any of the New World. They were not surpassed by anyone in America; equaled by few in the rest of the world.

What we call the Classical Period of the Maya culture goes from the year 250 to the 900 of our time. The great cities of the Peten, like Tikal and Uaxactún, reached then their maximum splendor, just as Copan, located in the Eastern corner of the Mayan country, in what is today Honduras.

In Yucatan flourished Palenque and Bonampak, along with the cities built on what we know today as the state of Campeche, inside the zones called Río Bec and Chenes. To the north of the peninsula, Chichen Itza, Coba, Dzibilchaltún and other cities saw their days of glory.

Towards the end of this cultural and constructive apogee, near the year 800 A.D., the cities of the lowlands were all in decadence. But between the years 800 and 900, on a region located close to the Gulf of Mexico, in the Yucatan peninsula, the Puuc style was developed, with Uxmal, Kabah, Sayil and Labna as its best exponents.

After that, forced by causes we don't yet clearly understand, between the years 900 and 1000 the cultural push slowed to almost a stop. Their civilization did not vanish, but it never reached the heights attained in the past. The ritual of erecting stone estelas to commemorate significant dates, with the so called "long count" of the days, fell into disuse. The ceremonial centers were abandoned, and the creators went away.

The center of power moved to the north of the Yucatecan peninsula, and Chichen Itza dominated the scene for some years, to later pass the sceptre to Mayapan. Maya history becomes much more political than cultural at this time, a novelty that was already common in almost every other part of the world.

And then they arrived, the whites from the East.

"Just because of the crazy times, because of the crazy priests, is it that sadness overtook us, that 'Christianity' overcame us. Because the 'very Christians' came here with the true God, but that was the beginning of our misery, the beginning of the tribute... the cause of the hidden discord to come out, the beginning of the fighting with firearms, the beginning of the outrages... Oh! Let us grieve, because they arrived!"

"They [the Spanish] taught us to fear; and they came to fade the flowers. For their flowers to live, they damaged and sucked dry the flowers of the others... There was no High Knowledge, nor Sacred Language, neither Divine Teachings in the substitutes of the gods that came here. To castrate the Sun! That is what the foreigners came here for. And the sons of their sons stayed here, among the people, and they receive their bitterness."

The Maya resisted with a persistence and force the conquerors did not expect to encounter. Mexico Tenochtitlan fell in 1521. Hernan Cortes himself organized and headed an expedition in 1524 that crossed the Guatemalan Peten, in the heart of the Mayan country. But the conquest of the Maya was long and difficult. Fray Diego de Landa, in his *Relación de las cosas de Yucatan*, tells us

> "That the Indians heavily felt the yoke of the servitude; but the Spaniards had their towns, which embraced their land, well under control."

It was not until 1546 that the two young Montejo, under the command of the Adelantado Cortes, managed to suffocate the resistance put up by the coalition of the Maya chiefs of the East. With this victory the conquest of the Yucatecan peninsula came to an end.

There was only one independent Mayan group left: the powerful and well organized Itza nation, settled in the surroundings of the Peten-Itza lake, inside the dense tropical forest of the Guatemalan Peten. The capital of the Itza, Tayasal, rested upon an island in the middle of the lake itself. The city kept its freedom for another 150 years. After a bloody fight in 1697, the last independent Mayan political entity was finally taken and subdued to the power of the Spanish Crown.

That did not bring peace to the territory. Revolts, insurrections and riots kept being the daily bread in the Mayan country. The official records of the Cabildo in Merida, December 1761, tell,

> "... of the generalized and bloody ravages that threaten the Province because of the insurrection of the indians who live here, them being precipitated into the reckless audacity of proclaiming one of them, with the name of Canek, as king."

Ermilo Abreu Gómez, in his poetic *Canek*, put in words of the hero the feelings of rebellion that had never left this land, just as the well rooted hatred against powerful and unjust landlords has never died:

> "Canek said: White people made this land foreign to the Indian; they forced the Indian to buy with his own blood the wind that he breaths. That is why the Indian follows the endless trail, being sure that the end, the only attainable end, the one that frees him and allows him to find the lost trail, is where Death lies."

After the independence of Mexico in 1821, the situation of the Maya, far from improving, became even worse. The War of the Castes that tore the Mayan country apart from 1847 to 1849, provoked sequels and consequences that led to the so called Continuation of the War of the Castes, between 1853 and 1901. There were armed *cruzobs* (as the Mayan rebels of that time were called, after the "miraculous cross" which spoke to them, foreseeing the holy war against the white oppressors) in the jungle as late as 1935.

And the story goes on and on, up to this day. This war is not a problem caused by today's Mexico. The war in Chiapas is but just another wave in the sea of irreconcilable differences that has always flooded the relationship between the Maya and the white people and its descendants.

From the glorious past of the Maya we have the ruins of their cities, the written codexes, the *estelas*, the brilliant ideas. After reaching their zenith, the ceremonial centers were abandoned. As the builders left, nature claimed her rights. The old cities were swallowed by the jungle, and in many cases even their names were forgotten. In 1696, Father Andres de Avendaño, Franciscan missionary detached in Guatemala, took part in an expedition which got lost in the tropical forest of the Peten. After days of terrible hardships, Father Avendaño stumbled upon the ruins of an ancient city:

> "Among these high mountains that we passed through there is a variety of ancient buildings, except several of them that I recognized as dwellings, inside, and although they were very tall, and my strength quite diminished, I climbed (although with difficulty) them."

The description that accompanies the story leaves no room to doubt: the Franciscan Father was the first European to see Tikal, the biggest of all ancient Maya centers.

Since the conquest of the Peten, very little was added to the history of the Mayan cities. But between 1839 and 1841, John Lloyd Stephens, American traveler and amateur archaeologist, along with Frederick Catherwood, an English artist, twice visited the Mayan country, to later publish two extraordinary books,

*Incidents of Travel in Central America, Chiapas and Yucatan* (1841), and *Incidents of travel in Yucatan* (1843). Both volumes were adorned with the superb engravings made by Catherwood. According to Professor Sylvanus G. Morley, a famous scholar and archaeologist dedicated to the Mayan world, *"until today, after 100 years, these are the most pleasant books yet written about the Maya region."*

The publishing of these books aroused a great interest throughout the world for the Maya and their culture, and inaugurated the era of the modern expeditions and investigations of the most important civilization of our indigenous America.

A lot has been said and studied and written about ancient Maya. But modern Maya still live in conditions that throw them into violence, be it a valid response or not. The temptation to simplify things and to forget history and to find somebody to blame is great.

The war in Chiapas cannot be explained just by naming a couple of "opportunistic manipulators", or "Marxist guerrillas."

It is not enough to get acquainted with the merciless oppression and the terrible material need suffered in the country.

All these ingredients are present in the stew, yes, but this is a cauldron that has been over the fire for centuries. The fire of racial differences, of discrimination of the indian and of discrimination of the white, of hatred between castes, of confrontation between two radically opposed cultures.

If we want a solution for Chiapas and for the rest of the Maya, we will have to look for and find these solutions in solidarity and mutual understanding, in the notions of person and fellowship. The answers to the problems that are today harassing the inheritors of this great culture are in there somewhere.

Meanwhile, in the traces on the stone and in the stucco mortar the evidence of this ancient civilization is still alive. The images of the past that we present here today may bring to mind the first lesson of History:

Nothing is forever in this world.

Everything passes away.

## GEOGRAPHY AND LANDSCAPE

The ancient Maya civilization occupied the eastern third of Mesoamerica, primarily the Yucatan Peninsula. The topography of the area greatly varied from volcanic mountains, which comprised the highlands in the South, to a porous limestone shelf, known as the Lowlands, in the central and northern regions. The southern portion of the Lowlands were covered by a rain forest with an average height of about 150 feet. Scattered savannas and swamps, or bajos, appeared sporadically, interrupting the dense forests. The northern Lowlands were also comprised of forests but they were drier than their southern counterparts, mainly growing small thorny trees. February to May was the dry season characterized by air that was intensely hot and uncomfortable. At this time of year, the fields had recently been cut and had to be burned in accordance with their slash and burn form of agriculture. The skies filled with a smoky grit, making the air even more unbearable until the rains came in late May to clear the murky atmosphere.

Many dangerous animals occupied this region of the peninsula including the jaguar, the caiman (a fierce crocodile), the bull shark, and many species of poisonous snakes. These animals had to be avoided as the Maya scavenged the forest for foods including deer turkey, peccaries, tapirs, rabbits, and large rodents such as the peca and the agouti. Many varieties of monkeys and quetzal also occupied the upper canopy. The climate of the Highlands greatly contrasted with that of the Lowlands as it was much cooler and drier.

Both the Highlands and the Lowlands were important to the presence of trade within the Mayan civilization. The lowlands primarily produced crops which were used for their own personal consumption, the principle cultigen being maize. They also grew squash, beans, chili peppers, amaranth, manioc, cacao, cotton for light cloth, and sisal for heavy cloth and rope.

The volcanic highlands, however, were the source of obsidian, jade, and other precious metals like cinnabar and hematite that the Mayans used to develop a lively trade. Although the lowlands were not the source of any of these commodities, they still played an important role as the origin of the transportation routes. The rainfall was as high as 160 inches per year in the Lowlands and the water that collected drained towards the Caribbean or the Gulf of Mexico in great river systems. These rivers, of which the Usumacinta and the Grijalva were of primary importance, were vital to the civilization as the form of transportation for both people and materials.

## THE MAYA CULTURE

Contrary to popular beleif, the Mayan civilization was not one unified empire, but rather a multitude of separate entities with a common cultural background. Similar to the Greeks, they were religiously and artistically a nation, but politically sovereign states. As many as twenty such states existed on the Yucatan Peninsula, but although a woman has, on rare occasions, ascended to the ruling position, she has never acquired the title of 'mah kina'.

### Mayan Writing

An elaborate system of writing was developed to record the transition of power through the generations. Maya writing was composed of recorded inscriptions on stone and wood and used within architecture. Folding tree books were made from fig tree bark and placed in royal tombs. Unfortunately, many of these books did not survive the humidity of the tropics or the invasion of the Spanish, who regarded the symbolic writing as the work of the devil.

Four books are known today:

The Dresden Codex

The Madud Codex

The Paris Codex

The Grolier Codex.

The priests followed the ruling class in importance and were instrumental in the recordings of history through the heiroglyphs. The two classes were closely linked and held a monopoly on learning, including writing. The heiroglyphs were formed through a combination of different signs which represented either whole words or single syllables. The information could be conveyed through inscriptions alone, but it was usually combined with pictures showing action to facilitate comprehension.

## Political Organization

In both the priesthood and the ruling class, nepotism was apparently the prevailing system under which new members were chosen. Primogeniture was the form under which new kings were chosen as the king passed down his position to his son. After the birth of a heir, the kings performed a blood sacrifice by drawing blood from his own body as an offering to his ancestors. A human sacrifice was then offered at the time of a new king's installation in office. To be a king, one must have taken a captive in a war and that person is then used as the victim in his accession ceremony. This ritual is the most important of a king's life as it is the point at which he inherits the position as head of the lineage and leader of the city. The religious explanation that upheld the institution of kingship asserted that Maya rulers were necessary for continuance of the Universe.

## Mayan Art

The art of the Maya, as with every civilization, is a reflection of their lifestyle and culture. The art was composed of delineation and painting upon paper and plaster, carvings in wood and stone, clay and stucco models, and terra cotta figurines from molds. The technical process of metal working was also highly developed but as the resources were scarce, they only created ornaments in this media. Many of the great programs of Maya art, inscriptions, and architecture were commissioned by Mayan kings to memorialize themselves and ensure their place in history. The prevailing subject of their art is not anonymous priests and unnamed gods but rather men and women of power that serve to recreate the history of the people. The works are a reflection of the society and its interaction with surrounding people.

One of the greatest shows of Mayan artistic ability and culture is the hieroglyphic stairway located at Copan. The stairway is an iconographical complex composed of statues, figures, and ramps in addition to the central stairway which together port ray many elements of Mayan society. An alter is present as well as many pictorial references of sacrifice and their gods. More importantly than all the imagery captured with in this monument, however, is the history of the royal descent depicted in the heiroglyphs and various statues. The figurine of a seated captive is also representative of Mayan society as it depicts someone in the process of a bloodletting ceremony, which included the accession to kingship. This figure is of high rank as depicted by his expensive earrings and intricately woven hip cloth. The rope collar which would usually mark this man as a captive, reveals that he is involved in a bloodletting rite. His genitals are exposed as he is just about to draw blood for the ceremony.

In the Indian communities, as it was with their Mayan ancestors, the basic staple diet is corn. The clothing worn is as it was in the past. It is relatively easy to determine the village in which the clothing was made by the the type of embroidery, color, design and shape. Mayan dialects of Qhuche, Cakchiquel, Kekchi, and Mam are still spoken today, although the majority of Indians also speak Spanish.

## MYSTERIES OF THE MAYANS

Unraveling the mystery of who the Maya were, how they lived—and why their civilization suddenly collapsed.

The crowd at the base of the enormous bloodred pyramid has been standing for hours in the dripping heat of the Guatemalan jungle. No one moves; every eye stays fixed on the building's summit, where the king, his head adorned with feathers, his scepter a two-headed crocodile, is about to emerge from a sacred chamber with instructions from his long-dead ancestors. The crowd sees nothing of his movements, but it knows the ritual: lifted into the next world by hallucinogenic drugs, the king will take an obsidian blade or the spine of a stingray, pierce his own penis, and then draw a rope through the wound, letting the blood drip onto bits of bark paper. Then he will take the bark and set it afire, and out of the rising smoke a vision of a serpent will appear to him.

When the king finally emerges, on the verge of collapse, he reaches under his loincloth, displays a bloodstained hand and announces the ancestors' message—the same message he has received so many times in the past: "Prepare to go to war." The crowd erupts in wild cheers. The bloodletting has barely begun.

Who were the Maya, the people who built and later abandoned these majestic pyramids scattered around Central America and who enacted these bizarre rites? The question has piqued scientists across a broad swath of disciplines ever since an American lawyer and explorer named John Lloyd Stephens stumbled across something strange in the Honduran jungle.

In Incidents of Travel in Central America, Chiapas and Yucatan (1841), Stephens impressionistically described what was later identified as the ruined Maya city of Copan: "It lay before us like a shattered bark in the midst of the ocean, her masts gone, her name effaced, her crew perished, and none to tell whence she came, to whom she belonged, how long on her voyage, or what caused her destruction."

More than 150 years later, the Maya seem less inscrutable than they did to Stephens, the man who discovered, or rediscovered, what they had left behind. Archaeologists have long known that the Maya, who flourished between about A.D. 250 and 900, perfected the most complex writing system in the hemisphere, mastered mathematics and astrological calendars of astonishing accuracy, and built massive pyramids all over Central America, from Yucatan to modern Honduras. But what researchers have now found among these haunting irruptions of architecture may be, among other things, reasons for admonishing today's world: at a time when tribal fratricide is destroying Bosnia and farmers are carving through the rain forest, the lessons yielded by the Maya have a disturbing resonance.

The latest discovery, announced just this week, underscores how quickly Maya archaeology is changing. Four new Maya sites have been uncovered in the jungle-clad mountains of southern Belize, in rough terrain that experts assumed the Maya would have shunned. Two of the sites have never been looted, which will provide researchers with a wealth of clues to the still largely unsolved puzzle of who the Maya were—and the mystery of how and why their civilization collapsed so catastrophically around the year 900. Of course, considerable mysteries persist and always will. "I wake up almost every morning thinking how little we know about the Maya," says George Stuart, an archaeologist with National Geographic. "What's preserved is less than 1% of what was there in a tropical climate."

Such limited and often puzzling physical evidence has not deterred growing legions of archaeologists, art historians, epigraphers, anthropologists, ethnohis torians, linguists and geologists from making annual treks to Maya sites. Propelled by a series of dramatic discoveries, Mayanism has been transformed over the past 30 years from an esoteric academic discipline into one of the hottest fields of scientific inquiry—and the pace of discovery is greater today than ever.

Among the already addicted, Mayamania is easy to explain. Says Arthur Dem arest, a Vanderbilt University archaeologist who for the past four years has led a team of researchers unearthing the remains of Dos Pilas, a onetime Maya metropolis in northern Guatemala: "You've got lost cities in the jungle, secret inscriptions that only a few people can read, tombs with treasures in them, and then the mystery of why it all collapsed."

The explosion of information has led to a comparable explosion of theorizing about the Maya, along with inevitable, often vehement, disagreements over whose ideas are right. Nevertheless, a consensus has begun to emerge among Mayanists. Among the first myths about this population to be debunked is that they were a peaceful race. Experts now generally agree that warfare played a key role in Maya civilization. The rulers found reasons to use torture and human sacrifice throughout their culture, from religious celebrations to sporting events to building dedications. "This has come as something of a shock to many Mayanists," says Carlos Navarrete, a leading Mexican anthropologist.

Uncontrolled warfare was probably one of the main causes for the Maya's eventual downfall. In the centuries after 250—the start of what is called the Classic period of Maya civilization—the skirmishes that were common among competing city-states escalated into full-fledged, vicious wars that turned the proud cities into ghost towns.

Among the first modern Westerners to be captivated by the Maya were the American Stephens and English artist Frederick Catherwood, who started in 1839 to bushwhack their way into the Central American rain forest to gaze at the monumental ruins of Copan, Palenque, Uxmal and other Maya sites. The book Stephens wrote about his trek was an enormous popular success and sparked others to follow him and Catherwood into the jungle and into musty Spanish colonial archives. Over the next half-century, researchers uncovered, among other things, the Popol Vuh (the sacred book of the Quiche Maya tribe) and the Relacion de las Cosas de Yucatan, an account of Maya culture during and immediately after the 16th century Spanish conquest written by the Roman Catholic bishop Diego de Landa. By the 1890s, Alfred Maudslay, an English explorer, was compiling the first comprehensive catalog of Maya buildings, monuments and inscriptions in the major known cities, and the first excavations were under way.

With all this data, 19th century scholars began trying to decipher the hieroglyphic script, reconstruct Maya history and figure out what caused the civilization to fall apart. In the absence of any historical context, though, speculation tended to run a little wild. Some ascribed the monumental buildings to survivors of the lost continent of Atlantis; others insisted they were the work of the Ten Lost Tribes of Israel, or the Egyptians, the Phoenicians, the Chinese, or even the Javanese.

The first half of the 20th century brought more excavations and more cataloging—but still only scratched the surface of what was to come. By 1950 the field was dominated by J. Eric Thompson and Sylvanus Morley of the Carnegie Institution of Washington. Both are still revered as brilliant archaeologists, but some of their theories have been overturned by new evidence. Among their now outdated ideas: that the city centers of the Classic Maya were used primarily for ceremonial purposes, not for living; hieroglyphic texts described esoteric calendrical, astronomical and religious subjects but never recorded anything as mundane as rulers or historical events; slash-and-burn agriculture was the farming method of choice; and, of course, the Maya lived in blissful coexistence with one another.

Morley and Thompson presumed that certain practices of the ancient Maya could be deduced from those of their descendants. Modern scientists are more rigorous; besides, they have the advantage of sophisticated technology, like radiocarbon dating, which can help test their theories.

Near the Mexican border of Guatamala, in the Maya city of Dos Pilas and the surrounding Petexbatun region, Arthur Demarest's excavations have put him at the forefront of the revisionists. He divides the history of the region into two periods: before 761 and after. Before that year, he says, wars were well-orchestrated battles to seize dynastic power and procure royal captives for very public and ornate executions. But after 761, he notes, "wars led to wholesale destruction of property and people, reflecting a breakdown of social order comparable to modern Somalia." In that year the king and warriors of nearby Tamarindito and Arroyo de Piedra besieged Dos Pilas. Says Demarest: "They defeated the king of Dos Pilas and probably dragged him back to Tamarindito to sacrifice him." The reason for the abrupt change in the Maya's battleground behavior, he suspects, was that the ruling elite had grown large enough to produce intense rivalries among its members. Their ferocious competition, which exploded into civil war, may have been what finally triggered the society's breakdown. Similar breakdowns, he believes, happened in other areas as well.

Arlen and Diane Chase, archaeologists at the University of Central Florida, believe their work at Caracol, in present-day Belize, also shows that escalating warfare was largely responsible for that ancient city's abrupt extinction. Among the evidence they cite: burn marks on buildings, the uncharacteristically unburied body of a six-year-old child lying on the floor of a pyramid, and an increase in war imagery on late monuments and pottery. "Of course we found weapons too," says Arlen.

While many Mayanists agree that wars contributed to the collapse, no one thinks they were the whole story. Another factor was overexploitation of the rain-forest ecosystem, on which the Maya depended for food. University of Arizona archaeologist T. Patrick Culbert says pollen recovered from underground debris shows clearly that "there was almost no tropical forest left."

Water shortages might have played a role in the collapse as well: University of Cincinnati archaeologist Vernon Scarborough has found evidence of sophisticated reservoir systems in Tikal and other landlocked Maya cities (some of the settlements newly discovered this week also have reservoirs). Since those cities depended on stored rainfall during the four dry months of the year, they would have been extremely vulnerable to a prolonged drought.

Overpopulation was another problem. On the basis of data collected from about 20 sites, Culbert estimates that there were as many as 200 people per sq km in the southern lowlands of Central America. Says Culbert: "This is an astonishingly high figure; it ranks up there with the most heavily populated parts of the pre-industrial world. And the north may have been even more densely populated."

One inevitable consequence of overpopulation and a disintegrating agricultural system would be malnutrition—and in fact, some researchers are beginning to find preliminary evidence of undernourishment in children's skeletons from the late Classic period. Given all the stresses on Maya society, says Culbert, what ultimately sent it over the edge "could have been something totally trivial—two bad hurricane seasons, say, or a crazy king. An enormously strained system like this could have been pushed over in a million ways."

What sorts of lessons can be drawn from the Maya collapse? Most experts point to the environmental messages. "The Maya were overpopulated and they overexploited their environment and millions of them died," says Culbert bluntly. "That knowledge isn't going to solve the modern world situation, but it's silly to ignore it and say it has nothing to do with us." National Geographic archaeologist George Stuart agrees.

The most important message, he says, is "not to cut down the rain forest." But others are not so sure. Says Stephen Houston, a hieroglyphics expert from Vanderbilt University: "I think we should be careful of finding too many lessons in the Maya. They were a different society, and the glue that held them together was different."

Just how different the Maya were is clear from their everyday lives, on which archaeologists are increasingly focusing. From the contents of graves and burial caches, the architecture of ordinary houses, and scenes painted on pottery, Demarest and others are learning what an average Maya day was like.

The typical Maya family (averaging five to seven members, archaeologists guess) probably arose before dawn to a breakfast of hot chocolate—or, if they weren't rich enough, a thick, hot corn drink called atole—and tortillas or tamales. The house was usually a one-room hut built of interwoven poles covered with dried mud. Meals of corn, squash and beans, supplemented with the occasional turkey or rabbit, were probably eaten on the run.

During the growing season, men would spend most of the day in the fields, while women usually stayed closer to home, weaving or sewing and preparing food. At the end of the day the family would reconvene at home, where the head of the household might perform a quick bloodletting, the central act of piety, accompanied by prayers and chanting to the ancestors.

Days that were not devoted to agriculture might be spent building pyramids and temples. In exchange for their toil, the people expected to attend royal marriages and ceremonies marking important astrological and calendrical events. At these occasions the king might perform a bloodletting, sacrifice a captive or preside over a ball game—the losers to be beheaded, or sometimes tied in a ball and bounced down the stone steps of a pyramid. Like modern-day hot-dog vendors, craftsmen and farmers might show up for these games to set up stands and barter for pots, cacao and beads.

The Maya also had a highly developed—and to modern eyes, highly bizarre—aesthetic sense. "Slightly crossed eyes were held in great esteem," writes Yale anthropologist Michael Coe in his book The Maya. "Parents attempted to induce the condition by hanging small beads over the noses of their children." The Maya also seemed to go in for shaping their children's skulls: they liked to flatten them (although this may have simply been the inadvertent result of strapping babies to cradle boards) or squeeze them into a cone. Some Mayanists speculate that the cone head effect was the result of trying to approximate the shape of an ear of corn. The Maya filed their teeth (it's unclear whether they used an anesthetic), sometimes into a T shape and sometimes to a point. They also inlaid their teeth with small, round plaques of jade or pyrite. According to Coe, young men painted themselves black until marriage and later engaged in ritual tattooing and scarring.

Information about the Maya has come not just from physical objects but also from the elaborate hieroglyphics they left behind. Indeed, the study of Maya writing has become a coequal—and sometimes competitive—path of inquiry. For some reason it has attracted more than its share of amateurs. In the early 1970s, "discoveries came at the pace of a raging prairie fire," writes Coe in his latest book, Breaking the Maya Code. Former University of South Alabama art teacher Linda Schele burst into the epigraphical world. On a 1970 visit to Mexico, she was mesmerized by the ruins at Palenque. Three years later, she was accomplished enough to collaborate with two others in a mind-boggling feat of decipherment: during a conference at modern Palenque, the trio took a mere 2 1/2 hours to decode the history of Palenque and its rulers from the beginning of the 7th century to its fall around the late 8th century—and got it right.

How was this possible? Because, say the professionals, deciphering glyphs depends as much on intuition and instinct as it does on knowledge of a given writing system. Insight can strike like lightning. Says Schele, now an art historian at the University of Texas at Austin: "These moments of clarity are just extraordinary. The greatest thrills of my career came in those moments when the inscription becomes clear and we suddenly understand the humans who created this legacy for the first time."

The Palenque decipherment work began an epigraphic revolution. Since then, the field has been blessed with a number of young, gifted epigraphers, including Stephen Houston, 34, and David Stuart, 28, who began his career as a child. The son of Maya archaeologists George and Gene Stuart, he made his first trip to Maya ruins at the age of three, and by 1984, at 18, was so skilled at deciphering glyphs that he became the youngest recipient ever of a MacArthur Foundation "genius" grant. Stuart's next project is nothing less than cataloging every known Maya inscription, a task he guesses could take him the rest of his life. "There is at least another century of work; it will go on long after I'm gone," he says.

Like most official records, glyphs undoubtedly contain a healthy dose of propaganda. Imagine, argues Richard Leven thal, director of UCLA's Institute of Archaeology, that you tried to understand the Gulf War by reading Saddam Hussein's pronouncements. Says Arlen Chase: "You get this real warped view of what Maya politics and Classic society look like if you just use epigraphy. It's important, but archaeology is the only way to test it." Observes Houston: "Of course it's propaganda, but to jump from that to a blanket dismissal is preposterous."

The argument over how to interpret Maya writing—along with arguments over just about every other aspect of Maya archaeology—won't be resolved anytime soon. New discoveries are constantly reinventing the conventional wisdom. At Caracol, for example, the Chases have uncovered an unprecedented 74 relic-filled tombs; their location, in living areas, supports the idea of ancestor worship, and the number of burial chambers provides evidence, the Chases think, that the Maya had a large, prosperous "middle class."

In Dos Pilas, Arthur Demarest is turning his attention to garbage piles. "Those are the most important finds," he says, "not the tombs, because you find everything they ate, their tools—a real cross-section of life, in really good preservation." A colleague plans to study the chemical composition of ancient soil and pollen samples and exhumed human bones to learn more about the Maya diet, common diseases, agricultural practices and even what the climate was like.

As they excavate deeper into the Maya past, archaeologists and other scientists are still struggling to make sense of this legacy of triumph and self-destruction. And there usually comes a point when a Mayanist has to decide how to draw joyful inspiration from the culture's destiny. "It's a very rare thing for the past to be a source of deep-seated pessimism," says David Freidel, an anthropologist at Southern Methodist University. So Freidel has come up with this way to think of the Maya: "When I see the past, what I see are not just the failures of human effort, of human imagination, but that unquenchable desire to make of life a meaningful thing."

A tour guide at the legendary ruins of Palenque in Chiapas, Mexico, likes to tell the story. A tourist, after staring in awe at the towering pyramids, turned to the guide and said, "The buildings are beautiful, but where did all the people go?" "Of course, she was talking to a Maya," the guide says, shaking his head at the irony. "We're still here. We never left."

The exchange illustrates a living paradox at the heart of the Maya puzzle: even as scientists continue to investigate the mysterious eclipse of the classic Maya empire, the Maya themselves are all around them. An estimated 1.2 million Maya still live in the southern Mexican state of Chiapas, and nearly 5 million more are spread throughout the Yucatan Peninsula and the cities and rural farm communities of Belize, Guatemala, Honduras and El Salvador. Ethnically, they are derived from the same people who created the most exalted culture in Mesoamerica. Yet the thousands of visitors who come each year to admire the imposing temples of Palenque might be shocked to know the ignominious fate of the Maya's modern-day descendants.

Centuries of persecution and cultural isolation have turned the Maya into impoverished outcasts in their own land. At best, they are often reduced to tourist attractions; for a little money, Mexico's Lacandon Indians, for instance, will display their traditional white cotton shikur and long black hair. But condescension is the mildest of the abuses suffered by today's Maya. In a 1992 report on the indigenous peoples of the Americas, Amnesty International cited dozens of human-rights violations carried out by Mexican authorities against the Maya people of Chiapas: they include an incident in 1990 when 11 Maya were tortured after being arrested during a land dispute, and another one two years ago when 100 Maya were beaten and imprisoned for 30 hours without food or medical attention.

In Guatemala's 30-year-old civil war, it has been the Maya who have been the primary victims of the military's antiguerrilla campaigns in the highlands, which have left 140,000 Guatemalans dead or missing. In some cases, government troops have burned entire Maya villages.

The systematic subjugation of the Maya dates back to the Spanish Conquest of the early 16th century, when Catholic missionaries outlawed the Maya religion and burned all but four of their sacred bark-paper books. Indians who were not killed in battle or felled by European diseases were forced to work on colonial plantations, often as slaves. Bands of Maya rebels, known to be ferocious fighters, resisted pacification for almost 400 years, first under the Spanish occupation and then under the Mexican army after Mexico became independent.

Despite this history of defiance—or maybe, in some cases, because of it—the Maya continued to be targets of abuse even after being incorporated into the family of Central American nations. As recently as 20 years ago, Maya peasants carrying chickens or peanuts to the town market in San Cristobal de las Casas were in danger of having their wares snatched away by non-Indian women, or "Black Widows." And though the town's economy depended on trade with the Indians, Maya found walking the streets at night would be thrown into jail and fined.

Today, despite government decrees that guarantee equal rights for Indians and the new presidency in Guatemala of human-rights champion Ramiro de Leon Carpio, indigenous peoples like the Maya remain at the bottom rung of the political and economic ladder. In Chiapas, where the natives speak nine different languages, literacy rates are about 50%, compared with 88% for Mexico as a whole. Infant mortality among the Maya is 500 per 1,000 live births, 10 times as high as the national average. And 70% of the Indians in the countryside lack access to potable water.

In these sorry conditions, many Maya have seized on their old ways to make sense of their modern lives. In the remote highlands of Guatemala and Mexico, where the rugged terrain has held the outside world at bay, contemporary Maya still practice many of the same rituals that were performed by their ancestors 4,000 years ago. Maya weavers embroider their wares with diamond motifs that are virtually identical to the cosmological patterns depicted on the lintels of ancient temples at Yaxchilan and other

Maya sites. By marking their clothing with the symbols of their ancestors, the Maya artisans build a material link to pre-Columbian gods—and the indelible spirit of their cultural past. "Depictions of everyday life do not occur in the weaving," notes Walter F. Morris Jr., a Seattle-based anthropologist and author of Living Maya. "It's always something supernatural, something dreamt, something you can only see in dreams."

Chiapas, Yaqui Indians follow two brothers who, guided by the spirit voices of macaws, retake the high country from the Hispanics who scorn and oppress them. In Alaska, a Yupik woman knows how to down airplanes by hexing television sets with a fox pelt. Near Tucson, two half-breed witches, elderly twin sisters, import cocaine to undermine the enemy and buy guns to store at their fortified ranch. Wherever it is shown, the white society is murderous, corrupt, mad with greed and hideously perverted. Among the white characters, and quite typical of the rest, are a federal judge who has sex with his basset hounds and a reptilian homosexual who steals the baby of a drug-soaked stripteaser for use in a torture video.

The ruling society has gone septic and sterile. Lecha, one of the twin witches, who can find lost objects and dead bodies, notices that "affluent, educated white people...sought [her] out in secret. They all had come to her with a deep sense that something had been lost...lottery tickets, worthless junk bonds or lost loved ones; but Lecha knew the loss was their connection with the earth." Later an Indian orator picks up the theme. Spirit voices direct white mothers "to pack the children in the car and drive off hundred-foot cliffs or into flooding rivers...The spirits whisper in the brains of loners, the crazed young white men with automatic rifles who slaughter crowds in shopping malls or school yards as casually as hunters shoot buffalo."

The author's sentences have a drive and a sting to them. But the receptacle of her crowded, raging, enormously long book swirls with half-digested revulsion, half-explained characters and, a white elitist must add, more than a little self-righteousness. The novel's long first half is a dull headache, because most of the dozen or more narrators, none of whom knows what is going on, are drunk, doped or crazy.

Yet angry prophets can't be expected to write neat, button-down denunciations. Old Indian legends, the author relates, say that after a very long time, the cruel and greedy white conquerors will weaken and vanish. Her intention is to bring readers to the point at which this is about to happen, and her success is far more troubling than her failure.

Chiapas, Mexico, for instance, are not threatened by native Lacandon practices but by the more commercial agricultural practices of encroaching peasants, according to James Nations of Conservation International in Washington. Many indigenous farmers in Asia and South America manage to stay on one patch of land for as long as 50 years. As nutrients slowly disappear from the soil, the farmers keep switching to hardier crops and thus do not have to clear an adjacent stretch of forest.

Westerners have also come to value traditional farmers for the rich variety of crops they produce. By cultivating numerous strains of corn, legumes, grains and other foods, they are ensuring that botanists have a vast genetic reservoir from which to breed future varieties.

The genetic health of the world's potatoes, for example, depends on Quechua Indians, who cultivate more than 50 diverse strains in the high plateau country around the Andes mountains in South America. If these natives switched to modern crops, the global potato industry would lose a crucial line of defense against the threat of insects and disease.

Anthropologists studying agricultural and other traditions have been surprised to find that people sometimes retain valuable knowledge long after they have dropped the outward trappings of tribal culture. In one community in Peru studied by Christine Padoch of the Institute of Economic Botany, peasants employed all manner of traditional growing techniques, though they were generations removed from tribal life.

Padoch observed almost as many combinations of crops and techniques as there were households. Similarly, a study of citified Aboriginal children in Australia revealed that they had far more knowledge about the species and habits of birds than did white children in the same neighborhood. Somehow their parents had passed along this knowledge, despite their removal from their native lands. Still, the amount of information in jeopardy dwarfs that being handed down.

### Lending a Hand

There is no way that concerned scientists can move fast enough to preserve the world's traditional knowledge. While some can be gathered in interviews and stored on tape, much information is seamlessly interwoven with a way of life. Boston anthropologist Jason Clay therefore insists that knowledge is best kept alive in the culture that produced it. Clay's solution is to promote economic incentives that also protect the ecosystems where natives live. Toward that end, Cultural Survival, an advocacy group in Cambridge, Mass., that Clay helped establish, encourages traditional uses of the Amazon rain forest by sponsoring a project to market products found there.

Clay believes that in 20 years, demand for the Amazon's nuts, oils, medicinal plants and flowers could add up to a $15 billion-a-year retail market—enough so that governments might decide it is worthwhile to leave the forests standing. The Amazon's Indians could earn perhaps $1 billion a year from the sales. That could pay legal fees to protect their lands and provide them with cash for buying goods from the outside world.

American companies are also beginning to see economic value in indigenous knowledge. In 1989 a group of scientists formed Shaman Pharmaceuticals, a California company that aims to commercialize the pharmaceutical uses of plants. Among its projects is the development of an antiviral agent for respiratory diseases and herpes infections that is used by traditional healers in Latin America.

An indigenous culture can in itself be a marketable commodity if handled with respect and sensitivity. In Papua New Guinea, Australian Peter Barter, who first came to the island in 1965, operates a tour service that takes travelers up the Sepik River to traditional villages. The company pays direct fees to villages for each visit and makes contributions to a foundation that help cover school fees and immunization costs in the region. Barter admits, however, that the 7,000 visitors a year his company brings through the region disrupt local culture to a degree. Among other things, native carvers adapt their pieces to the tastes of customers, adjusting their size to the requirements of luggage. But the entrepreneur argues that the visits are less disruptive than the activities of missionaries and development officials.

There are other perils to the commercial approach. Money is an alien and destabilizing force in many native villages. A venture like Barter's could ultimately destroy the integrity of the cultures it exhibits if, for example, rituals become performances tailored to the tourist business.

Some villages in New Guinea have begun to permit tourists to visit spirit houses that were previously accessible only to initiated males. In Africa villages on bus routes will launch into ceremonial dances at the sound of an approaching motor. Forest-product concerns like those encouraged by Cultural Survival run the risk of promoting overexploitation of forests, and if the market for these products takes off, the same settlers who now push aside natives to mine gold might try to take over new enterprises as well.

Still, economic incentives already maintain traditional knowledge in some parts of the world. John and Terese Hart, who have spent 18 years in contact with Pygmies in northeastern Zaire, note that other tribes and villagers rely on Pygmies to hunt meat and collect foods and medicines from the forests, and that this economic incentive keeps their knowledge alive. According to John Hart, the Pygmies have an uncanny ability to find fruits and plants they may not have used for years. Says Hart: "If someone wants to buy something that comes from the forest, the Pygmies will know where to find it."

## Restoring Respect

Preserving tribal wisdom is as much an issue of restoring respect for traditional ways as it is of creating financial incentives. The late Egyptian architect Hassan Fathy put his prestige behind an attempt to convince his countrymen that their traditional mud-brick homes are cooler in the summer, warmer in the winter and cheaper than the prefabricated, concrete dwellings they see as modern status symbols.

Balick has made it part of his mission to enhance the status of traditional healers within their own communities. He and his colleagues hold ceremonies to honor shamans, most of whom are religious men who value respect over material reward. In one community in Belize, the local mayor was so impressed that American scientists had come to learn at the feet of an elderly healer that he asked them to give a lecture so that townspeople could learn about their own medical tradition. Balick recalls that this healer had more than 200 living descendants, but that none as yet had shown an interest in becoming an apprentice. The lecture, though, was packed. "Maybe," says Balick, "seeing the respect that scientists showed to this healer might inspire a successor to come forward."

Such deference represents a dramatic change from past scientific expeditions, which tended to treat village elders as living museum specimens. Balick and others like him recognize that communities must decide for themselves what to do with their traditions. Showing respect for the wisdom keepers can help the young of various tribes better weigh the value of their culture against blandishments of modernity. If young apprentices begin to step forward, the world might see a slowing of the slide toward oblivion.

# 3

# Maya Mythology

Maya mythology refers to the pre-Columbian Maya civilization's extensive polytheistic religious beliefs. These beliefs had most likely been long-established by the time the earliest-known distinctively Maya monuments had been built and inscriptions depicting their deities recorded, considerably pre-dating the 1st millennium BC. Over the succeeding millennia this intricate and multi-faceted system of beliefs was extended, varying to a degree between regions and time periods, but maintaining also an inherited tradition and customary observances. The Maya shared many traditions and rituals with the other civilizations and cultures in the Mesoamerican region, both preceding and contemporary societies, and in general the entire region formed an interrelated mosaic of belief systems and conceptions on the nature of the world and human existence. However, the various Maya peoples over time developed a unique and continuous set of traditions which are particularly associated with their societies, and their achievements.

Despite the ca. early 10th century "Terminal collapse", during which Maya monument construction and inscription recording effectively ceased over large areas and many centers were subsequently abandoned, the Maya peoples themselves endured and continued to maintain their assorted beliefs and traditions. The maintenance of these traditions can be seen in the relics and products of those centers which flourished during the Post-Classic phase, such as in the northern YucatÃ¡n Peninsula, occasionally combined with other influences more characteristic of the Gulf coast and central Mexican regions. Although the southern lowland

and highland Maya regions of present-day Guatemala saw very little further monument building during this period, the maintenance of traditional beliefs among the local Maya is attested by the accounts and reports of the 16th and 17th century Spanish.

During and after the Spanish conquest, the stories and traditions of the Maya coninued to be handed down to succeeding generations, albeit much influenced and restricted by the influx of European practices and beliefs, Roman Catholicism in particular. Many Maya have experienced considerable persecution for their beliefs and political oppression over the centuries since the first European arrivals; although there can be no doubt that Maya society and tradition has undergone substantial change, many Maya people today maintain an identity which is very much informed by their collective history, traditions and beliefs– a heritage which is distinctively Maya even where substantially combined with the widespread adoption of Christianity.

Apart from epigraphic inscriptions on monuments (which deal primarily with commemorations and dynastic successions), only three complete Maya texts and a fragment of a fourth have survived through the years. The majority of the Maya codices were burned by Europeans like Bishop Diego de Landa during their conquest of Mesoamerica and subsequent efforts to convert the Maya peoples to Christianity. Available knowledge of Maya mythology, as such, is rather limited. What is known is drawn largely from 16th - 17th century accounts of post-conquest Maya beliefs and traditions, which do not necessarily correspond with the traditions which were maintained in earlier times.

## Overview

In common with other Mesoamerican civilizations, each of the cardinal (or world-) directions were ascribed certain properties and associations. These attributes held a particular significance, and they provided one of the major frameworks which interlinked much of Maya religion and cosmology. The Maya world-view recognized the four primary compass directions, and each of these was consistently associated with a particular color— east with red, north with white, west with black and south with yellow. These associations and their respective glyphs are attested from at least the Early Classic period, and also figure markedly in the Postclassic Maya codices.

A fifth 'direction', the "center", also formed a part of this scheme. Associated with a blue-green color, this was most frequently represented by a great ceiba tree, conceptualized as the "tree of life". In Maya cosmology this formed a kind of *axis mundi* which connected the Earth's center with the layers of both the underworld and the heavens. It is believed that living ceiba trees were maintained at the center of many pre-Columbian Maya settlements in symbolic representation of this connection, and alternatively one was placed at each of the four cardinal directions as well.

Maya deities each displayed different aspects based on these five directions as well as a number of other natural and symbolic cycles observed by the Maya.

Maya deities also had dualistic natures associating them with day or night, life or death. There were thirteen gods of the thirteen heavens of the Maya religion and nine gods of the nine underworlds. Between the upperworlds of the heavens and the underworlds of the night and death was the earthly plane which is often shown in Maya art as a two-headed caiman or a turtle lying in a great lake. Natural elements, stars and planets, numbers, crops, days of the calendar and periods of time all had their own gods. The gods' characters, malevolence or benevolence, and associations changed according to the days in the Maya calendar or the positions of the sun, moon, Venus, and the stars.

The QuichÃ Maya creation story is outlined in the *Popol Vuh*. This has the world created from nothing by the will of the Maya pantheon of gods. Man was made unsuccessfully out of mud and then wood before being made out of maize and being assigned tasks which praised the gods — silversmith, gem cutter, stone carver, potter, etc. Some argue this story adds credence to the belief that the Maya did not believe in art *per se;* all of their works were for the exaultation of the gods.

After the creation story, the Popol Vuh tells of the struggles of the legendary hero twins, Hunahpu and Ixbalanque, in defeating the lords of Xibalba, the underworld. The twins descend into the underworld, perish, and are eventually miraculously reborn. This myth provides a metaphor for the agricultural cycle and the annual rebirth of the crops. These two stories are focal points of Maya mythology and often found depicted in Maya art.

## THE CREATION MYTH

In Maya mythology, Tepeu and Gucumatz (also known as Kukulkan, and as the Aztec's Quetzalcoatl) are referred to as the Creators, the Makers, and the Forefathers. They were two of the first beings to exist and were said to be as wise as sages. Huracan, or the *Heart of Heaven*, also existed and is given less personification. He acts more like a storm, of which he is the god.

Tepeu and Gucumatz hold a conference and decide that, in order to preserve their legacy, they must create a race of beings who can worship them. Huracan does the actual creating while Tepeu and Gucumatz guide the process. Earth is created, but the gods make several false starts in setting humanity upon the earth. Animals were created first; however, with all of their howling and squawking they did not worship their creators and were thus banished forever to the forest.

Man is created first of mud, but they just crumbled and dissolved away. Other gods are summoned and man is next created of wood but has no soul, and they soon forgot their makers, so the gods turned all of their possessions against them and brought a black resinous rain down on their heads. Finally man is formed of masa or corn dough by even more gods and their work is complete. As such, the Maya believed that maize was not just the cornerstone of their diet, but they were also made of the same stuff.

### *Notable Gods*

* Ah Puch - God of Death

* Chaac - God of Rain and Thunder

* Camazotz - Bat god, tries to kill the Hero Twins in the *Popol Vuh.*

* Gucumatz - Snake god and creator.

* Hunahpu - One of the Maya Hero Twins.

* Huracan - Storm and fire god, one of the creator deities.
* Ixbalanque - One of the Maya Hero Twins.
* Ixchel - Earth and Moon goddess.
* Ixtab - Goddess of suicide.
* Zipacna - Underworld demon.

*Bacabs*

The Bacabs were four brothers, the sons of Itzamna and Ixchel. A creator god placed these skybearers at the four corners of the universe. Because each stands at one of the four cardinal directions, each is associated with a color and with a specific segment in the Maya calendar.

* Hobnil (later replaced by Chaac) - bacab of the east, is assigned the color red and the Kan years.
* Can Tzicnal - bacab of the north, is assigned the color white, and the Muluc years.
* Zac Cimi - bacab of the west, is assigned the color black and the Ix years.
* Hozanek - bacab of the south, is assigned the color yellow and the Cauac years.

References to the Bacabs are found in the writings of sixteenth-century historian Diego de Landa and the various Maya histories known as the Chilam Balams. At some point, the brothers became associated with the figure of Chac, a Maya rain god. In the YucatÃ¡n, the Maya of Chan Kom referred to the four skybearers as the four Chacs. They were also believed to be jaguar gods, and are associated with beekeeping. Like many other deities, the Bacabs were important in divination ceremonies, being approached with questions about crops, weather or the health of bees.

## THE FIRST HUMANS

### THE MEN

B'alam Agab:Meaning "night jaguar," he was the second of the men created from maize after the Great Flood sent by Hurakan. He married Choimha.

B'alam Quitze:Meaning "jaguar with the sweet smile," was the first of the men created from maize after the Great Flood sent by Hurakan. The gods created Caha-Paluma specifically for him to marry. Alernative names: Balam Quitze, Balam QuitzÃ

Iqi B'alam:Meaning "moon jaguar," he was the third of the men created from maize after the Great Flood sent by Hurakan. The gods created Cakixia specifically to be his wife.

Mahucatah:Meaning "distinguished name," he was the fourth of the men created from maize after the Great Flood sent by Hurakan. The woman Tzununiha was created just for him.

### *Their Wives*

Caha-Paluma:Meaning "falling water," she was a woman created specifically to be the wife of Balam-QuitzÃ.

Cakixia:Meaning "water of parrots," she was a woman created specifically to be the wife of Iqi-Balam.

Choimha:Meaning "beautiful water", she was a woman created by the gods specifically to marry B'alam Agab.

Tzununiha:Meaning "house of the water," she was a woman created specifically to be the wife of one of the first men, Mahucatah.

### *Gods and Supernatural Beings*

Ac Yanto:Considered responsible for the creation of European immigrants and their products. He appeared in the latter days of Maya civilization. His brother is the creator god Hachacyum and his name means 'our helper.'

Acan:The god of wine. His name means 'groan.'

Acat:The god of tattoo artists.

Ah Bolom Tzacab: Meaning "the lead-nosed god," he was a god of agriculture, thunder and rain. He was depicted with a leaf in his nose. Alternative names: Ah Bolon Dz'acab, God KAh

Cancum:A god of hunting.

Ah Chun Caan:The patron deity of the city of T'ho, modern MÃrida, YucatÃ¡n.

Ah Chuy Kak:A god of war.

Ah Ciliz:A god of solar eclipses.

Ah Cun Can:A god of war.Ah Cuxtal:A god of childbirth.

Ah Hulneb:Associated with the island of Cozumel, he was a god of war. Ah Hulneb means "he the spear thrower."

Ah Kin:Meaning "he of the sun," he was a solar deity and controlled disease and drought.

Ah Kumix Uinicob:Minor water gods.

Ah Mun:A maize god.

Ah Muzencab:The gods of bees.

Ah Patnar Uinicob:Minor water gods.

Ah Peku:The god of thunder.

Ah Tabai:The god of the hunt.

Ah Uincir Dz'acab:A god of healing and medicine.

Ah Uuc Ticab:A chthonic god of the Earth.

Ahau Chamahez:A god of medicine and good health.

Ahau-Kin: Meaning "lord of the sun face," he was a sun god and moon god; he had two manifestations. At night, he became a jaguar god and lord of the underworld.

Ahmakiq:An agriculture god who protected crops from the wind.

Ahulane:A war god, also called the archer. The island Cozumel was the location of Ahulane's shrine.

Ajbit:One of the thirteen creator gods who helped construct humanity from maize.

Ajtzak:One of the thirteen creator gods who helped construct humanity from maize.

Akhushtal:The goddess of childbirth.

Akna:Meaning "mother," she was a goddess of fertility and childbirth.

Alaghom Naom:A goddess of wisdom, consciousness, education and the intellect. Also known as Alaghom Naom Tzentel and the Mother of Mind.

Alom:A sky god and one of the creator deities who participated in the last two attempts at creating humanity.

Backlum Chaam:The god of masculine sexual prowess.

Balam:Any of a group of jaguar gods who protected people and communities against threats.

Balam-Agab:Meaning "night jaguar," he was the second of the men created from maize after the Great Flood sent by Hurakan. He married Choimha.

Bitol:A sky god and one of the creator deities who participated in the last two attempts at creating humanity.

Bolontiku:A group of underworld gods.

Buluc Chabtan:Sometimes referred to as "God F," he was a war god who received human sacrifices.

Cabaguil:A sky god.

Cabrakan:A god of mountains and earthquakes. He was a son of Vucub Caquix and Chimalmat. He had six children, though only the name of one survives: Chalybir.

Cacoch:A creator god.

Cakulha:A lightning god, an underling of Yaluk. His brother was Coyopa.

Camaxtli:A god of hunting, war, fate and fire (which he invented). He was one of the four creator gods, who made the Earth. The Chichimec considered him their tribal deity.

Camulatz:A bird that ate the heads of the first men.Cay:A water deity.

Chac Uayab Xoc:A fish god and the patron deity of fishermen. He blessed their catches, yet also ate them if they drowned.

Chalybir:The son of Cabrakan. He is only mentioned once in the surviving literature, in the epic "On the Shores of the Dead".

Chamer:A god of death, particularly popular in Guatemala. He was married to Ixtab.

Chaob:The four wind gods.

Chibirias:A goddess of the earth.

Chiccan:A group of four rain gods who live in lakes and make rain clouds from the water in those lakes. Each of the rain gods was associated with a cardinal direction, similar to the Bacabs. Chiccan was also the name of a day in the Tzolkin cycle of the maya calendar.

Chirakan:A fertility goddess.

Cit-Bolon-Tum:A boar-headed god of medicine and healing.

Chimalmat:A giant who, by Vucub Caquix, was the mother of Cabrakan and Zipacna.

Cizin:A god of death who lived in Metnal.

Colel Cab:A mother and fertility goddess.

Colop U Uichkin:A god of the sky.

Coyopa:The god of thunder and brother of Cakulha.

Cum Hau:A god of death and the underworld.

Ekchuah:Also spelled Ek Chuah, the "black war chief" was the patron god of warriors and merchants, depicted carrying a bag over his shoulder. In art, he was a dark-skinned man with circles around his eyes, a scorpion tail and dangling lower lip. In early modern studies of Maya art and iconography, he was sometimes referred to as God M before his identity was firmly established.

Ghanan:An agricultural and fertility god.

Hacha'kyum:Worshipped by the Lacandon people, he was their patron deity.

Hun Came:A demonic lord of the underworld Xibalba who, along with Vucub Caquix, killed Hun Hunahpu. They were killed by his sons, the Maya Hero Twins.

Hun Hunahpu:The father of the Maya Hero Twins Ixbalanque and Hun-Apu by a virgin. He was beheaded in Xibalba, the underworld, by the rulers of Xibalba, Hun Came and Vucub Caquix. His sons avenged his death.

Hunab Ku:The highest god. He rebuilt the world after three Great Floods, which came from the mouth of a sea monster. He is father of Itzamna and husband of Ixazalvoh.

Hunahpu-Gutch:One of the thirteen creator gods who helped construct humanity.

Itzamna:The founder of the Maya culture, he taught his people to grow maize and cacao, as well as writing, calendars and medicine. With Ixchel, he was the father of the Bacabs. He was associated with snakes and mussels. His father was Kinich Ahau or Hunab Ku. The city of Izamal was sacred to him.

Itzananohk'u:The patron god of the Lacandon people.

Ixmucane:One of the thirteen creator gods who helped construct humanity.

Ixpiyacoc:One of the thirteen creator gods who helped construct humanity.

Ixzaluoh:A goddess of water and weaving.

Kan-u-Uayeyab:A protector of cities.

Kan-xib-yui:A creator god.

Kianto:The god of foreign aliens, and the disease they brought with them.

K'in:Meaning "Sun" or day, he was a solar deity.

Kinich Ahau:A solar deity and father of Itzamna.

Kinich Kakmo:A solar deity represented by a macaw.

Nacon:A god of war.

Naum:The god who invented the mind and consciousness.

Nohochacyum:A creator god, he is the most important deity of the Lacandon. His name means "Our True Lord".

Qaholom :one of the second set of creator gods.

Tecumbalam:A bird that dearly injured the first men.

Tepeu:A sky god and one of the creator deities who participated in all three attempts at creating humanity.

Tlacolotl:A god of evildoers and villains.

Tohil:Tohil is the QuichÃ name for Huracan and was their patron deity. There was a great temple to him at their ancient capital of Rotten Cane (Q'umaraq aj or Gumarcaj).

Voltan:An earth and drum god (originally a human hero who was deified), married to Ixchel.

Vucub Caquix:A powerful ruling demon in the underworld, Xibalba, and, by Chimalmat, the father of the demonic giants Cabrakan and Zipacna. He and his children were arrogant and the divine twins Hunahpu and Ixbalangue killed Vucub Caquix and Zipacna, along with Vucub Caquix's co-regent in the underworld, Hun Came, as revenge for the beheading of their father Hun Hunahpu.

Xaman Ek:A god of travelers and merchants, who gave offerings to him on the side of roads while traveling.

Xecotcovach:A bird which tore the eyes out of the first men.

Xmucane and Xpiayoc:A deific creator god couple who helped creat the first humans. They are also the parents of Hun Hunahpu (one hunahpu) and Vucub Hunahpu (seven hunahpu). They were called Grandmother of Day, Grandmother of Light and Bearer twice over, begetter twice over and given the titles midwife and matchmaker.

Yaluk:The chief lightning god, and ruled over the lesser ones, such as Cakulha.

Yum Caax:The personification of maize and a god of agriculture and nature. Alternative names: Yum Kaax, God

EZotz:The god of bats, caves and the patron of the Tzotzil people. Zotz was also the name of one of the months of the Maya calendar. Alternative name: Zotzilaha, Sotz'

## Locations

Metnal:The lowest and most horrible of the nine hells of the underworld. It was ruled by Ah Puch. Ritual healers would intone healing prayers banishing diseases to Metnal.Xibalba:Also known as XibalbÃ¡ or Xibalbay, is a dangerous underworld ruled by the demons Vucub Caquix and Hun Came.

The road to it is said to be steep, thorny and very forbidding. Much of the Popol Vuh describes the adventures of the Maya Hero Twins in their struggle with the evil lords of Xibalba.

## PRE-COLUMBIAN MAYA DANCE

In pre-Columbian Maya civilization, ritual dance had great importance. However, since dance is a transient art, it is inherently difficult for archeologists to find and evaluate evidence of its role. There is little material information left behind, beyond a few paintings on murals and vases. This poverty of facts causes a wide range of interpretions by different archeologists.

Dance was a central component of social, religious, and political endeavors for the ancient Maya. The entire community danced, including kings, nobles, and common people. Dance served many functions such as creating sacred space, closing the gap between here and the otherworld, and releasing the dead from the grasp of the Xibalbans.

### Research

In 1966, Micheal Coe and Elizabeth Benson recognized the depiction of important lords standing with one heel raised was indicative of dancing. Even after this pose meaning was identified, most of the examples were either dismissed or not understood in the larger context of Maya history and religion.

In the spring of 1990, Nikolai Grube deciphered the glyph for "dance" (read as ak'ot) in Maya hieroglyphics. After this decipherment, it was clear that dance was one of the public actions most often depicted by Maya court artisans. The many representations of dancing people in the artwork show that the Maya kings and their courts were public performers. All of theses discoveries let archeologists know that dance was central to most of the public rituals of the ancient Maya.

Some interesting depictions of Maya dance of the Classic era are found on Maya ceramics and in the famous murals of Bonampak.

#### *Technique*

Ancient Maya dance is characterized by transformations of human beings into supernatural beings by means of visionary trance. Some think that hallucinogenic drugs or entheogenic medicines were used to put the performer into an altered state of mind. Once in this state of mind the participants were transformed into their *wayob* or soul companions. These soul companions were depicted through the masks and the costumes people wore in the dance. Some scenes are painted on pottery such as that from the myriad ritual meals of Classic festivals. These vessels depict humans, both kings and nobles, dressed in costumes. Their human faces are shown in cutaway view inside the costumes of the fantastic creatures they have become through the transformation of the dance. Some of these wayob are recognizable as animals like jaguars and birds of prey, but others just look like strange monsters.

For the Maya, dance was a very public affair. It induced visionary trances where either individuals or groups went into an altered state of mind that allowed them to communicate with the other world. Those who were strong enough to travel there, told stories about how the land had things like rivers and trees in this world. Some of the great Maya lords even depicted themselves dancing out over the abyss that leads into the otherworld.

One of the problems researchers have encountered is that the boundaries between humans dancing as supernatural beings and supernatural beings materializing in human rituals. The distinction between the two was never sharply made. Through dance, people became gods and gods became people even if it was only for a moment. It is important to note that these were more than just acts of civic pride or piety. They were considered to be direct connections to the otherworld.

## Meanings within Dances

One particular dance that has been discovered is called the Snake Dance. It was depicted on a panel that was looted from an unknown site. It depicted King Bird-Jaguar of Yaxchilan dancing with a snake. It also depicted the ruler of the town participating in important rituals with his king. Both men are wearing elaborate headdresses, personified wings, long feathers that arched behind them and they danced with snakes. The Snake Dance was also celebrated by the lords of Palenque. This time the dance was done with a male who has an ax in one hand and a serpent in the other, and a women who is grasping the lower body of the snake. These dancers wore costumes of First Father and First Mother, the deities whose actions enabled the final Creation and the birth of all the gods. This depiction is thought to point toward the role of dance in the story of Creation.

The importance of dance in the story of Creation is crucial because of its capacity to regenerate life. The story of the Popol Vuh exhibits examples of this idea. After the Hero Twins are killed they come back to life as vagabonds and quickly enchant the people of Xibalba wiih their dancing and magic.

The Twins danced such dances as the Dance of the Poorwill, the Weasel and the Armadillo and they are able to bring things back to life.

All of this fame caught the attention of the Lords of Death who command the Twins to perform. As the twins perform, the Lords are amazed by their powers and finally ask the Twins to sacrifice them. The Twins do, but this time they do not bring them back to life, limits the Xibalbans power over humans forever.

## MAYAN LANGUAGES

Mayan languages constitute a language family of related languages which are spoken in Mesoamerica, from southeastern Mexico to northern Central America, and as far south as Honduras. As a group of related languages, their collective origins can be reconstructed over at least some 5000 years of pre-Columbian habitation in the region. Although Spanish is an official language of the region's present-day countries (except for Belize, where English is official), many Mayan languages are still spoken as a primary or secondary language by more than 3 million indigenous Maya. As part of the 1996 Peace Accords, Guatemala recognized 21 Mayan languages by name.[1]

In pre-Columbian times, several forms and regional variants of Mayan languages were reflected in the writing system adopted and developed by peoples of the Maya civilization. Particularly from the period of Mesoamerican chronology known as the Classic period (c. 250-900 CE) and up to as late as the Spanish Conquest, this logosyllabic script was written on buildings, monuments, pottery and bark-paper codices.

## Note on Terminology

In the field of linguistic studies, it has become conventional to use the form *Mayan* when referring to the languages, or an aspect of the language. In other academic fields, the form *Maya* is the preferred usage, serving both as a singular and plural noun, and for the adjectival form.

In the Guatemalan highlands the Mayan language with the largest population, K'iche' (earlier spelled QuichÃ), is spoken by more than two million speakers (Ethnologue 2004). This language is the language in which the famous Maya mythological document the Popol Wuj was written. It is centered around the towns Chichicastenango and Quetzaltenango, and in the CuchumatÃ¡n Highlands. The K'iche' culture was at its pinnacle at the time of the Spanish conquest.

The most commonly spoken Maya language in Mexico is called Yucatec Maya by linguists but known simply as Maya to its speakers. It is currently spoken by approximately 900,000 people in the YucatÃ¡n Peninsula (Ethnologue 2004). It has a rich literature through the Spanish Colonial era, and remains common as the first language in rural areas in Yucatan today, where in many towns even Yucatecans of Spanish ancestry have a working knowledge of the tongue.

Another historically important Mayan language is Chol, formerly widespread, but only spoken today in pockets in Chiapas and Guatemala. A closely related language, Chorti, is spoken in a region around the boundaries of Honduras, Guatemala, and El Salvador. These particular languages are believed to be the most conservative in vocabulary and phonology, and are closely related to the language of the inscriptions of the ancient sites of the Classic era Central Lowlands.

The Classic Maya language is quite closely related to modern Chol and Yucatec, and the split between these two languages may be observed in Maya inscriptions.

In the Highlands of Guatemala are the QuichÃan-Mamean Maya languages and dialects, including K'iche, Cakchiquel, K'ekchi, Tz'utujil, Poqomam, and Mam. In the western highlands around Huehuetenango, Jacaltec is spoken.

The Huastec language, spoken in east-central Mexico, is part of the Mayan language family, although it is distant both linguistically and geographically from the rest of the language family.

Poqomchi' language is spoken in PurulhÃ¡, Baja Verapaz, and in the following municipalities of Alta Verapaz: Santa Cruz Verapaz, San CristÃ³bal Verapaz, Tactic, TamahÃº and TucurÃº.

Awakateko language is native only to 20,000 inhabitants of central AguacatÃ¡n, a municipality in the Department of Huehuetenango. It is also spoken by some immigrant Guatemalan households in Tuscarawas County, Ohio.

Sikapense language is spoken in Sipacapa, San Marcos (department).

Uspanteko language is native only in municipio UspantÃ¡n, in the department El QuichÃ.

Achi is spoken in Cubulco and Rabinal, two municipios of Baja Verapaz. Achi is one of Guatemala's 22 official languages. Linguist Raymond G. Gordon, Jr., considers the dialects spoken in Cubulco and Rabinal to be distinct languages, two of the eight languages of the Quiche-Achi family. [2]

Jakalteko language is also called Popti.[3] It is spoken in the following municipalities of Huehuetenango: Jacaltenango, La Democracia, ConcepciÃ³n, San Antonio Huista, Santa Ana Huista and in parts of NentÃ³n. Gordon recognizes Eastern and Western dialects of Jakalteko. [4]

Akateko language is spoken in the following municipalities of Huehuetenango: San Miguel AcatÃ¡n and San Rafael La Independencia.

*Language Families*

* Cholan-Tzeltalan languages

**Chol language

**Chorti language

**Chontal language

**Tzeltal language

**Tzotzil language

* Huastecan languages

**Huastec language

**Chicomuceltec language

* Kanjobalan-Chujean languages

**Chuj language

**Tojolabal language

**Jacaltec language

**Kanjobal language

**Mocho language

**Akateko language

* Quichean-Mamean languages

**Mam language

**Tektiteko language

**Ixil language

**Awakateko language

**Kekchi language

**Pocomam language [poqomam]

**Poqomchi' language

**Quichean languages

***QuichÃ language

***Cakchiquel language

***Tz'utujil language

***Quiche-Achi languages

***Sikapense language

***Sakapulteko language

***Uspanteko language

*Yucatecan languages

**Itza language

**Lacandon language

**Mopan language

**Yucatec Maya language

*Mayan Sign Languages

**Yucatec Maya Sign Language

## RELATION TO MESOAMERICAN WRITING

The pre-Columbian Maya civilization developed and used an intricate and versatile writing system which, out of the various historical Mesoamerican scripts known, displays the highest degree of correspondence to a spoken language. Earlier-established civilizations to the west and north of the Maya homelands also had scripts which are recorded in lasting~~surviving~~ inscriptions, such as those of the Zapotec, Olmec, as well as the Zoque-speaking peoples of the southern Veracruz - western Chiapas area. There is however insufficent available evidence to demonstrate whether these earlier scripts were also able to fully record all, or only some, aspects of their languages (or even to be sure which language they are associated with).

It is generally agreed that the Maya writing system was adapted from one or more of these preceding versions, many references (such as Schele & Freidel, 1990; Soustelle, 1984) identifying the Olmec script as the most likely precursor. The spoken language of the Olmec is unknown, and its relationship to early Maya spoken languages is still unclear.

The Maya writing system, known generally as Maya hieroglyphics, has however been confirmed as a fully-functioning writing system, in which it was possible to unambiguously express any statement of the spoken language. The script is a type best classified as logosyllabic, whose symbols (glyphs, or more formally *graphemes*) include both logograms and syllables. The script contains within it a complete syllabary (although not all possible syllables have been identified so far), and a Maya scribe could write an expression completely phonetically using these syllables. In practice however, almost all inscriptions of any length were written using a combination of logograms and syllabic signs.

Of the various Mayan languages, two major ones at least have been securely identified in the script, and at least one other is likely. An 'archaic' form known as Classic Maya appears predominantly, particularly in the Classic-era inscriptions of the southern and central lowland areas.

This language is most closely related to the Cholan branch of the language family, whose modern-day descendants include Ch'ol, Chorti and Chontal. Inscriptions in an early Yucatecan language (antecedent to the prevalent surviving Yucatec language) are also known or proposed, particularly from the YucatÃ¡n Peninsula region and from a later period; three of the four extant Maya codices are based on Yucatec.

It has also been surmised that some inscriptions found in the Chiapas region are in a Tzeltalan tongue, whose modern forms are Tzeltal and Tzotzil. Apart from these, regional variations and dialects are also presumed to have been used, but so far not securely identified.

## YUCATEC MAYA LANGUAGE

Yucatec Maya (or Yukatek in the revised orthography of the *Academia de Lenguas Mayas*, now preferred by scholars) is a Mayan language spoken in the YucatÃ¡n Peninsula, northern Belize and parts of Guatemala. To native speakers, it is known only as Maya - Yucatec is a tag linguists use to distinguish it from other Mayan languages (such as the QuichÃ language and the Lacandon language).

Yucatec Maya is written in the Latin script. This was introduced during the Spanish Conquest of Yucatan and the old Spanish orthography of that time was used (which included the use of "x" for the postalveolar fricative sound spelled "kh" in English, a sound that in Spanish has since turned into a uvular fricative nowadays spelled "j", except in a few orthographic archaisms such as "MÃxico"). In colonial times a reversed "c" was often used for the sound now more usually written "dz". The Maya were literate in pre-Columbian times, when the language was written using Maya hieroglyphs. The language itself can be traced back some 5000 years, derived from the Classic Maya language dialect Yucatecan.

A distinctive feature of spoken Yucatec (and other Mayan languages) is the use of ejective consonants - /p'/, /k'/, /t'/. These are often pronounced with a glottal stop just after the consonant release, resulting in a small popping sound as the sound is spoken. This is written using an apostrophe right after the letter, for example, *k'ux k'a k'al* (It's hot out.) The apostrophes indicating these sounds were not common in written Maya until the 20th century but are now preferred.

Yucatec is an agglutinative language and so many words in Yucatec can end up being very long. There are a great number of root words, prefixes, suffixes and affixes in Yucatec Mayan.

Like all Mayan languages, Yucatec is "Verb Subject Object"-language and an ergative language.

In the Yucatan it is many speakers' first language today, especially in rural areas.

### Vision Serpent

The Vision Serpent is an important creature in Pre-Columbian Maya mythology.

The serpent was a very important social and religious symbol, revered by the Maya. Maya mythology describes serpents as being the vehicles by which celestial bodies, such as the sun and stars, cross the heavens. The shedding of their skin made them a symbol of rebirth and renewal.

They were so revered, that one of the main Mesoamerican deities, Quetzalcoatl, was represented as a feathered serpent. The name means "quetzal serpent" ( Coe 1992:79).

The Vision Serpent is thought to be the most important of the Maya serpents. "It was usually bearded and had a rounded snout. It was also often depicted as having two heads or with the spirit of a god or ancestor emerging from its jaws". During Maya bloodletting rituals, participants would experience visions in which they communicated with the ancestors or gods. These visions took the form of a giant serpent "which served as a gateway to the spirit realm". The ancestor or god who was being contacted was depicted as emerging from the serpent's mouth. The vision serpent thus came to be the method in which ancestors or Gods manifested themselves to the Maya. Thus for them, the Vision Serpent was direct link between the spirit realm of the gods and the physical world. (Schele and Friedel, 1990:395)

The Vision Serpent goes back to earlier Maya conceptions, and lies at thecenter of the world as they conceived it. "It is in the center axis atop the World Tree. Essentially the World Tree and the Vision Serpent, representing the king, created the center axis which communicates between the spiritual and the earthly worlds or planes. It is through ritual that the king could bring the center axis into existence in the temples and create a doorway to the spiritual world, and with it power". (Schele and Friedel, 1990: 68)

The Vision Serpent is prevalent in Bloodletting ceremonies, in Maya religious practices, Maya jewelry, pottery and their architecture.

### Bloodletting Rituals

Many have attempted to explain the manifestation of the Vision Serpent in association with Maya bloodletting. One conclusion is "that massiveblood loss causes the brain to release an abundance of natural endorphins,which are chemically related to opiates.

As the body goes into shock, ahallucinatory vision occurs". Once the actual bloodletting was over, the bloodsoaked ceremonial papers were burned, releasing a column of smoke.The smoke provided the perfect medium for the Vision Serpent to appear. Every major political or religious event involved bloodletting because it provided a medium by which the gods could be called upon to witness and actually participate in the ceremony. Sometimes the spirits of ancestors were also called upon to give guidance. The Hauberg Stela (A. D. 199) from the Maya Lowlands "is one of the first dated monuments that depict the Vision Serpent's connection to bloodletting".

Lintel 25 depicts one of the bloodletting rituals. "One of Shield Jaguar's wives, is seen gazing up towards an enormous bicephalous Vision Serpent. In her left hand, she holds a bowl containing a stingray spine, an obsidian lancet, and papers spattered with blood. The Vision Serpent appears to be emanating from the bowl. From the jaws of the Vision Serpent, spews forth an ancestral Tlaloc warrior complete with spear and shield" (Graham and von Euw, 1977).

Lintel 17 refers to "Bird Jaguars as Blood Lord of Yaxchilan" and shows himpreparing to draw blood from his penis with a stingray spine. Opposite BirdJaguar is Lady Balam-Ix, who proceeds to pass course rope through a gouge in her tongue. The blood is being collected in the vessel near Bird Jaguar'sfeet. The Vision Serpent's mouth is green and, the trickles of bloodcharacteristic of bloodletting are red" (Graham and von Euw, 1977).

Lintel 15 depicts the appearance of this Vision Serpent. "The serpent can beseen rising out of the bowl with trickles of blood along a column of bloodscrolls. This lintel shows the queen of Yaxchilan involved in a visionaryexperience following an elaborate bloodletting ceremony. She holds the ritualparaphernalia in her arms while the vision serpent rises from a bowl of bloodstained paper".(Graham and von Euw, 1977).

## Maya Religious Rites

There was a Vision Serpent named Och-Kan, lord of Kalak'mul. One of the most common rituals associated with the Vision serpent involved invoking ancestral sprits. Especially during coronation rites, the kings would contact the spirits for guidance and blessings. It is the Vision Serpent who provides the medium for contacting these deities.

It is believed that Lord Pakal's sarcophagus lid, which was located at Palenque, is probably "the single most comprehensive image which relates the Vision Serpent to Maya religion". It depicts the death of Pakal and his descent into the Underworld. "The bicepalous serpent bar is placed horizontally on the World Tree and is the conduit for this transition. In the same way that the Vision Serpent represents a conduit between the physical world and the spirit realm of the ancestors, this bicephalous serpent bar represents a conduit between the realm of the living and the realm of the dead".

## Maya Jewelry and Pottery

A piece of Maya jewelry depicts an "anthropomorphic, bicephalous serpent". It is believed to have been worn during a bloodletting ceremony. It clearly shows the arrival of an ancestor from the spirit realm.

The portrayal of the Vision Serpent was very prevalent in Maya pottery. Vessels used during bloodletting ceremonies, depict the Vision serpent. The vessels below are excellent examples. They are carved in stone and are "some of the earliest depiction of Vision Serpent iconography. Blood spews forth from the open jaws of the front head. Although the rear is not physically attached, it sits just above the serpent's tail and also represents blood" (Schele and Miller, 1986).

## Maya Architectural Motifs

The Vision Serpent also finds a place in Maya architecture and is especially prominent in the decoration of pillars on the interior and exterior of Maya temples.

"In the palace at Labna, serpents adorn the corners of the principle facade. Characteristic of the Vision Serpent, there appears to be either an anthropomorphic deity or the spirit of an ancestor emanating from the gaping jaws of the serpent's mouth" (Ivanoff, 1973).

## Contemporary Observances

Remnants of the Vision Serpent have survived until modern times. Asrecently as "60 years ago, a documentary was done in San Antonio, Belize,revealing that the Q'eqchi Maya still perform a ritual very similar to thevision quest of the classic Maya. The ritual marks the initiation of a newshaman for the village. Although there are not many remnants of thebloodletting ceremony, the participant comes into direct contact with a giantserpent, Ochan (Och-Kan)" (National Geographic Society, 1982). It is through this experience that he completes his initiation rites and gains the knowledge that is needed to become a powerful shaman. Thus, modified vision quests still include contact with the Vision Serpent, among the Maya today.

### *The Ancient Maya*

The Maya occupied a vast area covering southeast Mexico and the Central American countries of Guatemala, Belize, Honduras and El Salvador. Mayan culture began to develop in the Pre-Classic period, around 1000 B.C. and was at its heyday between 300 and 900 A.D. The Maya are well known for their writing, of which a great part can now be read, as well as for their advanced mathematics, astronomy and calendrical calculations.

Despite sharing a common history and certain cultural attributes, ancient Mayan culture was extremely diverse, largely due to the range of geographic and environmental conditions in which it developed.

### *Mayan Writing*

The Maya devised an elaborate writing system which was largely deciphered in the 1980s. Prior to this, many archaeologists believed that Mayan writing dealt strictly with calendrical and astronomical themes, which went hand-in-hand with the concept that the Mayas were peaceful, studious stargazers. When Mayan glyphs were finally deciphered it became clear that the Maya were as interested in earthly matters as other Mesoamerican groups.

### *Mayan Mathematics, Calendar and Astronomy*

The Ancient Maya used a numerical system based on just three symbols: a dot for one, a bar for five and a shell which represented zero. Using zero and place notation, they were able to write large numbers and perform complex mathematical operations. They also formulated a unique calendar system with which they were able to calculate the lunar cycle as well as predict eclipses and other celestial events with great precision.

### *Mayan Religion and Mythology*

The Maya had a complex religion with a huge pantheon of gods. In the Mayan worldview, the plane on which we live is just one level of a multi-layered universe made up of 13 heavens and nine underworlds. Each of these planes is ruled by a specific god and inhabited by others. Hunab Ku was the creator god and various other gods were responsible for forces of nature, such as

Chac, the rain god. Mayan rulers were considered to be divine and traced their geneologies back to prove their descendence from the gods. Mayan religious ceremonies included the ball game, human sacrifice and blood-letting ceremonies in which nobles pierced their tongues or genitals to shed blood as an offering to the gods.

### *Mayan Ruins*

Coming upon impressive abandoned cities covered by vegetation in the middle of the jungle caused early archaeologists and explorers to wonder - who built these spectacular cities only to abandon them? Some surmised that the Romans or the Phoenecians were responsible for these magnificent constructions - from their racist perspective it was difficult to believe that the native people of Mexico and Central America could be responsible for such amazing engineering, architecture and artistry.

### *The Collapse of Mayan Civilization*

There is still much speculation about the decline of the ancient Mayan cities. Many theories have been put forward, ranging from natural catastrophes (epidemic, earthquake, drought) to warfare. Archaeologists today generally believe that a combination of elements brought about the collapse of the Mayan empire, probably brought on by severe drought and deforestation.

### *Present-day Mayan Culture*

The Maya did not cease to exist when their ancient cities went into decline. They live on today in the same areas their ancestors inhabited. Although their culture has changed over time, many Mayas maintain their language and traditions. There are over 750 000 speakers of Mayan languages living in Mexico today (according to INEGI). Present-day Mayan religion is a colorful hybrid of Catholicism and ancient beliefs and rituals. Some Lacandon Maya still live in a traditional manner in the Lacandon jungle of Chiapas.

## MAYAN RUINS OF THE YUCATAN PENINSULA

The Yucatan Peninsula offers many attractions: exquisite beaches along the Caribbean coastline, resort areas like Cancun and the Mayan Riviera, ecological reserves and waterparks, and the lovely colonial city of Merida. But among the Yucatan's most fascinating attractions are the amazing Mayan ruins which can be found throughout the area.

### Chichen Itza

"The edge of the well of the Itzaes"

One of Mexico's most important sites, for centuries Chichen Itza was the political, religious and military center of the North of the Yucatan Peninsula. The city flourished from 300 to 900 A.D., was abandoned, then re-established from 1000 to 1250 under Toltec rule. This is why there are two areas of Chichen, the "old" and the "new." The most well-known building of Chichen Itza is the Castillo, or "Castle," which was dedicated to Kukulcan, the Plumed Serpent. On the equinoxes a play of light and shadow on the stairs appears to take the form of a serpent.

Location: 75 miles (120 km) east of Merida and 60 miles (195 km) west of Cancun.

### Mayapan

"Mayan flag"

The site was part of a triple alliance with Chichen Itza and Uxmal, but was at its peak after the fall of Chichen Itza, between 1250 and 1450. It is considered the last great Mayan stronghold. The archaeological zone covers 4 square km and that area contains vestiges of nearly 4000 structures, mostly residential buildings. Several of the constructions contain mural paintings. Mayapan has a *Castillo* which is a replica of the one in Chichen Itza.

Location: 27 miles (43 km) south east of Merida

### Uxmal

"Three harvests" or "Three times built"

This is the most important site of the Puuc region and was at its peak between 600 and 1000 A.D. The legend of the city's founding involves a dwarf who outwitted the king, became the new ruler and magically constructed the buildings of Uxmal. The Pyramid of the Dwarf (also known as the Pyramid of the Magician) dominates the site. Many of the buildings are arrayed in ornate stone carvings.

Location: Uxmal is located 48 miles (77 km) south of Merida on federal highway 261.

### El Rey

"The king"

The original name of this site is unknown. The present name refers to a stone sculpture that was found on-site that depicts a head with an elaborate headdress. This stone is on exhibit in the Cancun Archaeology Museum. The excavated area contains 47 ancient structures which formed the center of a small city devoted to maritime trade and fishing.

Location: within Cancun's tourist resort area.

### Xcaret

"Little inlet"

This is an eco-park which encloses a small Mayan archaeological zone. Due to its location on one of the most important coves in the area, this site was a leading commercial port.

Location: 35 miles (72 km) south of Cancun

### San Gervasio

Inhabited from 200 A.D. until the Spanish conquest in the 1500s, this is the largest of 30 Maya sites found on Cozumel Island. It was the political and economical center of the island and also the sanctuary of the Mayan moon goddess Ixchel, deity of childbirth and fertility. Pilgrims from the entire Mayan world may have come to worship her.

Location: On the northern part of Cozumel island, Transversal highway Km 7.5

### Coba

"Ruffled water"

Functioning between 400 and 1000 A.D., Coba was built around four small lakes. Only a few of its estimated 6,500 structures have been uncovered. It was the hub of a complex network of causeways called *sacbeoob* (plural of *sacbe*- meaning white road). The Nohuch Mul Pyramid, the tallest in the area, has 120 steps and if you don't suffer from vertigo, from the top you can enjoy a breathtaking view of the surrounding jungle.

Location: 95 miles (150 km) from Cancun, 28 miles (45 km) from Tulum

### Xel-Ha

"Where the water is born"

A water park with ruins on-site, Xel-Ha's archaeological zone is only partially excavated. This was once an important sacred site where a variety of gods were honored. It was also a key ocean port and trade center. It went through two periods of flourishing, from 100 to 600 and again from early 12th century until the arrival of the Spaniards in the 1500s.

Location: 75 miles (122 km) south of Cancun

### Tulum

"Wall"

It is believed that the original name of this city meant dawn. The most spectacular aspect of Tulum is its stunning location right on a cliff by the clear turquoise water of the Caribbean Sea. The fortress city of Tulum had a population of only five to six hundred people within its walls, probably only nobles, and commoners dwelled outside the walls.

The site was at its peak between 1200 and 1520 and was one of the first sites mentioned by the Spaniards. The most important structures within the site are *El Castillo*, which functioned as a navigational aid, directing Mayan craft through the break in the reef to the beach, and the Temple of the Frescoes.

Location: 81 miles (131 km) south of Cancun on Highway 307.

## MAYA SITE FOUND

A newly discovered stone panel at the Classic Period Maya (AD 250-900) center of La Corona in Guatemala has confirmed the identification of that site as the long-sought Maya center once only known as "Site Q".

During the 1960s, between 30 and 35 stone panels carved with Maya hieroglyphic symbols became known to scholars. The panels had apparently been looted from an unknown classic period Maya capital city and acquired by museums all over the world. The panels were of high quality limestone and contained references to a previously unidentified city marked with a snakehead glyph emblem.

Peter Mathews, then a Yale graduate student and now at LaTrobe University, gave the unidentified Maya city the name of Site Q (short for 'Site ¿Que?' or 'which site?' in Spanish). Several of the glyphs on the panels illustrate athletes, ball players of the ancient Mesoamerican ball game in which players bet their lives. One athlete in particular is named on at least two panels; his name translates to Red or Great Turkey, and he appears on this panel from Site Q now in the Chicago Art Institute.

## MYSTERY OF SITE Q

The location of Site Q has been one of the great mysteries for scholars of the Maya civilization. Because it seemed unlikely that a Maya capital city would go undiscovered for so long, candidates for Site Q included the known sites of Calakmul and El Peru, also called Waka. But neither really fit the bill, for stylistic reasons: the steles and glyph panels recovered from Calakmul and El Peru simply did not compare well enough to the mysterious looted panels. There was clearly a connection between Calakmul and Site Q, but it didn't appear that they were one and the same. In 1996, a previously unknown Maya capital named La Corona was discovered in the jungles of the Peten peninsula, near Río San Pedro in northern Guatemala in the Laguna del Tigre region. La Corona had been severely looted, but scholars began to think that it was possible that the site represented Site Q.

## A CROWN OF FIVE TEMPLES

The La Corona site, as reported in Archaeology magazine when it was discovered in 1996, was called that because it had a row of five temples that looked like a crown to researchers Ian Graham and David Stuart of the Peabody Museum at Harvard. Although La Corona has experienced extensive looting, enough of the site remains to identify a main plaza about half the size of a football field. Two tall structures and an acropolis make up most of the intact portion of the site.

The west side of the plaza has mounds and two Maya altars, one of which is inscribed with the date May 2, AD 636, the 20th anniversary of the ascension of one of Maya rulers of Calakmul. Although there are no ballcourts, a typical feature of Maya cities, there are ballplayers illustrated on the stele, including one called Red or Great Turkey—the same Red or Great Turkey mentioned on the looted stele now at the Art Institute.

# 4

# The Role of the Plaza in Maya Festivals

Like many pre-modern societies, the Classic period Maya (AD 250-900 AD) used ritual and ceremony performed by the rulers or elites to appease gods, repeat historical events, and prepare for the future. But not all ceremonies were secret rituals; in fact, many were public rituals, theatrical performances and dances played in public arenas to unite communities and express political power relationships. Recent investigations of public ceremonialism by University of Arizona archaeologist Takeshi Inomata reveal the importance of these public rituals, both in the architectural changes made in the Maya cities to accommodate the performances, and in the political structure which developed alongside the festival calendar.

## MAYA CIVILIZATION

The 'Maya' is a name given to a group of loosely associated but generally autonomous city states, each led by a divine ruler. These small states were spread throughout the Yucatan peninsula, along the gulf coast and into the highlands of Guatamala, Belize and Honduras. Like small city centers anywhere, the Maya centers were supported by a network of farmers who lived outside the cities but were held by allegiances to the centers. At sites such as Calakınul, Copan, Bonampak, Uaxactun, Chichen Itza, Uxmal, Caracol, Tikal and Aguateca, festivals took place within the public view, bringing together the city residents and the farmers and reinforcing those allegiances.

## Festivals of the Maya

Many of the Maya festivals continued to be held into the Spanish colonial period, and some of the Spanish chroniclers such as Bishop Landa described festivals well into the 16th century. Three types of performances are cited in the Maya language: dance (okot), theatrical presentations (baldzamil) and illusionism (ezyah). Dances followed a calendar, and ranged from performances with humor and tricks to dances in preparation for war and dances mimicking (and sometimes including) sacrificial events. During the colonial period, thousands of people came from all around northern Yucatan to see and participate in the dances.

Music was provided by rattles; small bells of copper, gold and clay; tinklers of shell or small stones. A vertical drum called the pax or zacatan was made of a hollowed tree trunk and covered with an animal skin; another u- or h-shaped drum was called the tunkul. Trumpets of wood, gourd, or conch shell, and clay flutes, reed pipes and whistles were also used.

Elaborate costumes were part of the dances as well. Shell, feathers, backracks, headdresses, body plates transformed the dancers into historical figures, animals, and gods or other-worldly creatures. Some dances lasted all day, with food and drink brought to the participants who kept dancing. Historically, preparations for such dances were substantial, some rehearsal periods lasting for two or three months, organized by an officer known as a holpop. The holpop was a community leader, who set the key for the music, taught others and played an important role in festivals throughout the year.

## Audiences at Maya Festivals

In addition to Colonial period reports, murals, codices, and vases illustrating royal visits, court banquets, and preparations for dances have been the focus for archaeologists to understand the public ritual which predominated the classic period Maya. But in recent years, Takeshi Inomata has turned the study of ceremonialism at Maya centers on its head—considering not the performers or the performance but rather the audience for the theatrical productions. Where did these performances take place, what architectural properties were constructed to accommodate the audiences, what was the meaning of the performance for the audience?

Inomata's study involves a closer look at a somewhat less-considered piece of monumental architecture at classic Maya sites: the plaza. Plazas are big open spaces, surrounded by temples or other important buildings, framed by steps, entered via causeways and elaborate doorways. Plazas in Maya sites have thrones and special platforms where performers acted, and stelae—rectangular stone statues such as those at Copan—representing past ceremonial activity are also found there.

## Plazas and Spectacles

Plazas at Uxmal and Chichen Itza include low square platforms; evidence has been found in the Great Plaza at Tikal for the construction of temporary scaffoldings. Lintels at Tikal illustrate rulers and other elites being carried on a palanquin—a platform on which a ruler sat on a throne and was carried by bearers. Wide stairways at plazas were used as stages for the presentations and dances.

The plazas held thousands of people; Inomata reckons that for the smaller communities, nearly the entire population could be present at once in the central plaza. But at sites such as Tikal and Caracol, where over 50,000 people lived, the central plazas could not hold so many people. The history of these cities as traced by Inomata suggests that as the cities grew, their rulers made accommodations for the growing populations, tearing down buildings, commissioning new structures, adding causeways and building plazas exterior to the central city. These embellishments indicate what a crucial part performance for the audience was for the loosely structured Maya communities.

While carnivals and festivals are known today throughout the world, their importance in defining the character and community of governmental centers is less considered. As the focal point for gathering people together, to celebrate, prepare for war, or watch sacrifices, the Maya spectacle created a cohesion that was necessary for ruler and common people alike.

## MAYA CODICES

**Definition:** There are three surviving Maya codices known in the world: Dresden, Madrid, and Paris, named because that's where the codices ended up, in museums in those cities. The codices, essentially painted books made of bark cloth, were made in central America, by the Maya civilization and they illustrate towns, legends, kingly descent and other information that the Maya held sacred.

Originally there were probably hundreds of codices; the Spanish clerics burned most of them in 1521. How the codices from Central America got to Europe is unknown, although they were probably sent to Spain by the Spanish conquistador Hernan Cortes. One additional fragment, called the Grolier codex, was found in Mexico in 1965.

## MAYA RELIGION

The Mayan civilization arose in Mesoamerica around 250 AD, influenced by the culture and religion of the Olmecs. The Mayan urban culture especially flourished until about 900 AD, but continued to thrive in various places until the Spanish conquest.

During this first 650 years, which scholars call the Classic Period, the Mayan civilization consisted of more than 40 sizeable cities spread across modern-day Mexico, Guatemala, and northern Belize.

At its peak, the total population may have reached 2 million people, the majority of whom lived in modern-day Guatemala. The cities seem to have been mainly ceremonial centers, with the majority of the Maya living a rural, agricultural life around the cities.

Sometime after 900 AD, the Mayan culture declined dramatically and most of the cities were abandoned. Latest scholarship attributes this decline to the loss of trade routes due to war.

The great southern cities became depopulated, but the cities of the Yucatan peninsula in Mexico (such as Chichen Itza, Uxmal, and Mayapan) continued to thrive in the early part of the "Post-

Classic Period" (900–1519). By the arrival of the Spanish in the early 16th century, however, most of the Maya were village-dwelling farmers.

The remaining Maya were conquered by the Spanish and converted (at least nominally) to Roman Catholicism. The present-day Mayan peoples are spread mainly across southern Mexico, with small numbers in Guatemala and Belize. They practice a religion that combines Roman Catholicism with Mayan cosmology, deities, and domestic rituals.

The Maya had a highly sophisticated culture, and this included a written hieroglyphic language. Mayan hieroglyphics were carved into stone monuments or pieces of bone, painted on pottery, and written on books (codices) of bark paper.

Mayan texts describe religious rituals, astronomy, and divination, and are the most valuable source of information on the ancient civilization. Many of them were destroyed by the Spanish because of their pagan religious content, but three main codices have survived. Named for the cities in which they are now kept, these are the Dresden, Madrid, and Paris codices. The Dresden Codex contains very precise tables of Venus and the moon and describes a method of predicting solar eclipses.

Other important texts are those written by learned Indians who transcribed or summarized Mayan hieroglyphic records into Latin script. One of these is the *Books of Chilam Balam,* written in Yucatec Maya and consisting of historical chronicles mixed with myth, divination, and prophecy. Another text, *The Ritual of the Bacabs,* covers religious symbolism, medical incantations, and similar matters.

Perhaps the most famous of these texts is the *Popol Vuh* (1554-1558), which was written in Quiche, a highland Maya language, and translated into Spanish by a priest. This tells of the mythology and cosmology of the Postclassic Guatemalan Maya, and shows central Mexican influences. It chronicles the creation of man, the actions of the gods, the origin and history of the Quiche people, and the chronology of their kings down to 1550.

These Mayan texts were not regarded as sacred or authoritative in themselves (they are not revelations from the divine like the

Bible or Quran), but rather as important records of religious rituals and knowledge.

### Beliefs

The Maya worshipped a pantheon of nature gods, each of which had both a benevolent side and a malevolent side. The most important deity was the supreme god Itzamna, the creator god, the god of the fire and god of the hearth.

Another important Mayan god was Kukulcan, the Feathered Serpent, who appears on many temples and was later adopted by the Toltecs and Aztecs as Quetzalcoatl. Also important was Chac, a hooked-nose god of rain and lightning.

A third god that frequently appears in Mayan art is Bolon Tzacab, who is depicted with a branching nose and is often held like a sceptre in rulers' hands. He is thought to have functioned as a god of royal descent.

Mayan rulers were seen as intermediaries between the gods and the people, and as semi-divine themselves. They were buried in elaborate tombs filled with valuable offerings.

The Mayan view of the afterlife consisted primarily of a dangerous voyage of the soul through the underworld, which was populated by sinister gods and represented by the jaguar, symbol of night. The majority of Maya, including the rulers, went to this underworld. Heaven was reserved for those who had been sacrificed or died in childbirth.

To the Maya, science and religion were one and the same. The Maya developed an impressive system of mathematics and astronomy, which was initimately related to religious rituals. Their mathematical achievements included positional notation and the use of zero; in astronomy, they accurately calculated a solar year, compiled precise tables of positions for the Moon and Venus, and were able to predict solar eclipses.

The Maya were obsessed with time; to understand and predict various cycles of time allowed them to adapt to and best make use of their natural world. Mayan cosmology had it that the world had been created five times and destroyed four times. On a more temporal scale, the various days of the year were considered appropriate to specific activities, while some were entirely unlucky.

### Practice

The Maya practiced a form of divination that centered on their elaborate calendar system and extensive knowledge of astronomy. It was the job of the priests to discern lucky days from unlucky ones, and advising the rulers on the best days to plant, harvest, wage war, etc. They were especially interested in the movements of the planet Venus — the Maya rulers scheduled wars to coordinate with its rise in the heavens.

The Mayan calendar was very advanced, and consisted of a solar year of 365 days. It was divided into 18 months of 20 days each, followed by a five-day period that was highly unlucky. There was also a 260-day sacred year (tzolkin), divided into days named by the combination of 13 numbers and 20 names.

For longer periods, the Maya identified an elaborate system of periods and cycles of various lengths. In ascending order, these were: *kin* (day); *uinal* (20 days); *tun* (18 uinals/360 days); *katun* (20 tuns/7,200 days); *baktunbaktun* (20 katuns/144,000 days), and so on, with the highest cycle being the *alautun* (23,040,000,000 days).

These units were used in the Maya Long Count, which calculated the time elapsed from a zero date set at 3114 BC. In the Postclassical Period, the method of notation was somewhat simplified, and the Long Count *katuns* end with the name *Ahau* (Lord), combined with one of 13 numerals; and their names form a Katun Round of 13 *katuns*.

This change makes it difficult to correlate the Mayan count with the Christian calendar, but scholars are fairly confident that the *katun* 13 Ahau, which seems to have had great significance for the Mayan, ended on November 14, 1539. It has been calculated that the next *katun*, which the *Popul Vuh* describes as the catastrophic end of the world, will end on December 21, 2012. Naturally, this has inspired quite a bit of speculation as to what might happen on this date.

Until the mid-20th century, scholars believed the Maya to be a peaceful, stargazing people, fully absorbed in their religion and astronomy and not violent like their neighboring civilizations to the north. This was based on the Maya's impressive culture and scientific discoveries and a very limited translation of their written texts.

But since then, nearly all of the Mayan hieroglyphic writings have been deciphered, and a much different picture has emerged. The texts record that the Mayan rulers waged war on rival Mayan cities, took their rulers captive, then tortured them and ritually sacrificed them to the gods.

In fact, human sacrifice seems to have been a central Mayan religious practice. It was believed to encourage fertility, demonstrate piety, and propitiate the gods. The Mayan gods were thought to be nourished by human blood, and ritual bloodletting was seen as the only means of making contact with them. The Maya believed that if they neglected these rituals, cosmic disorder and chaos would result.

At significant ceremonies, the sacrificial victim was held down at the top of a pyramid or raised platform while a priest made an incision below the rib cage and ripped out the heart with his hands. The heart was then burned in order to nourish the gods.

It was not only the captives who suffered for the sake of the gods: the Mayan aristocracy themselves, as mediators between the gods and their people, underwent ritual bloodletting and self-torture. The higher one's position, the more blood was expected. Blood was drawn by jabbing spines through the ear or penis, or by drawing a thorn-studded cord through the tongue; it was then spattered on paper or otherwise collected as an offering to the gods.

Other Mayan religious rituals included dancing, competition, ball games, dramatic performances, and prayer to the gods.

Most of us are not archaeologists or astronomers, anthropologists or astrologers. Yet the majority of what is written about one of the most exciting and relevant subjects of our day - the approaching Winter Solstice 2012 end-date of the Mayan Calendar - appears in words aimed at specialists and couched in language that can be hard to read. This article is written for the Everyday Earthling who may be hearing a lot about the Mayans, their calendars, hieroglyphs and mysterious temples scattered throughout the jungles of Mexico, Guatemala, Belize and Honduras.

Let us begin with some questions. Why is there so much talk about the "end of the Mayan calendar" and what does it mean? Is there something significant we should know about the Winter Solstice date of December 21, 2012? How were the Mayans able to track long periods of time and why would they want to? Why should we care about the Mayans today? Is there anything we can learn from them? I'll begin by sharing how my own interest in the subject developed and go on from there.

I first learned about the Mayans in 1987 from Jose Arguelles' book The Mayan Factor. It was during the months leading up to the event known as Harmonic Convergence that Arguelles, artist and visionary, introduced me to the 20 Mayan daysigns and the thirteen Mayan numbers - and to the wonderfully engaging and mysterious 260 day Mayan ceremonial calendar, called the Tzolkin (pronounced chol-kin). My pursuit of knowledge about pre-Columbian culture had begun.

A great deal of scientific and visionary research work has been done about the Mayans, so I started reading. I learned that the Mayans tracked cycles within cycles within cycles of time. Their calendar acted as a harmonic calibrator, linking and coordinating the earthly, lunar, solar and galactic seasons in an aesthetically simple and elegant manner. The provocative simplicity of the daysigns and the sheer harmony of the calendar drew me in. Then a landmark article by John Major Jenkins appeared in Mountain Astrologer magazine in 1994, revealing for the first time in our era the true meaning of the end-date.

Is there something significant we should know about the Winter Solstice date of December 21, 2012? Yes. On this day a rare astronomical and Mayan mythical event occurs. In astronomic terms, the Sun conjuncts the intersection of the Milky Way and the plane of the ecliptic. The Milky Way, as most of us know, extends in a general north-south direction in the night sky. The plane of the ecliptic is the track the Sun, Moon, planets and stars appear to travel in the sky, from east to west. It intersects the

Milky Way at a 60 degree angle near the constellation Sagittarius. The cosmic cross formed by the intersecting Milky Way and plane of the ecliptic was called the Sacred Tree by the Maya. The trunk of the tree, the Axis Mundi, is the Milky Way, and the main branch intersecting the tree is the plane of the ecliptic. Mythically, at sunrise on December 21, 2012, the Sun - our Father - rises to conjoin the center of the Sacred Tree, the World Tree, the Tree of Life..

This rare astronomical event, foretold in the Mayan creation story of the Hero Twins, and calculated empircally by them, will happen for many of us in our lifetime. The Sun has not conjoined the Milky Way and the plane of the ecliptic since some 25,800 years ago, long before the Mayans arrived on the scene and long before their predecessors the Olmecs arrived. What does this mean?

Due to a phenomenon called the precession of the equinoxes, caused by the Earth's wobble that lasts almost 26,000 years, the apparent location of the Winter Solstice sunrise has been ever so slowly moving toward the Galactic Center. Precession may be understood by watching a spinning top. Over many revolutions the top will rise and dip on its axis, not unlike how the Earth does over an extremely long period of time. One complete rise and dip constitutes the cycle of precession.

The Mayans noticed the relative slippage of the positions of stars in the night sky over long periods of observation, indicative of precession, and foretold this great coming attraction. By using an invention called the Long Count, the Mayans fast-forwarded to anchor December 21, 2012 as the end of their Great Cycle and then counted backwards to decide where the calendar would begin. Thus the Great Cycle we are currently in began on August 11, 3114 B.C. But there's more.

The Great Cycle, lasting 1,872,000 days and equivalent to 5,125.36 years, is but one fifth of the Great Great Cycle, known scientifically as the Great Year or the Platonic Year - the length of the precession of the equinoxes. To use a metaphor from the modern industrial world, on Winter Solstice A.D. 2012 it is as if the Giant Odometer of Humanity on Earth hits 100,000 miles and all the cycles big and small turn over to begin anew. The present world age will end and a new world age will begin.

Over a year's time the Sun transits through the twelve houses of the zodiac. Many of us know this by what "Sun sign" is associated with our birthday. Upping the scale to the Platonic Year - the 26,000 year long cycle - we are shifting, astrologically, from the Age of Pisces to the Age of Aquarius. The Mayan calendar does not really "end" in 2012, but rather, all the cycles turn over and start again, vibrating to a new era. It is as if humanity and the Earth will graduate in the eyes of the Father Sun and Grandmother Milky Way.

Why should we care about the Mayans today? Is there anything we can learn from them? The trees give us oxygen to breathe and help create the nourishing rains upon which we depend, sustaining life. We are missing these rains in places where the trees have been cut down or burned. Fires begin that nature can no longer extinguish. For the Mayans, trees were intermediaries between the physical and spiritual worlds, and absolutely essential to life. They believed that without the tree man could not survive and that "with the death of the last tree comes the death of the human race."

The ancient carved stones and the stars themselves tell us we are on the brink of a new world age. There is no reason not to take a leap of faith into imagining what may be in store. We may trust that it is time for humanity to awaken into a true partnership with each other, with the Earth, and the Cosmos. By accepting this partnership we may claim our birthright and become Galactic Citizens who care for and sustain the planet, thus sustaining ourselves. This is clearly the challenge of our times. Yet, arriving just in time and on schedule is the Winter Solstice dawn on the day we may remember that we are truly Children of the World.

## ON MAYAN ASTROLOGY

People have used astrology for thousands of years to learn about themselves and link their existence to a larger whole. Astrology is used to put life into perspective, to explain what is happening and what might happen. I am going to tell you a bit about how the Mayan calendar is used, and can be used by you, astrologically.

Astrology is both art and science, allowing for creativity within a defined system. Traditional western astrology is based on the 365-day solar calendar and depends on counting days as the zodiac is navigated over the course of a year. The Maya keep a 260-day calendar named the Tzolkin (pronounced chol-kin), their most basic module of time that plugs into the circuitry of their entire fantastically harmonic calendar system. Of course the Maya also keep a 365-day calendar, named the Haab. And there is the Tun, a 360-day cycle.

The Tzolkin (meaning Book of Days) runs its 260-day cycles over and over again. There are Mayan daykeepers living today who continue to count a sequence of days unbroken for well over 2000 years. Each day one of the 20 Mayan daysigns combines with one of thirteen Mayan numbers, weaving the ceremonial cycle. While there is much to say about the Maya and their time-keeping, we are going to focus on the basic 260-day cycle that happens to be the length of the human gestation period.

As the same combination of daysign and number arrives every 260 days, I would like you to consider that you experience a "ceremonial birthday" every 260 days. The daysign and number unique to your day of birth are imprinted deep in the template of your existence. Thus the Tzolkin gives us information about ourselves, individually, and serves to place us within a greater whole, like astrology does with its sun and moon signs, rising signs and other aspects.

The Tzolkin goes as far as to place us within a galactic context, but now we are getting ahead of ourselves. The larger wheels of the Mayan calendar will be discussed in future installments, and we will talk then about the Winter Solstice A.D. 2012 end-date of the Mayan Great Cycle, an event that will happen, for many of us, in our lifetimes. I find it is often most helpful to begin by discovering our own personal relationship with the Tzolkin. Then we can relate easier to larger cycles.

If you were born into certain Mayan tribes the daysign and number on your birthday could be part of your name. You might be 3 Rain, 4 Wind, 1 Deer or 13 Flower. There are particular qualities, predispositions, strengths and weaknesses implied and, some would say, encoded, in each combination of daysign and number. The daysigns are generally named after aspects of nature and have both earthly qualities and esoteric connotations. Thus Wind is also Spirit, House is also Heart, Death is also Revelation, and Flower is also Knowledge and Wisdom.

The numbers are equally curious. Some numbers make logical sense, such as One representing Unity and two, Polarity. Other numbers are understood by deduction, such as Five, the number of Center, around which the four directions turn. Some numbers such as Eleven and Twelve may ask you to spend some time with them before you can receive their message. Both the daysigns and numbers have reciprocal relationships, just as opposite houses of the zodiac relate to each other.

As this web page grows, we will talk about each of the daysigns and numbers, and learn what the Tzolkin looks like and how it operates. You will be able to find out what your Mayan birthday is and I'll show you how to set up your own Ceremonial Calendar to run side-by-side your yearly solar calendar.

Learning about Mayan calendrics and cosmology (of course they are intertwined) has added a depth to my life and a perspective on our times that I feel has great value, and I want to share it with others. The wisdom of our ancestors, whether we have direct blood connections with them or not, is here for us - provided we bring it into our lives in a respectful manner with a right intent.

Humanity is on the brink of ending one millennium and beginning another. An astrological shift from the Age of Pisces to the Age of Aquarius is in our midst. And the Mayan Great Cycle turns over in 2012, ending one world age and beginning another. This is such an exciting time to be alive! To be continued!

# 5

# The Mayan Connection—Los Cimientosalliance

## INTRODUCTION

Since 1991, The Mayan Connection-Los Cimientos Alliance has served the Maya K'iche landowners of Los Cimientos and their families as humanitarian resource development and human rights advocates.

The community of Los Cimientos was displaced from their land after large scale massacres during the Guatemalan civil war in the 1980´s, becoming one group among many of Guatemala´s internally displaced peoples. During the long years of stuggle, the people of Los Cimientos endured hardships and attempted to regain their land as part of a widespread movement across Guatemala to build a functioning civil society and seek justice for the victims of the war, as promised in the Peace Accords that ended the fighting in 1996.

In 1991 elders from the Los Cimientos community asked a representative from the Mayan Connection for international help. Driven from their land and suffering as refugees, the women in the community asked for help in finding food and medicine for their children; the men asked for assistance in their struggle to regain their land. The Mayan Connection responded and has since raised funds, provided human rights accompaniment, organized food supplies and helped to develop an artisans project. This assistance became crucial to the community's survival when they were violently driven from their land in 2001. The network created during Mayan Connection's presentations has proved to be essential to the process of negotiating a just resolution in this case. Their daily struggle for survival continues today on their new land in San Vicente. We invite you to learn more about the on-going story of Los Cimientos. This community is one among thousands of Guatemalan Mayan communities confronting the abyss of cultural annihilation.

## HISTORY

### Origins

The ancestors of today's Los Cimientos Maya K'iche community moved to the land known as Los Cimientos in the late 1800s. Situated in the municipality of Chajul, in the department of Quiche, in the Cuchamatanes Mountains, the land is rich and productive, allowing for a traditional highland Guatemala agricultural life. After suffering military oppression dating back to the times of the conquistadors the community decided to try and find a safe place to settle in the mountains Cuchumatan Mountains, where they engage in subsistence agriculture rather than work on Latino owned plantations.

So as to avoid potential conflict with the neighbouring Maya Ixil people, community leaders approached the Maya Ixil council in Chajul to ask if they could move their families to an area of land that was then uninhabited. The Ixil elders gave them their blessing along with a document from the Chajul Town Council that gave the community of Los Cimientos the right to settle on the land. The people of Los Cimientos began to rebuild their community while living peacefully with their Ixil neighbors.

In 1900 the president of Guatemala, Manuel Estrada Cabrero, initiated a process of giving land titles for those areas of land outside municipality holdings. In 1909 an elder on behalf of the community of Los Cimientos received title to the land from the president. This title was inscribed in the Second Registry of Property in Quetzaltenango. In the mid 1930s Diego Itzep Rojop, a respected leader, inherited the title to the land from his father. In 1973 he decided to give land titles to a further 65 members of the community. Each of these titles were registered with the Registry of Property in Quetzaltenango.

## Massacres in the Mountains

After the 1954 coup which overthrew the democratic government of Jacob Arbenz, Guatemala suffered a string of military dictatorships and civil war against revolutionary liberation movements. In the early 1980´s the dictatorships of Lucas García and Rios Montt engaged in widespread massacres of indigenous populations in an effort to eradicate the social support for the rebel movements. The people of Los Cimientos were not spared.

On May 24th 1981, fifteen members of the community went to the market in Finca San Francisco to sell produce. On that day the army surrounded the market and slaughtered many of the innocent men, women and children, including fourteen residents of the Los Cimientos community. The only survivor from Los Cimientos was a nine year old child who had been hidden under the bodies.

Shortly after this attack the army invaded Los Cimientos and accused the people of being sympathizers with the guerilla. The army found two elders, Mayan priests in their 70´s lighting candles and praying in the cemetery. The soldiers brutally killed them in front of the rest of the community. The families of the community were told by the army to leave before they were killed by the bombing that would shortly commence. The community fled their land and headed through the mountain paths witnessing friends and neighbors being tortured and burnt as homes and villages were destroyed.

The Los Cimientos families only managed to take a handful of personal belongings with them. Some families later returned to their land to try and salvage what they could, but they found everything burnt to the ground. The community thus began a stretch of thirteen years living as refugees while being exploited as a cheap source of labor in the surrounding fincas-large export oriented plantations.

## The Struggle for Land

In 1985 the people of Los Cimientos presented a petition to the Guatemalan President Venicio Cerezo. He referred the case to INTA (Instituto Nacional de Transportacion de la Agricultura) and after an investigation that organization concluded that the people of Los Cimientos were the rightful owners of the land. However, INTA lacked the apparatus to enforce such a finding and thus referred the case to the Court of First Instance in Santa Cruz de Quiche.

In a terrible reminder of the illegal influence of the military over the Guatemalan judicial system during that era, the court found that, due to the role of the military within the armed conflict the courts had no power to order the return of the land. Again in 1987 and 1989 the owners of Los Cimientos presented petitions to the President only to be referred again to INTA and the Court of First Instance and to be given similar responses.

In 1989 the community was told by the government that they could return to their land. The community returned to visit their land to find that their ancestral cemetery had been destroyed, and a army base had been built on that sacred site. As part of a widespread plan to bring indigenous communities under government and army control, the army had resettled fifty Maya Ixil families to live in Los Cimientos. They created a village on the former cemetery in 1989 that is known today as Xeputul. These families were part of the Civil Patrol, meaning they were armed and participated, without pay, in military patrols of the area. They were originally residents and land owners near the town of Chajul.

The original Los Cimientos Maya K´iche community persevered with their efforts to reclaim their land and hired a lawyer in 1990 who initiated a lawsuit in the Court of First Instance in Quiche. Again they received the same response that their titles to the land were valid but the court couldn't enforce their claim against the Minister of Defense. Later in 1992 representatives of the community approached CERJ (the Council of Ethnic Communities) one of the leading human rights organizations in Guatemala at that time. CERJ organized several meetings that were attended by all the relevant parties. In July 1992 INTA stated that the land was registered in the community members' names but that the involved parties should resolve the issue through the court system! CERJ continued to hold meetings with governmental agencies, the Ixil and the K'iche.

### Return Come what May

In August 1994 after receiving government approval the people of Los Cimientos took the decision to re-occupy their land, and take the risks involved in facing the hostility of the Ixil Civil Patrol. They returned and occupied approximately one-third of their rightfully owned land while the Ixil continued to live on the other two-thirds. This quickly led to government response, and by August 7th the army, two governmental agencies along with the K'iche and Ixil signed an agreement that a final study of the facts would be made and those who were not the legal owners would leave the land peacefully. The governmental agencies would purchase land for the non legal occupants to settle elsewhere. In February 1995 a presidential commission studied all documentation and published a report that again confirmed the legitimacy of the K´iche titles. The K'iche were to return to their legally owned land.

The government, however, continued to support the Ixil and refused to aid the K'iche, leaving them to petition again. The result has been incessant conflicts between the two ethnic groups, with the Ixil taking a variety of illegal and violent steps to stop the K´iche community from taking posession of the entirety of their lands. The Ixil have destroyed food crops, killed their horses and installed a water system that cut off the K'iches water supply. Moreover, the Ixil community has been able, through access to envangelical religious groups and donor organizations such as US AID, to strengthen their own infrustructure and power positions at the expense of the K´iche community. None the less, the K´iche community of Los Cimientos continued to live on the small part of their ancestral lands that they could.

### History Repeats Itself

On the 25th June 2001 the K´iche families of Los Cimientos were awoken at dawn by a group of men armed with machetes, guns and sharpened sticks the size of baseball bats. The community was told they had two hours to leave Los Cimientos or they would be killed. So as to reinforce this point, the armed men raped at least two K´iche women in front of their young children. Once again the K'iche landowners were forced to flee their homes and their land, leaving behind their possessions, food and crops, and becoming once again impoverished internal refugees.

The community fled to the lands of Xeputul II near Cotzal, a village of 29 houses which is on colder land, and not sufficient in size for the 230 families. Moreover, they were subject to further human rights abuses there. On December 29, 2001, the community again moved to Batzula Churrancho, Cunen, also in Quiche, where they are safer.

Police reports have been filed but to date the police have made no arrests nor helped to return the community to their land. This is even after the leaders of the Ixil community during negotiations admitted that they were responsible for the crimes and that the K'iche are the legal owners of the land. The Ixil continue to threaten further violence if the K'iche families of Los Cimientos try to return to their land.

The government response is that they are powerless to enforce the rule of law, and cannot move the Ixil from the land. The Government is now offering to buy other land for the K'iche. However, high population pressures make fertile land in Guatemala difficult to find, and lands of the beauty, fertility and value of Los Cimientos are rare. Since the attack in June the community has offered to sell part of their land to the government for a fair market price (estimated at US $7,500,000 based on similar property sales). However the government refuses to consider buying the land and insists that they accept other land in exchange. The lands that are being offered to the community are between ten and twenty times smaller than their own land.

## Conclusion

Today's Los Cimientos community consists of 230 Maya K'iche families who are again living as internal refugees within Guatemala. The community's leaders attend what seem to be endless resolution/negotiation meetings with the government and plead with humanitarian organizations to continue providing survival rations. While they are able to find some legal help with respect to their case before the Inter American Commission on Human Rights, they are severely lacking in resources to hire lawyers for help within the Guatemala legal system. The lack of education and Spanish fluency makes negotiating with the Guatemala government and with aid organizations difficult.

### Update - Recent Events: 2002 - 2004

On December 8th, 2002 Los Cimientos families abandoned all hope of returning home to their fields in Los Cimientos and relocated to new land in San Vicente. Forced by hunger, inadequate housing in a freezing climate and the prospect of being forcibly driven again from their tenuous refugee site, community leaders accepted the new land exchange offered by the government of president Alfonzo Portillo. The community sacrificed Los Cimientos (6000 acres with 5 pure water rivers, producing 3 to 4 harvests a year of a wide variety of organically grown crops) in trade for San Vicente (about 2000 acres with one polluted river and 2 to 3 harvests a year possible with the use of agricultural chemicals).

The government of Guatemalan president Portillo proclaimed this land exchange to be a great victory for the government's resolution of the Los Cimientos case - citing it as second in importance to the peace accords.

This governmental communications ministry announced around the clock on national T.V. that this was a reconciliation between the K'iche and the Ixil. In legally signed agreements, the Guatemalan government promised to give the community food support until their own food crops were established and on-site health care. The promises also included infrastructure and houses to replace those lost in the Ixil attack on Los Cimientos. All these promises remain unfulfilled - though government word games try to make legal channels believe they have fulfilled the agreements. Children have died from malnutrition and suffer from malnutrition-related illnesses. There are no medicines available.

On January 15th the newly elected government of Oscar Berger came into power. Now, the Berger government assumes responsibility for a Guatemala with an staggering legacy of problems on all levels, among them, the promises made by Portillo and his representatives to resolve the Los Cimientos land case justly and with dignity.

**TIMELINE**

Hundred Year Timeline of Events in Los Cimientos / Xetzununchaj

Sources: Community of Los Cimientos Archives, CONTIERRA History, Los Cimientos Alliance, Rights Actions.

1887: First known official acknowledgment that Los Cimientos belongs to the K'iche - Pedro and Maximo Ysep (Itzep) receive approval from the Chajul Ixil Town Council to claim the area known today as Finca Los Cimientos.

1909: Guatemalan President, Manuel Estrada Cabrero, in a national grant program, officially grants Pedro and Maximo Ysep (Itzep) land title to Los Cimientos after a witnessed survey, is ratified by majority of Ixil Town Council. Two members of the Town Council, Sr. Caba and Rivera object on the grounds that they believe that Chajul lands extend to the Putul River.

This idea is shown to be in error at the time of the survey after careful study of Chajul municipality title. Ysep (Itzep) title is recorded in the Public Register of Quetzaltenango. Pedro and Maximo Yzep apply for and receive Titulos Inmuebles Registrado.

1935: The K'iche (Ysep/Itzep) ownership re-inscribed in the Public Register under the names of descendants of the Ysep/Itzep brothers, Diego Itzep Rojop - (a respected, elected community leader) and Felipe Itzep Tum. These titles are Titulos Inmuebles Registrado.

1967: Municipalities of Cotzal and Chajul attempt to claim Finca Los Cimientos land through court actions. Court decisions are that the K'iche titles are affirmed and that the cases are considered Casos Juzgado - court decisions that are binding for all time - never to be retried or legally questioned.

1969: Ixil from Santa Rosa, Chajul invade Los Cimientos and kill two Los Cimientos landowners. Diego Itzep Rojop files court action and the killers are found guilty yet released due to a plea for mercy from K'iche community. Diego Itzep Rojop points out that the killers have wives and children who would suffer if they were imprisoned.

1973: More than 60 individual titles to Los Cimientos, originally registered to Diego Itzep Rojop and Felipe Tum, were distributed to members of the Los Cimientos K'iche community at the request of these two community leaders. Individual titles included in this "dismembration" were recorded in the 2nd Register of Property, (again Titulos Inmuebles Registrado - a classification that represents the highest level of a complicated and costly process that legally protects the Constitutionally guaranteed right of Private Property - a great effort for a Mayan campesino community.)

1976: Guatemalan Earthquake: Los Cimientos K'iche community generously contributes significant amount of food to neighboring Ixil communities and rescues several Ixil from the river. Descendants of some of those Ixil currently illegally occupy the K'iche owned Finca Los Cimientos.

1981-1983: The Guatemalan Army executes a scorched earth campaign that results in the massacre of thousands of non-combatant civilians and burning of hundreds of villages in several zones of Guatemala. Chajul, particularly the area of Chajul municipality in which Los Cimientos is located, suffers severe damages. The United Nations sponsored "Commission for Historical Verification" found that this Guatemalan military campaign was in truth a genocide.

Early 1982: Forced to flee from intense danger and direct military threats, 132 K'iche families of Los Cimientos, 672 people, settle in six Cunen Municipality villages near Nebaj. In six months these villages come under strong Army control and are given the identity of "Model Villages." (Villages closely controlled by the Army and "Civil Patrol" units as part of the Army's contra-insurgency policy.) Army units begin establishing themselves in Los Cimientos.

1985-87-89: the K'iche present three separate petitions to the Guatemalan government insisting that their land right be acknowledged. In each instance, their case is referred to INTA - National Institute of Agricultural Transformation, which finds the K'iche ownership of Los Cimientos is legitimate. However, also in each case, INTA lacks the means of enforcement and political power to order that the Army remove themselves from Los

Cimientos. INTA refers the case to the judicial branch, which fails to push for a return of Los Cimientos to the rightful owners.

Oct. 1989: The Guatemalan Army establishes a base in Los Cimientos in order to control the CPR - Communities of Population in Resistance. This base, established on the K'iche ancestral cemetery eventually becomes what is known today as "Cimientos Xeputul"- the home site of the illegal land occupiers. Army brings 50 Chajul Ixil Civil Patrol (paramilitary) families to live in Los Cimientos. Two of the four Civil Patrol "Military Commissioners" leading this Civil Patrol are descendants of Sr. Caba and Rivera who refused to accept the 1906 land survey. The Civil Patrol are heavily armed and given orders to shoot the K'iche landowners if they attempt to return to their legally owned land, Los Cimientos. Civil Patrol units throughout the area become infamous for atrocious human rights abuses.

1993: Council of Los Cimientos Traditional Priests and Elders request international assistance, food and funding from The Maya Connection. The Mayan Connection- Los Cimientos Alliance grew out of this requested partnership and continues to this day to accompany and advocate for the Los Cimientos community. With the help of CERJ, Comunidades Etnica Runujel Juman, a Mayan Guatemalan Human Rights organization that confronted the brutal Civil Patrols during the 1980s-1990s, Los Cimientos community files suit against the Minister of Defense, requesting the removal of the Army base. Decision is in favor of the Los Cimientos K'iche landowners. The UN sends an official to investigate. The investigation finds that the K'iche are being deprived of their legal, constitutional, land rights.

1994: 200 K'iche return to their land, accompanied by CERJ and international accompaniment. Army War Audit confirms K'iche ownership of Los Cimientos. K'iche appeal to the Inter-American Commission to remove the Army base in Los Cimientos. The returning group gradually became 97 families, nearly 500 people, by 2001.

1995: A Presidential Commission land study (February, 1995) confirms the K'iche titles and land rights. The Commission recommends-orders a land survey to locate the boundary between

Finca Los Cimientos and Chajul public lands. CPR living in Xaxboj, an Ixil village illegally created in Finca Los Cimientos, stop the survey by threatening the lives of the surveyors.

1998: An agricultural corporation, Agropecuaria Nabalija Anonima, arrives in court represented by a lawyer well known for his work on behalf of top military personnel. They claim to have a "pre-existing" title to Los Cimientos. Nabalija send two helicopters and 40 armed men to Los Cimientos to evict all inhabitants. The K'iche take the case to court and once again their titles and land rights are confirmed.

At this same time: The Guatemalan government, in a USAID funded project, demarcates " Caba Visis Bio Reserve" This amazingly large project includes nearly all land within the Chajul municipality. Los Cimientos is included in the "multi-use" zone - as an area where petroleum exploration and mining development are allowed. Los Cimientos owners are not consulted during the planning meetings even though all Ixil communities and political leaders within the target area are brought into meetings concerning the development of the Reserve.

Also in 1998: An agreement to give up the K'iche claim to Los Cimientos is sponsored by FONAPAZ. It is apparently fraudulently signed by four relatives of Los Cimientos landowners. The four were not elected nor appointed by K'iche landowners to make such an agreement. In a private arrangement, the group involved in the FONAPAZ agreement agree to accept a finca name El Soch. Before completing the transaction, the government has the leader of the four sign an agreement acknowledging that the government has informed him that El Soch will not support the needs of a community (minimal water, other residents competing to survive on the barren mountainous land) and that the government was not to be held responsible. (CONTIERRA History)

1998-1999: Los Cimientos leaders nationally and internationally protest the secret signing of the Dec. 8, 1998 FONAPAZ agreement. Community states that those families (24 titleholders) who wish to go to El Soch are free and welcome to do so and that the elected leadership, including the closest relatives of Diego Itzep Rojop and Miguel Tum, demand the right to maintain their claim to their land. This group includes the majority of Los Cimientos landowners and families. K'iche are represented before InterAmerican Commission by CALDH.

June, 2001: CONTIERRA announces they will present results of their extensive land study on June 26. 70 top level invitations are sent to governmental and international officials for a presentation in an exclusive Guatemala City hotel.

June 25, 2001: Chajul Ixil former Civil Patrol living in Xeputul and some CPR living in Xaxboj attack Los Cimientos community early in the morning. After allegedly raping two women in front of their children the Ixil force all families to flee. 67 landowning families are present in Los Cimientos - 30 more are working for survival money on the south coast fincas since the Ixil have not permitted the K'iche to successfully farm their own land since 1994. All local and national governmental law agencies ignore the plight of the K'iche landowners. All K'iche homes and buildings are destroyed or forcibly occupied. All belongings stolen, all K'iche food crops, ready to be harvested, are stolen and sold in Chajul markets by the outlaw Ixil. Local and national law enforcement agencies do nothing to stop the theft.

June 25-29, 2001: K'iche flee to San Marcos village near Los Cimientos trusting that law enforcement will facilitate their return to their legally owned land. Ixil threaten the leaders of San Marcos and the K'iche flee again, arriving in the Cotzal Ixil village of Xeputul II - a community of 29 permanent residents, who share their homesites with the 97 K'iche families until Dec 27 when Chajul Ixil threats and Cotzal Ixil fatigue again force the K'iche to flee. No investigation of Los Cimientos is ever made by official law enforcement or human rights observer organizations.

June 26, 2001: CONTIERRA land study, funded by USAID, World Bank and the Government of Denmark is presented in the InterContinental Hotel, confirming the titles of the Los Cimientos K'iche. The study shows clearly that the titles presented by Agropecuaria Nabalija are "ghost titles' - titles without land. Many such titles have been presented since the war and the Peace Accords were signed. During intensive K'iche negotiations with the government, the director of CONTIERRA attempts to claim that "new evidence" supports Agropecuaria's claim, even though the director of Agropecuaria acknowledged during three meetings with the K'iche that Agropecuaria land is not Los Cimientos.

June, July, August, Sept, October, November, December, 2001, January, February...2002: K'iche live as penniless, landless "displaced persons", begging for food from international aid organizations and the Guatemalan government. At the present time, (March 2002) the K'iche are on a small piece of land near Nebaj, an area known for overcrowded conditions and freezing cold nights. They have minimal survival shelter, less than sufficient blankets, and since mid-January, no food is forthcoming from international aid organizations. The K'iche negotiating team is meeting time and again, at their own financial cost, with the government in a heroic effort to keep their case alive.

July 2, 2001: Lawyer for the displaced K'iche files a complaint against the Ixil invaders for the crimes of June 25, 2001. A judge in Nebaj refuses to issue arrest warrants, citing "insufficient" evidence, despite the presentation of boxes of substantial documentation brought forth by the K'iche landowners.

July 6, 2001: With Bishop Julio Cabrera of Quiche as mediator, negotiations begin between the Landowners and the illegal land occupiers. The K'iche again are forced into defending their right to their land. Tables of negotiation take place over a period of several months, as the K'iche plead to return to their ancestral land. The Ixil admit the crimes committed on June 25 and that the K'iche are the legal owners of the land. The Ixil also threaten further violence if the K'iche return.

The Guatemalan government states that it is incapable of enforcing the rule of law in Chajul and states that if the K'iche return home they will be the cause of a "civil war." The K'iche present several offers of how to resolve the theft of their land, all including providing land to and sharing the area with the Ixil. The government states that if the K'iche will "be flexible"...give up their land, the government will give them new land and help them with each step of the relocation. Guatemalan governmental Conflict Resolution Agency, UPRECO, and MINUGUA (UN Verification Team,) are present. UPRECO is made up of

CONTIERRA- Guatemalan land conflict resolution commission, SEPAZ- Guatemalan Presidential Secretariat of the Peace, SAE - Secretariat of Civil Intelligence, COPREDEH - Presidential Human Rights Commission and SCEP - Presidential Executive Secretariat. The K'iche believe and eventually accept the offer of new land when it becomes clear that there is no support for the rule of law.

July, 2001: Plan Pueblo-Panama, an international economic project stretching from Southern Mexico to Panama is launched. Los Cimientos is within its geographical mandate that includes emphasis on "eco-tourism" projects.

Oct. 25, 2001: UPRECO publicly states its commitment to a rapid and permanent resolution to the land dispute. After repeated requests from the K'iche UPRECO issues a written statement promising to provide new land. Its goals are to search for adequate replacement land where the K'iche could live and economically sustain themselves, in return for giving up ownership for Los Cimientos. In fact, there no longer exists pieces of land available in Guatemala as large, fertile, productive and water rich as Los Cimientos.

The K'iche offer to accept 2 or 3 pieces of land to arrive at the extension of land taken from them. They now find themselves locked into a phrase in the UPRECO offer - stating that the government will give them "one finca" - the same extension as Los Cimientos. The community continues to suffer in refugee circumstances, without adequate housing and less than adequate food. Each week during the negotiations the Los Cimientos representatives also must attend Humanitarian Aid meetings in order to convince Guatemalan governmental and international agencies to provide the refugees with sufficient food to survive.

Nov. 13, 2001: CALDH, Guatemalan based Center for Human Rights Legal Action again presents the K'iche case against the Republic of Guatemala regarding the June 25, 2001 attack before the Inter-American Human Rights Commission in Washington DC. The Commission also has a K'iche case pending for the 1981-82 Army expulsion of the community and accumulated damages. Commission sends demands for the Guatemalan government to respond to within 15 days: 1. A public commitment on the part of the State to resolve the Los Cimientos issue by offering new land to the displaced K'iche landowners. 2. Compensation for damages since the original displacement in 1981-82. 3. Public admission of responsibility for that displacement. 4. On-going information to be provided to the Inter-American commission on progress in the criminal case against the June 25, 2001 invaders.

Nov.-Dec., 2001: Los Cimientos twice submits proposal to UPRECO describing acceptable land exchange details, inviting further discussion and negotiation.. Proposal includes:

1. a request that the government buy adequate, productive land with clear titles in return for the K'iche giving up their legal titles to Los Cimientos,
2. Creation of two committees - Government and K'iche, to search for and evaluate the new land.
3. Financial and technical assistance to make sustainable life possible on the new land.
4. Compensation for the million dollars worth of damages resulting from the June 25 attack.
5. Writing a verified history of Los Cimientos with the assistance of an NGO.

UPRECO promises response yet none is given to date. UPRECO continues to publicly state that it will be dangerous for the K'iche to attempt to return to their legally owned land as the Ixil land occupants continue threats of further violence.

Government representatives repeatedly insist that they are unable to do anything to establish rule of law in Los Cimientos, nor to bring about the arrest of the four leaders of the June 25 attack and that the K'iche will be the cause of violence if they attempt to return. K'iche continue to be forced to beg for food for their families.

Also in Dec., 2001: As a result of Ixil threats against the small village where the K'iche have lived as refugees since July, the host community demands that they leave. December 29 the K'iche relocate to Batzula, near Nebaj. A local land owner grants them 2 months residency on an open field. Nights are freezing cold. They arrive with no blankets and only rolls of plastic to create temporary shelters.

Jan., 2002: Two representatives from government - UPRECO and SEGEPLAN, agency coordinating humanitarian relief visit community making promises of food in return for work - building latrines, improving road, etc. Promise is also made to give food to families with children in school. Community is running out of food.

Feb. 7, 2002: Los Cimientos representatives present reports of community having fulfilled work for food projects. SEGEPLAN coordinator informs them that World Food Program will not accept the above described work projects and that only the children in school will receive food - if the Ministry of Education provides either a breakfast or a lunch. Community is out of food supplies.

Feb. 11, 2002: Community submits written request to UPRECO for them to initiate negotiations for a small but highly productive land the land search team has found. Land owner and Los Cimientos Alliance urge UPRECO to give a positive response as this small area will at least provide the K'iche with some land to be on and productive crops to sell. No response is given. Director of SCEP - (governmental ministry sponsoring UPRECO,) is fired for activities not related to Los Cimientos issue, new Director arrives.

Feb. 14, 2002: World Food Program visits refugee site. Describes work (educational programs) for food projects. WFP was notified in advance that key community leaders will not be present due to morning court hearing regarding June 25 attack leaders. When a representative from the Governors office insists on talking about resolution of land issue community becomes concerned due to past experiences and state that they are not authorized to sign any documents without the presence of community leaders. WFP delegation leaves before leaders return at noon. SEGEPLAN receives complaints regarding Los Cimientos leaders absence and refusal of community to sign documents.

Feb. 27, 2002: UPRECO meeting that should vote to initiate negotiations on new land. Los Cimientos request not voted on. The next day, UPRECO is disbanded, returning the case of Los Cimientos to CONTIERRA.

March 1, 2002: Los Cimientos community must leave refugee site - there is nowhere for them to go. There is no food forthcoming until WFP receives "cronograms" from the community regarding educational work for food projects. There is no confirmation from new SCEP director that the government will honor the October agreement to buy new land. Rumors from Los Cimientos say that a government helicopter arrived in February to tell the Ixil that now the government or a large business now owns Los Cimientos and the Ixil must prepare to leave. K'iche community is left in limbo with more than 400 children suffering from exposure related illnesses and malnutrition.

## VOLUNTEERING

Los Cimientos Alliance welcomes all those who wish to volunteer for this most worthy cause, but there are a number of characteristics which will enable both volunteers and the Alliance to get the maximum out of your time working with us:

Availability: The Los Cimientos case is a very complex issue. We want people to have time to get an understanding and make a valuable contribution to the cause, and so look for people to make a commitment of at least 14 days in Guatemala. The longer you can commit, the better. We can can also benefit from people who wish to help by providing shorter terms services such as translation, transportation, internet/Web Site or telephone/fax support.

Personality: Your personality is very important. Volunteers should be culturally sensitive, patient, understanding, and above all, have the flexibility to meet tasks as priorities change with rapidly changing events, frequently in crisis conditions. A spirit of forgiveness is essential and an earnest commitment to working as a Team.

Potentially useful: Skills such as Spanish (to help with translation of written materials or interacting with the community), computing skills (updating Web Page and computer based research of foundations for funding sources), the ability to drive (a car/truck to help with transport to meetings in Guatemala City and food aid deliveries to the north). Each of these services is of great value.

Longer Term Volunteers: We also accept those who wish to make a longer commitment of a month and more. This work is basically divided into 2 groups, though there may be a lot of crossover between work areas.

- Group 1. Administrative: This volunteer role may include:
  * Writing and editing documents sent out by the organization.
  * Translation of documents to or from English/Spanish.
  * Being international observers and note takers at meetings with the government and at refugee site.
  * Liaison and contacting other organizations, foundations and interested parties.
  * Helping raise awareness of the case both locally and internationally.
  * Helping in the generation of funds and aid for the community
  * Internet research and Web Page development.
- Group II. Field Worker: This volunteer role may include:
  * Liaison with the community on issues relating to aid relief and the land issue.
  * Observing living conditions of the refugee K'iche community, documenting and reporting them to the Alliance.
  * Helping deliver and oversee distribution of aid relief including the World Food Program "food for work" plan.
  * Liaison with national and international aid organizations working in the field.

## Recent Events: 2002 - 2004

On December 8th, 2002 Los Cimientos families abandoned all hope of returning home to their fields in Los Cimientos and relocated to new land in San Vicente. Forced by hunger, inadequate housing in a freezing climate and the prospect of being forcibly driven again from their tenuous refugee site, community leaders accepted the new land exchange offered by the government of president Alfonzo Portillo. The community sacrificed Los Cimientos (6000 acres with 5 pure water rivers, producing 3 to 4 harvests a year of a wide variety of organically grown crops) in trade for San Vicente (about 2000 acres with one polluted river and 2 to 3 harvests a year possible with the use of agricultural chemicals).

The government of Guatemalan president Portillo proclaimed this land exchange to be a great victory for the government's resolution of the Los Cimientos case - citing it as second in importance to the peace accords. This governmental communications ministry announced around the clock on national T.V. that this was a reconciliation between the K'iche and the Ixil. In legally signed agreements, the Guatemalan government promised to give the community food support until their own food crops were established and on-site health care. The promises also included infrastructure and houses to replace those lost in the Ixil attack on Los Cimientos. All these promises remain unfulfilled - though government word games try to make legal channels believe they have fulfilled the agreements. Children have died from malnutrition and suffer from malnutrition-related illnesses. There are no medicines available.

On January 15th the newly elected government of Oscar Berger came into power. Now, the Berger government assumes responsibility for a Guatemala with an staggering legacy of problems on all levels, among them, the promises made by Portillo and his representatives to resolve the Los Cimientos land case justly and with dignity.

# 6

# The How and Why of the Mayan End Date in 2012 A.D.

Why did the ancient Mayan or pre-Maya choose December 21st, 2012 A.D., as the end of their Long Count calendar? This article will cover some recent research. Scholars have known for decades that the 13-baktun cycle of the Mayan "Long Count" system of timekeeping was set to end precisely on a winter solstice, and that this system was put in place some 2300 years ago. This amazing fact - that ancient Mesoameri- can skywatchers were able to pinpoint a winter solstice far off into the future - has not been dealt with by Mayanists. And why did they choose the year 2012? One imme tely gets the impression that there is a very strange mystery to be confronted here. I will be building upon a clue to this mystery reported by epigrapher Linda Schele in Maya Cosmos (1994). This article is the natural culmination of the research relating to the Mayan Long Count and the precession of the equinoxes that I explored in my recent book Tzolkin: Visionary Perspectives and Calendar Studies (Borderlands Science and Research Foundation, 1994).

Just some basics to get us started. The Maya were adept skywatchers. Their Classic Period is thought to have lasted from 200 A.D. to 900 A.D., but recent archeological findings are pushing back the dawn of Mayan civilization in Mesoamerica. Large ruin sites indicating high culture with distinctly Mayan antecedents are being found in the jungles of Guatemala dating back to before the common era. And even before this, the Olmec civilization flourished and developed the sacred count of 260 days known as the tzolkin. The early Maya adopted two different time keeping systems, the "Short Count" and the Long Count. The Short Count derives from combining the tzolkin cycle with the solar year and the Venus cycle of 584 days. In this way, "short" periods of 13, 52 and 104 years are generated. Unfortunately, we won't have occasion to dwell on the properties of the so-called Short Count system here. The Long Count system is somewhat more abstract, yet is also related to certain astronomical cycles. It is based upon nested cycles of days multiplied at each level by that key Mayan number, twenty:

Number of Days / Term

1 / Kin (day)

20 / Uinal

360 / Tun

7200 / Katun

144000 / Baktun

Notice that the only exception to multiplying by twenty is at the tun level, where the uinal period is instead multiplied by 18 to make the 360-day tun. The Maya employed this counting system to track an unbroken sequence of days from the time it was inaugurated. The Mayan scholar Munro Edmonson believes that the Long Count was put in place around 355 B.C. This may be so, but the oldest Long Count date as yet found corresponds to 32 B.C. We find Long Count dates in the archeological record beginning with the baktun place value and separated by dots. For example: 6.19.19.0.0 equals 6 baktuns, 19 katuns, 19 tuns, 0 uinals and 0 days. Each baktun has 144000 days, each katun has 7200 days, and so on. If we add up all the values we find that 6.19.19.0.0 indicates a total of 1007640 days have elapsed since the Zero Date of 0.0.0.0.0. The much discussed 13-baktun cycle is completed 1872000 days (13 baktuns) after 0.0.0.0.0. This period of time is the so called Mayan "Great Cycle" of the Long Count and equals 5125.36 years.

But how are we to relate this to a time frame we can understand? How does this Long Count relate to our Gregorian calendar? This problem of correlating Mayan time with "western" time has occupied Mayan scholars since the beginning. The standard question to answer became: what does 0.0.0.0.0 (the Long Count "beginning" point) equal in the Gregorian calendar? When this question is answered, archeological inscriptions can be put into their proper historical context and the end date of the 13-baktun cycle can be calculated. After years of considering data from varied fields such as astronomy, ethnography, archeology and iconography, J. Eric S. Thompson determined that 0.0.0.0.0 correponded to the Julian date 584283, which equals August 11th, 3114 B.C. in our Gregorian calendar. This means that the end date of 13.0.0.0.0, some 5125 years later, is December 21st, 2012 A.D.1

The relationship between the Long Count and Short Count has always been internally consistent (both were tracked alongside each other in an unbroken sequence since their conception). Now it is very interesting to note that an aspect of the "Short Count", namely, the sacred tzolkin count of 260 days, is still being followed in the highlands of Guatemala. As the Mayan scholar Munro Edmonson shows in The Book of the Year, this last surviving flicker of a calendar tradition some 3000 years old supports the Thompson correlation of 584283. Edmonson also states that the Long Count was begun by the Maya or pre-Maya around 355 B.C., but there is reason to believe that the Long Count system was being perfected for at least 200 years prior to that date.

The point of interest for these early astronomers seems to have been the projected end date in 2012 A.D., rather than the beginning date in 3114 B.C. Having determined the end date in 2012 (for reasons we will come to shortly), and calling it 13.0.0.0.0, they thus proclaimed themselves to be living in the 6th baktun of the Great Cycle.

The later Maya certainly attributed much mythological significance to the beginning date, relating it to the birth of their deities, but it now seems certain that the placement of the Long Count hinges upon its calculated end point. Why did early Mesoamerican skywatchers pick a date some 2300 years into the future and, in fact, how did they pinpoint an accurate winter solstice? With all these considerations one begins to suspect that, for some reason, the ancient New World astronomers were tracking precession.

### The Precession

The precession of the equinoxes, also known as the Platonic Year, is caused by the slow wobbling of the earth's polar axis. Right now this axis roughly points to Polaris, the "Pole Star," but this changes slowly over long periods of time. The earth's wobble causes the position of the seasonal quarters to slowly precess against the background of stars.

For example, right now, the winter solstice position is in the constellation of Sagittarius. But 2000 years ago it was in Capricorn. Since then, it has precessed backward almost one full sign. It is generally thought that the Greek astronomer Hipparchus was the first to discover precession around 128 B.C. Yet scholarship indicates that more ancient Old World cultures such as the Egyptians (see Schwaller de Lubicz's book Sacred Science) and Babylonians also knew about the precession.

I have concluded that even cultures with simple horizon astronomy and oral records passed down for a hundred years or so, would notice the slow shifting of the heavens. For example, imagine that you lived in an environment suited for accurately demarcated horizon astronomy. Even if this wasn't the case, you might erect monoliths to sight the horizon position of, most likely, the dawning winter solstice sun. This position in relation to background stars could be accurately preserved in oral verse or wisdom teachings, to be passed down for centuries. Since precession will change this position at the rate of 1 degree every 72 years, within the relatively short time of 100 years or so, a noticeable change will have occurred. The point of this is simple. To early cultures attuned to the subtle movements of the sky, precession would not have been hard to notice.2

The Maya are not generally credited with knowing about the precession of the equinoxes. But considering everything else we know about the amazing sophistication of Mesoamerican astronomy, can we realistically continue to deny them this? Many of the as yet undeciphered hieroglyphs may ultimately describe precessional myths. Furthermore, as I show in my book Tzolkin: Visionary Perspectives and Calendar Studies, the Long Count is perfectly suited for predicting future seasonal quarters, indefinitely, and precession is automatically accounted for. Some of the most incredible aspects of Mayan cosmo-conception are just now being discovered. As was the case with the state of Egyptology in the 1870's, we still have a lot to learn. In addition, Mayanists like Gordon Brotherston (The Book of the Fourth World) consider precessional knowledge among Mesoamerican cultures to be more than likely.

## The Sacred Tree

We are still trying to answer these questions: What is so important about the winter solstice of 2012 and, exactly how were calculations made so accurately, considering that precession should make them exceedingly difficult?

If we make a standard horoscope chart for December 21st, 2012 A.D., nothing very unusual appears. In this way I was led astray in my search until Linda Schele provided a clue in the recent book Maya Cosmos. Probably the most exciting breakthrough in this book is her identification of the astronomical meaning of the Mayan Sacred Tree. Drawing from an impressive amount of iconographic evidence, and generously sharing the process by which she arrived at her discovery, the Sacred Tree is found to be none other than the crossing point of the ecliptic with the band of the Milky Way. Indeed, the Milky Way seems to have played an important role in Mayan imagery.

For example, an incised bone from 8th century Tikal depicts a long sinking canoe containing various deities. This is a picture of the night sky and the canoe is the Milky Way, sinking below the horizon as the night progresses, and carrying with it deities representing the nearby constellations. The incredible Mayan site of Palenque is filled with Sacred Tree motifs and references to astronomical events. In their book Forest of Kings, Schele and Freidel suggested that the Sacred Tree referred to the ecliptic. Apparently that was only part of the picture, for the Sacred Tree that Pacal ascends in death is more than just the ecliptic, it is the sacred doorway to the underworld. The crossing point of Milky Way and ecliptic is this doorway and represents the sacred source and origin. In the following diagram of the well known sarcophagus carving, notice that the Milky Way tree serves as an extension of Pacal's umbilicus. The umbilicus is a human being's entrance into life, and entrance into death as well:

*Diagram 1: Pacal and the Sacred Tree*

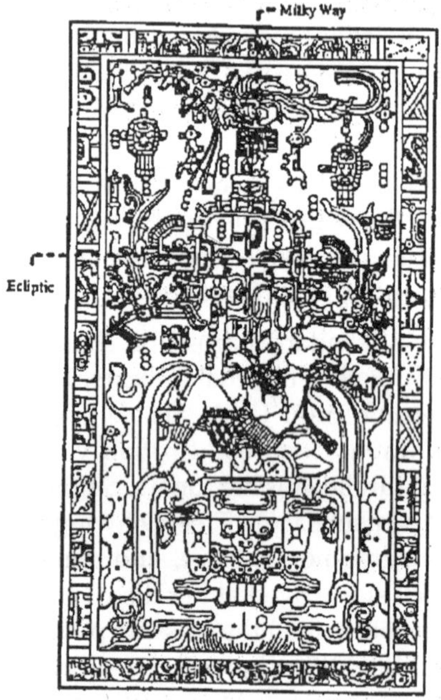


We may also remember at this point that the tzolkin calendar is said to spring from the Sacred Tree. The Sacred Tree is, in fact, at the center of the entire corpus of Mayan Creation Myths. We should definitely explore the nature of this astronomical feature.

The first question that came up for me was as follows. Since Lord (Ahau) Pacal is, by way of divine kingship, equated with the sun, and he is portrayed "entering" the Sacred Tree on his famous sarcophagus lid, on what day does the sun come around to conjunct the crossing point of ecliptic and Milky Way? This would be an important date. In the pre-dawn skies of this date, the Milky Way would be seen to arch overhead from the region of Polaris (Heart of Sky) and would point right at where the sun rises. This (and the corollary date 6 months later) is the only date when the Sun/ Lord could jump from the ecliptic track and travel the Milky Way up and around the vault of heaven to the region of Polaris, there to enter the "Heart of Sky." It should be mentioned that 1300 years ago, during the zenith of Palenque's glory, Polaris was much less an exact "Pole Star" than it is now. Schele demonstrates that it wasn't a Pole Star that the Maya mythologized in this regard, it was the unmarked polar "dark region" symbolizing death and the underworld around which everything was observed to revolve. Life revolves around death - a characteristically Mayan belief. The dates on which the sun conjuncts the "Sacred Tree" are thus very important. These dates will change with precession. Schele doesn't pursue this line of reasoning, however, and doesn't even mention that these dates might be significant. If we go back to 755 A.D., we find that the sun conjuncts the Sacred Tree on December 3rd. I should point out here that the Milky Way is a wide band, and perhaps a 10-day range of dates should be considered.

To start with, however, I use the exact center of the Milky Way band that one finds on star charts, known as the "Galactic Equator" (not to be confused with Galactic Center). Where the Galactic Equator crosses the ecliptic in Sagittarius just happens to be where the dark rift in the Milky Way begins. This is a dark bifurcation in the Milky Way caused by interstellar dust clouds. To observers on earth, it appears as a dark road which begins near the ecliptic and stretches along the Milky Way up towards Polaris. The Maya today are quite aware of this feature; the Quich» Maya call it xibalba be (the "road to Xibalba") and the Chorti Maya call it the "camino de Santiago". In Dennis Tedlock's translation of the Popol Vuh, we find that the ancient Maya called it the "Black Road". The Hero Twins Hunahpu and Xbalanque must journey down this road to battle the Lords of Xibalba. (Tedlock 334, 358). Furthermore, what Schele has identified as the Sacred Tree was known to the ancient Quich» simply as "Crossroads."

This celestial feature was not marginal in ancient Mayan thought and is still rec- ognized even today. In terms of how this feature was mythologized, it seems that when a planet, the sun, or the moon entered the dark cleft of the Milky Way in Sagittarius (which happens to be the exact center of the Milky Way, the Galactic Equator), entrance to the underworld road was possible, which could then take the journeyer up to the Heart of Sky.

Shamanic vision rites were probably involved in this scenario. In the Yucatan, underground caves were ritual places used by shaman to journey to the underworld. Schele explains that "Mayan mythology identifies the Road to Xibalba as going through a cave" (Forest of Kings, 209). Here we have a metaphorical reference to the "dark rift" in the Milky Way by way of its terrestrial counterpart, a syncretism between earth and sky which is characteristic of Mayan thinking. Above all, what is becoming apparent from the corpus of Mayan Creation Myths is that creation seems to have taken place at a celestial crossroads - the crossing point of ecliptic and Milky Way.

To clarify this ever growing picture, we should stop here and plot out some charts. In addition to the detailed star maps from Norton's 2000.0 Star Atlas which allowed me to pinpoint the crossing point of Galactic Equator and ecliptic, I use EZCosmos to plot these positions3. What I found answers the question of why the Maya chose the winter solstice of 2012, a problem seemingly avoided by astronomers and Mayanists alike. While it is true that the sun conjuncts the Sacred Tree on December 3rd in the year 755 A.D., over the centuries precession has caused the conjunction date to approach the winter solstice. So, how close are we to perfect conjunction today? Exactly when might we expect the winter solstice sun to conjunct the crossing point of Galactic Equator and ecliptic - the Mayan Sacred Tree? Any astronomer will tell you that, presently, the Milky Way crosses the ecliptic through the constellation of Sagittarius and this area is rich in nebulae and high density objects. In fact, where the Milky Way crosses the ecliptic in Sagittarius also happens to be the direction of the Galactic Center.

### The Charts

So the quest returns to identifying why December 21st, 2012 A.D. might represent some kind of astronomical anomoly. I'll get right to the heart of the matter. Let's look at a few charts.

Here is a full view of the sky at noon on December 21st, 2012 A.D. The band of the Milky Way can be seen stretching from the lower right to the upper left. The more or less vertical dotted line indicates the Galactic Equator. The planets can be seen tracing a roughly horizontal path through the chart, indicating the ecliptic. The sun, quite strikingly, is dead center in the Sacred Tree. Let's look closer.

*Chart 2.*

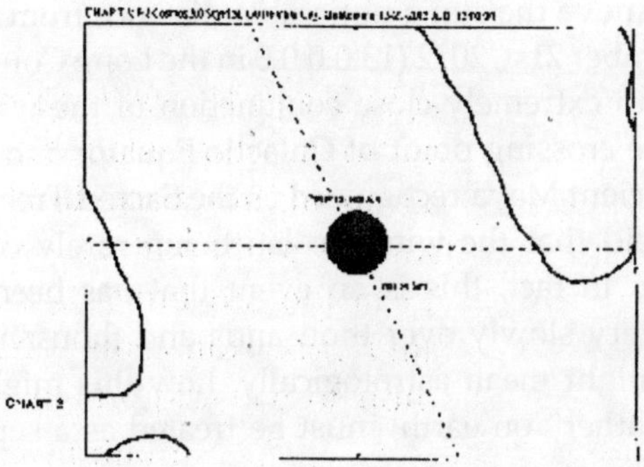

The field is now reduced from a horizon-to-horizon view to a field of 30 degrees. Part of the constellation of Sagittarius can be seen in the lower left portion of the chart. The planet in the middle-to-upper left portion of the chart is Pluto, which rarely travels directly along the ecliptic.

The center square near the sun is placed on the Trifid Nebula (M20). According to the star chart I used, this nebula is very close to the crossing point of Galactic Equator and ecliptic. However, a small star (4 Sgr) is even closer; it sits right on the Galactic Equator and its declination is only 00 .08' below the ecliptic. Let's look closer at these features.

*Chart 3.*

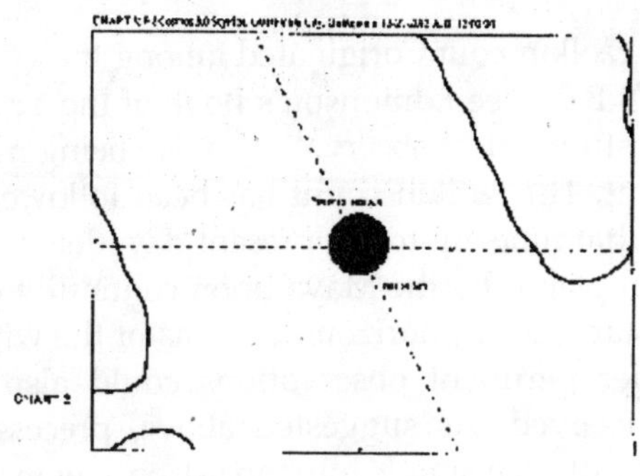

The field is now reduced to a 5-degree span, what astrology considers to be within conjunction. The dot to the lower right of the sun is the star 4 Sgr. Amazingly, the Sun is right on target. We couldn't have hoped for a closer conjunction. 1 day before or after will remove the sun a noticeable distance from the crossing point. December 21st, 2012 (13.0.0.0.0 in the Long Count) therefore represents an extremely close conjunction of the winter solstice sun with the crossing point of Galactic Equator and the ecliptic, what the ancient Maya recognized as the Sacred Tree. It is critical to understand that the winter solstice sun rarely conjuncts the Sacred Tree. In fact, this is an event that has been coming to resonance very slowly over thousands and thousands of years. What this might mean astrologically, how this might effect the "energy weather" on earth, must be treated as a separate topic.

But I should at least mention in passing that this celestial convergence appears to parallel the accelerating pace of human civilization. It should be noted that because precession is a very slow process, similar astronomical alignments will be evident on the winter solstice dates within perhaps 5 years on either side of 2012. However, the accuracy of the conjunction of 2012 is quite astounding, beyond anything deemed calculable by the ancient Maya, and serves well to represent the perfect mid-point of the process.

Let's go back to the dawn of the Long Count and try to reconstruct what may have been happening.

## Why: Winter Solstice Sun Conjuncts The Sacred Tree in 2012 A.D.

First, the tzolkin count originated among the Olmec at least as early as 679 B.C. (see Edmonson's Book of the Year). We may suspect that astronomical observations were being made from at least that point. The tzolkin count has been followed unbroken since at least that time, up to the present day, demonstrating the high premium placed by the Maya upon continuity of tradition. In this way, star records, horizon positions of the winter solstice sun, and other pertinent observations could also have been accurately preserved. As suggested above, precession can be noticed by way of even simple horizon astronomy in as little time as 100 to 150 years. (Hipparchus, the alleged "discoverer" of precession among the Greeks, compared his own observations with data collected only 170 years before his time.) Following Edmonson, the Long Count system may have appeared as early as 355 B.C. Part of the reason for implementing the Long Count system, as I will show, was probably to calculate future winter solstice dates.

We must assume that even at this early point in Mesoamerican history, the crossing point of ecliptic and Milky Way was understood as the "Sacred Tree". Since the Sacred Tree concept is intrinsically tied into the oldest Mayan Creation Myths, this is not improbable. At the very least, the "dark rift" was already a recognized feature. Early skywatchers of this era (355 B.C.) would then observe the sun to conjunct the dark ridge in the Milky Way on or around November 18th.5 This would be easily observed in the pre-dawn sky as described above: the Milky Way points to the rising sun on this date.

Over a relatively short period of time, as an awareness of precession was emerging, this date was seen to slowly approach winter solstice, a critical date in its own right in early Mayan cosmo-conception. At this point, precession and the rate of precession was calculated, the Long Count was perfected and inaugurated, and the appropriate winter solstice date in 2012 A.D. was found via the Long Count in the following way.

## How: Long Count and Seasonal Quarters

Long Count katun beginnings will conjunct sequential seasonal quarters every 1.7.0.0.0 days (194400 days). This is an easily tracked Long Count interval. Starting with the katun beginning of 650 B.C.:

Long Count Which Quarter? Year

6.5.0.0.0 Fall 650 B.C.

7.12.0.0.0 Winter 118 B.C.

8.19.0.0.0 Spring 416 A.D.

10.6.0.0.0 Summer 948 A.D.

11.13.0.0.0 Fall 1480 A.D.

13.0.0.0.0 Winter 2012 A.D.

Note that the last date is not only a katun beginning, but a baktun beginning as well. It is, indeed, the end date of 2012.[6]

The Long Count may have been officially inaugurated on a specific date in 355 B.C., as Edmonson suggests, but it must have been formulated, tried, tested, and proven before this date. This may well have taken centuries, and the process no doubt paralleled (and was perhaps instigated by) the discovery of precession. The Long Count system automatically accounts for precession in its ability to calculate future seasonal quarters - a property which shouldn't be underestimated

# 7

# 21st December 2012 in Present Discussion

## INTRODUCTION

One of the time periods of the Long Count of the Maya is the baktun, which lasts 144,000 days. In some texts of the Maya a new period of the Long Count is said to begin after 13 baktuns (exactly 1,872,000 days). Such a new period in the Long Count of the Maya will probably begin on 21 December 2012, when the Long Count returns to 0.0.0.0.0, and some people expect to see special things in the sky or on Earth then that would not otherwise be expected.

The interest for 21 December 2012 seems to have been spurred by publications by John Major Jenkins, who (if I understand correctly) is of the opinion that the Maya designed their Long Count in order that the coming special date 0.0.0.0.0 corresponds to a southern solstice (when the winter begins in the northern hemisphere) when the Sun stands in the Milky Way in the sky. Mr. Jenkins reached this opinion based on extensive research of Maya texts and other traces. See http://alignment2012.com for his opinion.

As far as I know, no text by the Maya has been found in which they explain (unambiguously) how they chose the day on which their Long Count should start (or on which the special date of 0.0.0.0.0 should return), so we cannot be sure why the Maya designed their calendar in that way. We can form opinions about this, based on other knowledge we have of the Maya culture and of other calendars, and depending on how much weight we assign to each fact and each opinion. Different people can form different opinions about this.

## BASIC ARGUMENTS

The basic arguments of many stories about 21 December 2012 seem to be as follows:

1. On exactly 21 December 2012 there is a certain special astronomical conjunction that is so rare that it doesn't repeat for a long period of time (centuries, or even millennia) before or after that date.
2. 21 december 2012 corresponds to the round date 0.0.0.0.0 in the Long Count of the Maya.
3. The Maya designed the Long Count in such a way that the special conjunction would correspond to the round date 0.0.0.0.0 in their Long Count, far into their future.
4. The Maya had the knowledge to predict that special conjunction precisely and accurately to one day.
5. Because of the conjunction, special phenomena are to be expected in the sky or on Earth on 21 December 2012.

## REACTION

My claim is that nothing will happen on 21 December 2012 that is tied to the conjunction and that is of interest to the physical sciences. I explain my arguments below.

1. The conjunction is not clearly limited to a single day, but covers a period of many years.

The Milky Way is a luminous band in the sky that can be seen only (sometimes) at night, outside, from dark locations far from city lights and other lights. The Milky Way has a fixed location amidst the stars in the sky. The annual path of the Sun between the stars in the sky crosses the Milky Way in two locations, near the constellations of the Archer and the Twins. So, the Sun passes through the Milky Way in the sky twice a year.

The southern solstice (the beginning of winter in the northern hemisphere, and of summer in the southern hemisphere) always falls around 21 December in the Gregorian calendar (around 11:13

UTC on 21 December 2012). The spot where the Sun then is between the stars slowly shifts between the stars, because of the precession of the equinoxes. In about 26,000 years that spot moves once around the whole sky (compared to the stars), roughly along the ecliptic (the annual path of the Sun between the stars in the sky), so the southern solstitial point moves through the Milky Way twice each 26,000 years.

The Milky Way has no very clear boundaries, but is on average about 12 degrees wide in the sky, and the solstitial point takes about 12°/360°*26000 = about 900 years to cover such a distance.

The Milky Way has no clear central line either, so there is uncertainty about when the solstitial point crosses that central line. Different groups of people can each use reasonable definitions for the central line that yet deviate from one another. If we estimate (for example) that the uncertainty about the "best" central line of the Milky Way is half a degree (which is only a small fraction of the width of the Milky Way), then the corresponding uncertainty in the date at which the solstitial point crosses the central line is 0.5°/360°*26000 = about 36 years.

The conjunction of the southern solstitial point and the Milky Way is therefore quite rare (it happens only once each about 13,000 years) but also lasts many years.

If you accept the central line that the IAU has defined for the Milky Way (see question 480), then (based on some experimenting with planetarium program *Redshift 5*) the southern solstitial point crossed the central line of the Milky Way already back in 1999.

2. It is quite likely but not entirely certain that the Long Count date of 0.0.0.0.0 corresponds to 21 December 2012.

The exact correspondence between the Long Count and modern calendars was lost when the Spanish conquistadors destroyed many Maya documents in the 16th century. In the course of time, the beginning of the Long Count has been proposed to correspond to dates in our calendars that varied by as much as 1000 years.

3. It seems unlikely to me that the Maya would be (almost?) the only people to define a calendar based on a date in their distant future.

It seems very unlikely to me that the Maya (or any other people) would design a calendar such that a certain round date in that calendar would correspond to some astronomical conjunction more than 2000 years into their future. All calendars that I know that have a certain specific day as a reference point have for that reference point a date in the past of the calendar makers that is important to them, such as the birth date or the date of the beginning of the reign of an important leader, or of the founding of an important city or of their country, or the (assumed) beginning of the world.

The idea that the Long Count was designed to have 0.0.0.0.0 on 21 December 2012 was invented when someone noticed not too long ago that the next beginning of a new period of 13 baktuns (on 21 December 2012) coincides with a solstice. Munro Edmonson writes [Edmonson, p. 119]:

There was, however, nothing arbitrary about the fixing of the end of the Long Count era. Victoria Bricker has pointed out to me that 13.0.0.0.0 4 Ahau 3 Kankin corresponds to an astronomically correct winter solstice: December 21, 2012 A.D. (Julian day number 2456283). Thus there appears to be a strong likelihood that the eral calendar, like the year calendar, was motivated by a long-range astronomical prediction, one that made a correct solsticial forecast 2,367 years into the future in 355 B.C.

(The mentioned 13.0.0.0.0 corresponds to the 0.0.0.0.0 that I mention elsewhere.) Absent from this description (and from its neighborhood in the book) is any indication about this from texts of the inventors or users of the Long Count. That we think that it fits so nicely doesn't say anything about what the inventors had in mind when they designed the Long Count.

4. I don't think that the Maya had the knowledge to be able to predict the date of such a conjunction over 2000 years into their future to an accuracy and precision of one day.

The Maya could of course pick a certain day over two thousand years into their future, just like anyone can do, but they did not have the knowledge to be very likely to predict the *correct* day for the conjunction. To be likely to calculate the correct day, the Maya would have had to be able to do the following:

* Define the central line of the Milky Way very accurately, and hence also measure the positions of stars very accurately.

If that central line is not clearly defined, then you cannot determine either when the solstitial point crosses that central line. The solstitial point shifts by only about 360/26000 = 1/70 degree per year, so, to be able to predict the exact year in which the conjunction was suposed to happen, the Maya would have to define the central line of the Milky Way at an accuracy of better than 1/70th of a degree. That angular distance is at about the limit of what the human eye can distinguish. However, I have never heard of a star map from the Maya that shows the central line of the Milky Way or even the positions of stars with that kind of accuracy.

* Accurately predict the motion of the solstitial point.

If you can determine from observations the time of a solstice or equinox accurately to one day (which seems reasonable if you have no modern equipment), then, to be able to make a prediction with a likely accuracy of one day, you need to have observations spanning as many years into the past as the number of years into the future for which you want to make a prediction. To correctly predict the date of a southern solstice 2367 years into the future in the 4th century BC, the Central Americans must then have had accurate records of observations of solstices and equinoxes from the preceding 2400 years, but no indications of such records for so many years have been found.

5. The conjunction has no astronomical or physical scientific significance.
   * The conjunction is not visible from Earth, because the Sun is then in the solstitial point so the solstitial point is then above the horizon only during the day.
   * There are no special forces associated with the conjunction, so the planets and other celestial bodies will continue in their orbits as usual.
   * The positions of the planets on 21 December 2012 are not remarkable. Here are the geocentric ecliptic longitude ë and the elongation *E* of the Sun and all planets on 21 December 2012, measured in degrees:

| Planet | λ | E |
|---|---|---|
| Sun | 269.3 | 0.0 |
| Mercury | 253.8 | "15.5 |
| Venus | 245.8 | "23.5 |
| Mars | 295.9 | +26.5 |
| Jupiter | 68.8 | +159.4 |
| Saturn | 218.4 | "50.9 |
| Uranus | 4.5 | +95.1 |
| Neptune | 330.6 | +61.3 |
| Pluto | 278.8 | +9.4 |

* For example, Mercury is then 15.5 degrees west of the Sun, and Jupiter 159.4 degrees east of the Sun. The planets aren't especially close together, and I see nothing special in their configuration on that date.
* Here is a picture (made using xplns) of the location of the Sun, Moon, and planets in the sky on 21 December 2012. The round white spot (below the name "Pluto") is the Sun, and the half round spot between Jupiter and Uranus is the Moon. The white lines indicate the approximate boundary of the Milky Way. I see nothing special here, either.

## OTHER CLAIMS

Besides the basic arguments that I mentioned above, I also encounter other claims related to 21 December 2012 or to astronomical knowledge of the Maya. I note a few of them below, with my response.

"The Sun is then in conjunction with the center of the Milky Way"

The Sun (and hence also the ecliptic) does not approach the center of the Milky Way to closer than about 5 degrees (which is ten times the apparent size of the Sun and the Moon in the sky), and that happens not on 21 December but around 18 December, and not just in 2012 but in every year.

It is of course possible that the Maya recognized some other point as the center of the Milky Way than we do today, but I don't know of any Maya text that clearly defines that point, so there is no evidence that the Maya regarded 2012 as a special year in this regard.

"The conjunction happens at sunrise"

This is total nonsense. Sunrise does not happen at the same moment everywhere on Earth, and the conjunction is of things outside of the Earth and does not depend on where you are on Earth, and not either on whether it is sunrise there at the time.

It may be that sunrise was a special time of day for the Maya and that such special conjunctions should be celebrated preferably at sunrise, but that does not say anything about the conjunction itself.

"We then pass through the plane of the Milky Way to the other side"

The Sun is now a few dozen lightyears north of the plane of the Milky Way. Not everybody agrees exactly how many dozen, which means that not everyone agrees where the plane of the Milky Way is near the Sun. See question 337.

If we are now a few dozen lightyears north of the plane of the Milky Way, then it is clear that we cannot pass through that plane in 2012, because to get to that plane would take a few dozen years even at the speed of light, and the Sun moves much slower than light does.

"The Maya knew the precession of the equinoxes and knew that five of their periods of 13 baktuns of the Long Count were equal to the period of the precession"

From J. Laskar et al., 1993: *Astronomy and Astrophysics,* volume 270, p. 522 I find that the (instantaneous) period of the precession of the equinoxes is on average about 25,678 Julian years but that it varies between about 24,820 and 26,550 years during the coming 500,000 years (ignoring the unknown influence of ice ages). Between the years -2000 and +3000 the period of the precession decreases at a rate of 0.100 year per year, and the period was 25,946 years in the year 0. (This linear approximation yields errors of at most 6 years compared to the full method, for years between "2000 and +3000.)

The period of the precession of the equinoxes is about equal to five periods of 13 baktuns, and 5 * 13 = 65 baktuns are exactly 9,360,000 days, or approximately (but not exactly) 25,626 Julian years.

Some people claim that the Maya (or their predecessors - for convenience, I refer to them all as Maya) knew about the precession of the equinoxes and tried to follow the precession using their Long Count, and that the period of the precession of the equinoxes was exactly 65 baktuns long according to the Maya. However, I have seen no indications that the Maya knew the precession, except for this rough correspondence between the period of the precession and 65 baktuns, and that correspondence could very well be a coincidence. (See at the bottom of this page for a discussion of coincidence.)

To detect precession, one needs to measure the position of the Sun between the stars in the sky very accurately and then compare those positions that were measured a century or more apart, because precession is very slow. 100 years of precession causes the phenomena of a particular star at a particular time of day to occur about one day sooner (compared to the solstices and equinoxes), or on the same day about 5 minutes earlier. However, I've not heard of any Maya texts that record measurements of the positions of one or more stars with sufficient accuracy to be able to make these kinds of comparisons.

Moreover, the period of the precession when the Long Count was invented was not equal to 65 baktuns = 25,626 Julian years, and the period of the precession is not constant anyway. In the year "500 the period of the precession was about 25,998 years and in the meantime it has declined to about 25,744 years. Only around the year 3176 will the period of the precession be equal to 65 baktuns.

The earliest recorded date in the Long Count that I know of is from the year "31, so the Long Count and the date of the end of the period of 13 baktuns on 21 December 2012 were already fixed then. If the Long Count is indeed based on the period of the precession, then the Maya would have had to measure the period of the precession already in or before the year "31 (and found 65 baktuns for it). The period of the precession was then about 25,951 years, which is 1.3 percent less than 65 baktuns, so the Maya would then have measured the period of the precession with an error of 1.3 percent.

Such seemingly small differences can have great consequences in the long run. According to the data of Laskar the vernal equinox (and hence also the southern solstitial point which is exactly 90 degrees removed from the vernal equinox) shifts over 28.46 degrees between the years "31 and 2012, but if the period of the precession were equal to 65 baktuns then the shift would have been 360/ 25626.28*(2012 - (-31)) = 28.70 degrees. The Maya would then have had to aim for a shift of 28.70 degrees for 2012, but in 2012 we've only had 28.46 degrees of that shift. It takes an additional 18 years (until the year 2030) before the shift has increased to 28.70 degrees.

How much extra time is needed to compensate for the difference between the true precession and the precession according to a period of 65 baktuns depends on when exactly the Long Count was fixed, because the period of the precession is not constant. The longer ago the Long Count was fixed, the more compensation is needed. If the Long Count was already fixed by the year "300, then 21 extra years would be needed.

"The Maya used very accurate astronomical knowledge to design their calendar, and that's why even today special things happen in the sky on nice round dates in their calendar."

The periods in the calendars of the Maya are always the same, and no extra periods are ever inserted or removed. Therefore, the calendars of the Maya cannot keep accurately in step with astronomical periods.

Most calendars attempt to follow one or more astronomically determined periods, such as the seasons or the phases of the Moon, but those periods are not a whole number of days long and are not equal either to some fixed ratio of whole numbers. That means that a calendar that always has the exact same periods that are always a whole number of days long cannot run in step with any astronomical period. For example, a calendar with always 365 days in a year (such as one of the calendars of the Maya) runs about (but not exactly) 1/4 day more out of step with the seasons each year, compared to the first year, so in the course of time the beginning of every season runs through all months of such a calendar.

To be able to follow an astronomical period reasonably well, a calendar must occasionally vary the length of a period, or occasionally include an extra period or omit a period. Lunar calendars, for example, have some months of 29 days and some months of 30 days. Solar calendars occasionally insert a bissextile (extra) day, and lunisolar calendars occasionally insert an embolistic (extra) month. In this way, the average length of the periods of those calendars can be a simple ratio that is close to the length of the astronomical period that that calendar tries to follow. The calendars of the Maya do not do this.

Also, astronomical periods are not constant, but slowly vary with time. For example, the length of the year of the seasons varies because of the influence of the gravity of the Sun and the other planets, and (through the precession) because of the influence of the distribution of mass in and on Earth (including the flow of matter under the surface, of water in the oceans, and of the air, and the distribution and melting of ice). The length of the synodical month increases because the Moon slowly recedes from the Earth. We can accurately predict some of these influences, but not others (including the distribution of matter in and on Earth and how that influences the rotation of the Earth).

A calendar that wants to follow an astronomically determined period must occasionally be adjusted because the length of the astronomical periods changes in a not entirely predictable way. Calendars such as those of the Maya that have fixed rules that are not adjusted based on observations cannot keep accurately following an astronomical period forever, even if they did so at the beginning.

So, the calendars of the Maya do not keep in step with any astronomically determined period.

## CONCLUSION

My conclusion is that a new period of 13 baktuns in the Long Count of the Maya probably begins on 21 December 2012, but that we should not expect any special phenomena in the sky that are tied to that beginning.

It seems unlikely to me that the Maya tried to design their Long Count in such a way that the new period would start on a southern solstice in the middle of the Milky Way in their distant future, though it is not impossible.

If the Maya did design their Long Count with that conjunction in mind, then I do not think that they had enough knowledge to be able to predict the correct day of the conjunction accurately to better than a few dozen years, so if any special phenomena could be expected on the exact day of the conjunction, then they would probably not be visible on (or not visible just one) 21 December 2012.

I think that the beginning of a new period in the Long Count of the Maya in 2012 is just as unimportant as the 6000th anniversary of the Biblical creation date (celebrated in 1996), or the planetary conjunction of May 2000, or all kinds of past dates for which the end of the world had been predicted. Someone who did not hear about the prediction in advance would not have noticed anything special on those dates, and I predict that December 2012 will be like that as well.

The only effects that can be expected associated with the conjunction of 21 December 2012 have to do with the attention that people draw to that conjunction and date. If people expect that unusual things will happen on a certain date, then on that date they'll behave differently than usual, and that in itself is already an unusual thing. In this way they can fulfill their own expectations.

## COINCIDENCE

It is believed that it is but a coincidence that 65 baktuns are approximately equal to the period of the precession of the equinoxes and that it is coincidence that the coming date of 0.0.0.0.0 in the Long Count falls on a southern solstice in the middle of the Milky Way.

You might think that it would have to be a very great coincidence, because if you choose the length of 65 baktuns at random then the chances of it happening to be about equal to the period of the precession of the equinoxes would be very small, and if you fix the date 0.0.0.0.0 at random (without regard to solstices or the Milky Way), then the chances of it happening to fall on a southern solstice in the middle of the Milky Way are also very small.

However, the probability of getting three sixes when casting three dies is also very small, but if someone does cast three sixes then that is not evidence of design or foul play.

After all, if you cast the dies, then you must get *some* result, and if the dies are honest, then any result is equally probable, with the same very small probability, so getting three sixes is then just as likely as getting, for example, a two, and then a four, and then a three. This shows that the improbability of an occurrence is not by itself proof of design or foul play.

The observation that 65 baktuns are roughly equal to the period of the precession of the equinoxes is by itself not evidence that the Maya knew the precession, and the observation that the real 0.0.0.0.0 falls on a southern solstice when the Sun is in the middle of the Milky Way is therefore by itself no proof that the Maya must have designed their Long Count with the solstice and the Milky Way in mind.

Without unambiguous evidence from the Maya themselves we'll never be certain why they designed their Long Count in exactly the way they did.

## PREDICTED AND SCHEDULED EVENTS

### *January*

- January 1 - Poland, Bulgaria, and Latvia are set to adopt the Euro.
- January 15 - Presidential elections in Finland.
- January 31 - 433 Eros, the second-largest Near Earth Object on record (size 13x13x33 km) will pass Earth at 0.1790 astronomical units (26,778,019 km/16,639,090 mi). NASA studied Eros with the NEAR Shoemaker probe launched on 1996-02-17.

*February*

- February 5 - Super Bowl XLVI will be played at Lucas Oil Field in Indianapolis, Indiana.
- February 6 - Queen Elizabeth II will celebrate her Diamond Jubilee. A series of festivities across the United Kingdom and Commonwealth of Nations will likely run throughout the year.

*April*

- April 1 - The United States Census of 1940 data is released to the public.
- April 17 - The United States will cede wartime control of the military of the Republic of Korea after 50 years and dissolve the Combined Forces Command. Two distinct military commands (South Korea and the United States) will operate in Korea during wartime, rather than one unified command under the Combined Forces Command.

*May*

- May - French Presidential election (if the incumbent's term had normally finished in May).
- May - Irish general election is due to be held if the current government remains in office for a full term.
- May 20 - Annular solar eclipse, a Sunday.

*June*

- June 6 - The second and last solar transit of Venus of the century. The next pair is predicted to occur in 2117 and 2125.
- June 9 – July 1 - The 2012 European Football Championship will be played in Poland and Ukraine.

*July*

- July 1 - Presidential Elections in Mexico.
- July 18–21 - The 2012 World Rowing Championships will be held at Plovdiv, Bulgaria.
- July 27 - Opening ceremony of the 2012 Summer Olympics begins in London at 7:30 pm UTC, 8:30pm BST.

*August*

- August 12 - Closing ceremony of the 2012 Summer Olympics in London, a Sunday.
- August 29 - Start of the 2012 Summer Paralympics.

*September*

- September 9 - End of the 2012 Summer Paralympics.

*October*

- October 19 - at 01:36 UTC, the Earth will be home to 7 billion people, according to the US Census Bureau.

*November*

- November 6 - The United States Presidential, Senate, and House of Representatives elections.
- November 6 - Puerto Rico general election.
- November 13 - Total solar eclipse (visible in northern Australia and the South Pacific).
- November 28 - Penumbral lunar eclipse.

*December*

- December - Presidential elections in South Korea to elect the 18th President.
- December 1 - The next President of Mexico will be inaugurated.
- December 3 - Jupiter oppositions.
- December 21 - 11:11 UTC. Winter Solstice in the Northern Hemisphere, Summer Solstice in the Southern Hemisphere.
- December 21 - The Mesoamerican Long Count calendar, notably used by the Maya civilization among others of pre-Columbian Mesoamerica, completes its thirteenth *b'ak'tun* cycle since the calendar's mythical starting point (equivalent to August 11, 3114 BC in the proleptic Gregorian calendar, according to the "GMT-correlation" JDN= 584283). The Long Count *b'ak'tun* date of this starting point (13.0.0.0.0) is repeated, for the first time in a span of approximately 5,125 solar years. The significance of this

period-ending to the pre-Columbian Maya themselves is unclear, and there is an incomplete inscription (Tortuguero Monument 6) that records this date. It is also to be found carved on the walls of the Temple of Inscriptions in Palenque, where it functions as a base date from which other dates are computed. This date figures prominently in the religious syncretism of New Age Mayanism.

- December 23 - The alternative date for the completion of the thirteenth *b'ak'tun* cycle in the Maya calendar, using a version of the GMT-correlation based on a JDN of 584285 (a.k.a. the "astronomical" or "Lounsbury correlation"), which is supported by a smaller number of Mayanist researchers.
- December 31 - The Kyoto Protocol will expire.

*Unknown Dates*

- Australia and Ireland will cease analogue television broadcasts.
- California's ban on the production of foie gras will take effect.
- China will launch the Kuafu spacecraft.
- Internet traffic is expected to exceed 44 Exabytes per month, according to a study by Cisco Systems.
- Jamaica will hold its general elections.
- *Pleiades*, a proposed super computer build by Intel and SGI for NASA's Ames Research Center, is expected to be completed, reaching a peak performance of 10 Petaflops (10 quadrillion operations per second).
- Sight & Sound magazine will conduct its Top Ten Films of All-Time poll for the seventh decade since 1952.
- Start of the commercial operation of the first unit from the Novovoronezh Nuclear Power Plant II.
- The 108-ft Elwha Dam and 210-ft Glines Canyon Dam will be removed from the Elwha River in Washington state, marking the largest dam removal project in history.
- The Canadian Navy receives the delivery of the first Joint Support Ship.

- The Canberra class light aircraft carriers/large amphibious ships, the largest ships ever to be operated by the Royal Australian Navy, will be in service.
- The Hallandsas Ridge Tunnel will be completed, 17 years behind the original plan.
- The Replacement Eastern Span of the San Francisco – Oakland Bay Bridge will open to traffic, replacing the old Eastern cantilever span that was damaged in the Loma Prieta Earthquake in 1989, almost a quarter century (23 years) after the span was damaged
- The sun will reverse its own magnetic poles as a result of reaching the end of the current 11-year sunspot cycle.
- The United Kingdom will complete a 5-year process to cease analogue television broadcasts region-by-region, with Meridian Broadcasting, ITV London, Tyne Tees Television and UTV being the last areas to switch off analogue.
- Trinidad and Tobago will hold their general elections.

*Major Religious Holidays*

- January 7 - Christmas Day by Julian Calendar (Celebrated by Eastern Orthodox Christians)
- February 1 - Imbolc, a Cross-quarter day (Celebrated on February 2 in some places)
- February 5 - Mawlid an Nabi - Islam
- March 8 - Purim - Judaism
- March 20 - Spring Equinox, also known as Ostara
- April 7 - Passover - Judaism
- April 8 - Easter - Christianity
- May 1 - Beltane, a Cross-quarter day
- May 27 - Shavuot - Judaism
- June 17 - Lailat al Miraj - Islam
- June 20 - Summer solstice, also known as Midsummer or Litha
- July 20 - Ramadan Begins - Islam
- August 1 - Lammas, a Cross-quarter day
- August 19 - Id al Fitr - Islam

- September 17 - Rosh Hashanah - Judaism
- September 21 - Fall Equinox, also known as Mabon
- October 1 - Sukkot - Judaism
- October 26 - Eid al-Adha, a religious festival in Islam
- November 1 - Samhain, a Cross-quarter day, Neopagan new year and Christian All Saints' Day
- November 15 - New Year - Islam
- December 9 - Hanukkah - Judaism
- December 21 - Winter solstice, also known as Yule
- December 25 - Christmas

*Metaphysical Speculations*

2012 is claimed by some with New age beliefs to be a great year of spiritual transformation (or alternatively an apocalypse). There is disagreement among believers as to whether 2012 will see an end of civilization, or humanity will be elevated to a higher level. Many esoteric sources interpret the completion of the thirteenth B'ak'tun cycle in the Long Count of the Maya calendar (which occurs on December 21 by the most widely held correlation) to mean there will be a major change in world order. Astrologer John Jenkins has determined that on this date, there will be "an extremely close conjunction of the northern hemisphere winter solstice sun with the crossing point of the Galactic equator and the ecliptic", an event that will not be repeated for thousands of years.

Several authors have published works which claim that a major, world-changing event will take place in 2012:

- The 1997 book *The Bible Code* by Michael Drosnin claims that, according to certain algorithms of the Bible code, an asteroid or comet will collide with the Earth.
- The 2006 book *2012: The Return of Quetzalcoatl* by Daniel Pinchbeck discusses theories of a possible global awakening to psychic connection by the year 2012, creating a noosphere.
- Riley Martin claims that *Biaviian* aliens will allow passage aboard their 'Great Mother Ship' when the Earth is 'transformed' in 2012.

- Terence McKenna's numerological novelty theory suggests a point of singularity in which humankind will go through a great shift in consciousness.

## 2012 in Fiction

### *Literature*

- *Methuselah's Children* (1941/1958) and *Time Enough for Love* (1973) by Robert A. Heinlein: A crucial meeting of the Howard Families takes place, following the election of Nehemiah Scudder for president of the USA. In both novels, viewpoint character Lazarus Long is asked what happened at this meeting as he is the last living eyewitness; in both novels he declines to answer. Nehemiah Scudder establishes a religious dictatorship in the USA.
- *Domain* (2002) and *Resurrection* (2000) by author Steve Alten: A fictional series that tells the events of the Gabriel twins after discovering the mystery behind 2012.
- *2012: The War for Soul* by author Whitley Strieber (2007) is a fictional novel about three parallel earths and the occurrences leading up to December 21, 2012 in each as the walls between them begin to thin and allow passage through gateways to the others. A film adaptation is proposed, produced by Michael Bay.

### *Comics*

- *The Invisibles* ("The Invisible Kingdom," 1999–2000): The Invisibles' "fictional" universe expands into the meta-context of the "higher universe," possibly our own.
- Jojo's Bizarre Adventure by Hirohiko Araki: In the 6th part of this manga, the protagonists Jolyne Kujo, Hermes, Emporio, Anasui and Weather Report have to stop the villain Enrico Pucci from erasing the universe. Pucci obtains the stand Stairway to Heaven, which has the power of rewriting the universe, and tries to use the stand to create the perfect world for his master Dio. All these events occur in 2012, with the current universe ending near the completion of the thirteenth cycle of the Mayan calendar.

*Music*

- "A Certain Shade of Green," a song from the Incubus album *S.C.I.E.N.C.E.*, references 2012 in the following lines: *Are you gonna stand around till 2012 A.D.? / What are you waiting for, a certain shade of green?*. December 21, 2012 also appears to be the date when the video for the song "Warning" is supposed to take place.
- Genesis's song *Get'em Out By Friday* from their 1972 album *Foxtrot*, sets "18/9/2012" (on the printed operistic-dialog lyrics) as the date when "Genetic Control" would set a height restriction on human beings so that twice as many people could fit on real estate properties.
- The Hed PE song "I.F.O." (to be found on their *self-titled album*), which is about UFO sightings and governmental conspiracies to cover them up, references the year 2012: "Prepare to meet your maker in the skies over the pyramids / Check Stonehenge / Go ask the Mayans / 2012 soon come / I will be waitin' sayin' I told you so / When the skies are ripped open / And the mothership lands on your cynical ass". Hed PE also references 2012 in "Killing Time" from their second album *Broke. Come Twenty Twelve, come twelve tribes, come twelve strands, come twelve lives Twelve steps, twelve months, twelve drug dealers*
- Stones Throw Reccrds artist Dudley Perkins released his LP, entitled 'Expressions (2012 A.U.)', in 2006
- The instrumental song "December 21, 2012" by Frodus, which appears as a B-side to their best-selling 7" vinyl single of their Devo cover "Explosions" (Released 1997).
- The Anaal Nathrakh song "Timewave Zero" is about the apparent end of the world on December 21, 2012. The lyrics are translated as "The 21st Of December, 2012, The time will come"
- The A Day To Remember song "Fast Forward to 2012" refers to the world ending in 2012 as a warning for friends to do something to prepare.
- British nu-rave outfit Klaxons sing about apocalyptic horsemen in their song "Four Horsemen Of 2012" from the 2007 album Myths of the Near Future.

- The song "2012 — Demise of the 5th Sun" by the melodic death metal band Scar Symmetry is a reference to the year 2012. *"For the lines on the fractal wave / Fit the course of history / They're created to work as one till the end / When the winter solstice comes / Actualizing the prophecy / The demise in 2012 realized"*
- The Testament song "3 Days in Darkness", off of The Gathering album is a song about 2012, and speaks of the earth being swallowed in molten fire.
- VNV Nation's album Praise The Fallen" has the subtitle "PTF 2012", which is also the name of a track in the album, which seems to be predominantly about an upcoming war. The song, "Honour" starts with the line, "Passive fields, January 2012..."
- Heavy metal band Burnt By The Sun's two albums both deal with prophecies concerning the year 2012.
- "2012" is the name of the 2005 album by the experimental rock band Old Time Relijun, and several songs make references to ancient Mayan culture, such as "Burial Mound" and "The King of Lost Light."
- On the band Hella's album There's No 666 in Outer Space there is a track called "2012 and Countless" in which the only words are "There's no 666 in Outer Space" repeated.
- Metal band Ewigkeit's album Radio Ixtlan has a track entitled "Live at Palenque 2012" referencing both the Mayan calendar date and the site at which the Temple of Inscriptions where it is carved.
- Canibus mentions the year 2012 and December 21, 2012 on his Poet Laureate Infinity vocals and on his 2007 album For Whom the Beat Tolls.
- Industrial metal band Hanzel und Gretyl's fifth album is called 2012: Zwanzig Zwölf referencing the belief that the world will end in this year, as foretold in the Mesoamerican Long Count calendar.
- On DJ Muggs & Sick Jacken's album *Legend of the Mask and the Assassin*, they "prophetize" armageddon and other catastrophic events occurring in "2012 (feat. Cynic)."

*Film*

- *I Am Legend*, set in this year.
- *2012*, based on significance of Mesoamerican Long Count calendar.
- *Death Race* references this year as the year when the U.S. economy falls.

*Television*

- *Doctor Who*
  * "Dalek," 2005: A Dalek breaks loose under the Utah salt plains, and plans to kill every living thing on Earth.
  * "Fear Her," 2006: The episode is set during the lead-up to the 2012 Summer Olympics in London.
- *Futurama*
  * Xmas Story," 1999: The War of 2012 occurs, during which talk-show host Conan O'Brien lost his "freakishly long legs.".
  * Jurassic Bark," 2002; Philip J. Fry's dog Seymour dies in this year.
- *The X-Files* ("The Truth," 2002): On December 22, Aliens invade Earth.

*Games*

- *Shadowrun*: With the sixth Mayan world beginning, magic returns to the world in an event called "The Awakening."
- *Escape 2012*: The player's mission is to escape from alien captivity.
- In Dark•Matter, a campaign setting for the Alternity and D20 Modern roleplaying games, the institute that the protagonists belong to believe that 2012 will be the end of the world.
- *S.T.A.L.K.E.R — Shadow of Chernobyl* is set in this year
- *Psychic Force 2012* is set during this year.
- In *Universe at War: Earth Assault*, the Hierarchy invasion on Earth begins.

- An in-game document from *The Secret World* contains the date 2012 circled and underlined but the significance of this is yet unknown.
- In *Shattered Union*, U.S. president David Jefferson Adams accepts his second term in office after the Supreme Court disqualifies all other presidential candidates.
- Events of Mega Man III, Mega Man's Soccer, Wily and Right's RockBoard and Mega Man V are set in this year.
- One of the puzzles later on in La Mulana (A freeware PC game based on many of the older MSX games released) states you need to 'walk the end year of the Aztec's Fifth Age.' The player must then light only the torches of the gates that correspond to the numbers in the year '2012'.
- The setting of *Assassin's Creed* is September, 2012.

*Radio*

- The sitcom *Deep Trouble*, set on a nuclear submarine, takes place in 2012.

# 8

# Maya Calendar

The Maya calendar is a system of distinct calendars and almanacs used by the Maya civilization of pre-Columbian Mesoamerica, and by some modern Maya communities in highland Guatemala.

These calendars can be synchronized and interlocked, their combinations giving rise to further, more extensive cycles. The essentials of the Maya calendric system are based upon a system which had been in common use throughout the region, dating back to at least the 6th century BCE. It shares many aspects with calendars employed by other earlier Mesoamerican civilizations, such as the Zapotec and Olmec, and contemporary or later ones such as the Mixtec and Aztec calendars. Although the Mesoamerican calendar did not originate with the Maya, their subsequent extensions and refinements of it were the most sophisticated. Along with those of the Aztecs, the Maya calendars are the best-documented and most completely understood.

By the Maya mythological tradition, as documented in Colonial Yucatec accounts and reconstructed from Late Classic and Postclassic inscriptions, the deity Itzamna is frequently credited with bringing the knowledge of the calendar system to the ancestral Maya, along with writing in general and other foundational aspects of Maya culture.

### General Overview

The most important of these calendars is one with a period of 260 days. This 260-day calendar was prevalent across all

Mesoamerican societies, and is of great antiquity (almost certainly the oldest of the calendars). It is still used in some regions of Oaxaca, and by the Maya communities of the Guatemalan highlands. The Maya version is commonly known to scholars as the *Tzolkin*, or *Tzolk'in* in the revised orthography of the Academia de las Lenguas Mayas de Guatemala. The Tzolk'in is combined with another 365-day calendar (known as the *Haab*, or *Haab'* ), to form a synchronized cycle lasting for 52 Haabs, called the *Calendar Round*. Smaller cycles of 13 days (the *trecena*) and 20 days (the *veintena*) were important components of the Tzolk'in and Haab' cycles, respectively.

A different form of calendar was used to track longer periods of time, and for the inscription of calendar dates (i.e., identifying when one event occurred in relation to others). This form, known as the *Long Count*, is based upon the number of elapsed days since a mythological starting-point. According to the correlation between the Long Count and Western calendars accepted by the great majority of Maya researchers (known as the GMT correlation), this starting-point is equivalent to August 11, 3114 BCE in the proleptic Gregorian calendar or 6 September in the Julian calendar ("3113 astronomical). The Goodman-Martinez-Thompson correlation was chosen by Thompson in 1935 based on earlier correlations by Joseph Goodman in 1905 (August 11), Juan Martínez Hernandez in 1926 (August 12), and John Eric Sydney Thompson in 1927 (August 13). By its linear nature, the Long Count was capable of being extended to refer to any date far into the future (or past). This calendar involved the use of a positional notation system, in which each position signified an increasing multiple of the number of days. The Maya numeral system was essentially vigesimal (i.e., base-20), and each unit of a given position represented 20 times the unit of the position which preceded it. An important exception was made for the second place value, which instead represented 18 × 20, or 360 days, more closely approximating the solar year than would 20 × 20 = 400 days. It should be noted however that the cycles of the Long Count are independent of the solar year.

Many Maya Long Count inscriptions are supplemented by what is known as the *Lunar Series*, another calendar form which provides information on the lunar phase and position of the Moon in a half-yearly cycle of lunations.

A 584-day *Venus cycle* was also maintained, which tracked the appearance and conjunctions of Venus as the morning and evening stars. Many events in this cycle were seen as being inauspicious and baleful, and occasionally warfare was timed to coincide with stages in this cycle.

Other, less-prevalent or poorly-understood cycles, combinations and calendar progressions were also tracked. An *819-day count* is attested in a few inscriptions; repeating sets of 9- and 13-day intervals associated with different groups of deities, animals and other significant concepts are also known.

*Maya Concepts of Time*

With the development of the place-notational Long Count calendar (believed to have been inherited from other Mesoamerican cultures), the Maya had an elegant system with which events could be recorded in a linear relationship to one another, and also with respect to the calendar ("linear time") itself. In theory, this system could readily be extended to delineate any length of time desired, by simply adding to the number of higher-order place markers used (and thereby generating an ever-increasing sequence of day-multiples, each day in the sequence uniquely identified by its Long Count number). In practice, most Maya Long Count inscriptions confine themselves to noting only the first 5 coefficients in this system (a *b'ak'tun*-count), since this was more than adequate to express any historical or current date (with an equivalent span of approximately 5125 solar years). Even so, example inscriptions exist which noted or implied lengthier sequences, indicating that the Maya well understood a linear (past-present-future) conception of time.

However, and in common with other Mesoamerican societies, the repetition of the various calendric cycles, the natural cycles of observable phenomena, and the recurrence and renewal of death-rebirth imagery in their mythological traditions were important and pervasive influences upon Maya societies. This conceptual view, in which the "cyclical nature" of time is highlighted, was a pre-eminent one, and many rituals were concerned with the completion and re-occurrences of various cycles. As the particular calendaric configurations were once again repeated, so too were the "supernatural" influences with which they were associated.

Thus it was held that particular calendar configurations had a specific "character" to them, which would influence events on days exhibiting that configuration. Divinations could then be made from the auguries associated with a certain configuration, since events taking place on some future date would be subject to the same influences as its corresponding previous cycle dates. Events and ceremonies would be timed to coincide with auspicious dates, and avoid inauspicious ones.

The completion of significant calendar cycles ("period endings"), such as a *k'atun*-cycle, were often marked by the erection and dedication of specific monuments (mostly stela inscriptions, but sometimes twin-pyramid complexes such as those in Tikal and Yaxha), commemorating the completion, accompanied by dedicatory ceremonies.

A cyclical interpretation is also noted in Maya creation accounts, in which the present world and the humans in it were preceded by other worlds (one to five others, depending on the tradition) which were fashioned in various forms by the gods, but subsequently destroyed. The present world also had a tenuous existence, requiring the supplication and offerings of periodic sacrifice to maintain the balance of continuing existence. Similar themes are found in the creation accounts of other Mesoamerican societies.

### *Tzolk'in*

Some Mayanists employ the name *Tzolk'in* (in modern Maya orthography; also and formerly commonly written *tzolkin*) for the Maya Sacred Round or 260-day calendar. Tzolk'in is a neologism coined in Yukatek Maya, to mean "count of days" (Coe 1992). The actual names of this calendar as used by Precolumbian Maya peoples are still debated by scholars. The Aztec calendar equivalent was called *Tonalpohualli*, in the Nahuatl language.

The Tzolk'in calendar combines twenty day names with the thirteen numbers of the *trecena* cycle to produce 260 unique days.

It is used to determine the time of religious and ceremonial events and for divination. Each successive day is numbered from 1 up to 13 and then starting again at 1. Separately from this, each day is given a name in sequence from a list of 20 day names:

### *Tzolk'in calendar: named days and associated glyphs*

| Tzolk'in calendar: named days and associated glyphs | | | | | | | | | |
|---|---|---|---|---|---|---|---|---|---|
| Seq. Nº.[1] | Day Name[2] | Glyph example[3] | 16th C. Yucatec[4] | reconstructed Classic Maya[5] | Seq. Nº.[1] | Day Name[2] | Glyph example[3] | 16th C. Yucatec[4] | reconstructed Classic Maya[5] |
| 01 | **Imix'** |  | Imix | Imix (?) / Ha' (?) | 11 | **Chuwen** |  | Chuen | (unknown) |
| 02 | **Ik'** |  | Ik | Ik' | 12 | **Eb'** |  | Eb | (unknown) |
| 03 | **Ak'b'al** |  | Akbal | Ak'b'al (?) | 13 | **B'en** |  | Ben | (unknown) |
| 04 | **K'an** |  | Kan | K'an (?) | 14 | **Ix** |  | Ix | Hix (?) |
| 05 | **Chikchan** |  | Chiccha n | (unknown) | 15 | **Men** |  | Men | (unknown) |
| 06 | **Kimi** |  | Cimi | Cham (?) | 16 | **K'ib'** |  | Cib | (unknown) |
| 07 | **Manik'** |  | Manik | Manich' (?) | 17 | **Kab'an** |  | Caban | Chab' (?) |
| 08 | **Lamat** |  | Lamat | Ek' (?) | 18 | **Etz'nab** |  | Etznab | (unknown) |
| 09 | **Muluk** |  | Muluc | (unknown) | 19 | **Kawak** |  | Cauac | (unknown) |
| 10 | **Ok** |  | Oc | (unknown) | 20 | **Ajaw** |  | Ahau | Ajaw |

*NOTES:*

1. The sequence number of the named day in the Tzolk'in calendar
2. Day name, in the standardised and revised orthography of the Guatemalan Academia de Lenguas Mayas[2]
3. An example glyph (logogram) for the named day. Note that for most of these several different forms are recorded; the ones shown here are typical of carved monumental inscriptions (these are "cartouche" versions)
4. Day name, as recorded from 16th century Yukatek Maya accounts, principally Diego de Landa; this orthography has (until recently) been widely used
5. In most cases, the actual day name as spoken in the time of the Classic Period (ca. 200–900) when most inscriptions were made is not known. The versions given here (in Classic Maya, the main language of the inscriptions) are reconstructed based on phonological evidence, if available; a '?' symbol indicates the

Some systems started the count with 1 Imix', followed by 2 Ik', 3 Ak'b'al, etc. up to 13 B'en. The *trecena* day numbers then start again at 1 while the named-day sequence continues onwards, so the next days in the sequence are 1 Ix, 2 Men, 3 K'ib', 4 Kab'an, 5 Etz'nab', 6 Kawak, and 7 Ajaw. With all twenty named days used, these now began to repeat the cycle while the number sequence continues, so the next day after 7 Ajaw is 8 Imix'. The repetition of these interlocking 13- and 20-day cycles therefore takes 260 days to complete (that is, for every possible combination of number/named day to occur once).

*Divination*

Each day of the Tzolk'in has a Patron Spirit who influences events. Ah K'in, the Maya shaman-priest, whose title means "Day Keeper", read the Tzolk'in to determine the answers to yes/no questions as well as more complex questions involving health, wealth and family. The Sacred Calendar is also used to set the most auspicious dates for household, lineage, and community rituals.

When a child is born, the day keeper interprets the Tzolk'in cycle to identify the baby's character (similarly done today with a natal chart). For example, a child born on the day of Ak'b'al is thought to be feminine, wealthy, and verbally skillful. The birthday of Ak'b'al (along with several other days) is also thought to give the child the ability to receive messages with the supernatural world through somatic twitches of "blood lightning", so he or she might become a Shaman-priest or a Marriage Spokesman.

There are several forms of Maya Calendar divination employing the sacred coral seeds which each Calendar diviner carries in a small bag with crystals and 'other small things' (Tozzer 1941).

The Precolumbian Maya practiced a form of Bibliomancy, in which they would cast the seeds upon a calendar to determine the good and bad days for the year.

Precolumbian Maya employed and Modern Maya Ah K'in employ Sortilage, in which piles of four or five beans are counted from the current calendar day of the Sacred Round to arrive at the result. Modern Maya Ah K'in also employ Cartomancy, in which the fifty two cards of the poker deck represent the fifty two Year Bearers of the Maya Calendar Round.

Maya shamans also perform a wide variety of divinatory arts which do not specifically depend upon a mastery of the sacred calendar, including crystal, mirror, and water gazing; and spirit possession, among others.

## *Origin of the Tzolk'in*

The exact origin of the Tzolk'in is not known, but there are several theories. One theory is that the calendar came from mathematical operations based on the numbers thirteen and twenty, which were important numbers to the Maya. The numbers multiplied together equal 260. Another theory is that the 260-day period came from the length of human pregnancy. This is close to the average number of days between the *first missed* menstrual period and birth, unlike Naegele's rule which is 40 weeks (280 days) between the *last* menstrual period and birth. It is postulated that midwives originally developed the calendar to predict babies' expected birth dates.

A third theory comes from understanding of astronomy, geography and paleontology. The mesoamerican calendar probably originated with the Olmecs, and a settlement existed at Izapa, in southeast Chiapas Mexico, before 1200 BCE. There, at a latitude of about 15° N, the Sun passes through zenith twice a year, and there are 260 days between zenithal passages, and gnomons (used generally for observing the path of the Sun and in particular zenithal passages), were found at this and other sites. The sacred almanac may well have been set in motion on August 13, 1359 BCE, in Izapa. Vincent H. Malmström, a geographer who suggested this location and date, outlines his reasons:

(1) Astronomically, it lay at the only latitude in North America where a 260-day interval (the length of the "strange" sacred almanac used throughout the region in pre-Columbian times) can be measured between vertical sun positions — an interval which happens to begin on the 13th of August — the day the peoples of the Mesoamerica believed that the present world was created; (2) Historically, it was the only site at this latitude which was old

enough to have been the cradle of the sacred almanac, which at that time (1973) was thought to date to the 4th or 5th centuries B.C.; and (3) Geographically, it was the only site along the required parallel of latitude that lay in a tropical lowland ecological niche where such creatures as alligators, monkeys, and iguanas were native — all of which were used as day-names in the sacred almanac.

Malmström also offers strong arguments against both of the former explanations.

A fourth theory is that the calendar is based on the crops. From planting to harvest is approximately 260 days.

*Haab'*

***Haab' Months***

| Name | Meaning† |
|---|---|
| Pop | mat |
| Wo | black conjunction |
| Sip | red conjunction |
| Sotz' | bat |
| Sek | ? |
| Xul | dog |
| Yaxk'in | new sun |
| Mol | water |
| Ch'en | black storm |
| Yax | green storm |
| Sac | white storm |
| Keh | red storm |
| Mak | enclosed |
| K'ank'in | yellow sun |
| Muwan | owl |
| Pax | planting time |
| K'ayab' | turtle |
| Kumk'u | granary |
| Wayeb' | five unlucky days |

† *Jones 1984*

The Haab' was the Maya solar calendar made up of eighteen months of twenty days each plus a period of five days ("nameless days") at the end of the year known as *Wayeb'* (or *Uayeb* in 16th C. orthography). Bricker (1982) estimates that the Haab' was first used around 550 BCE with the starting point of the winter solstice.

The Haab' month names are known today by their corresponding names in colonial-era Yukatek Maya, as transcribed by 16th century sources (in particular, Diego de Landa and books such as the *Chilam Balam* of Chumayel). Phonemic analyses of Haab' glyph names in pre-Columbian Maya inscriptions have demonstrated that the names for these twenty-day periods varied considerably from region to region and from period to period, reflecting differences in the base language(s) and usage in the Classic and Postclassic eras predating their recording by Spanish sources.

Each day in the Haab' calendar was identified by a day number in the month followed by the name of the month. Day numbers began with a glyph translated as the "seating of" a named month, which is usually regarded as day 0 of that month, although a minority treat it as day 20 of the month preceding the named month. In the latter case, the seating of Pop is day 5 of Wayeb'. For the majority, the first day of the year was 0 Pop (the seating of Pop). This was followed by 1 Pop, 2 Pop as far as 19 Pop then 0 Wo, 1 Wo and so on.

As a calendar for keeping track of the seasons, the Haab' was crude and inaccurate, since it treated the year as having 365 days, and ignored the extra quarter day (approximately) in the actual tropical year.

This meant that the seasons moved with respect to the calendar year by a quarter day each year, so that the calendar months named after particular seasons no longer corresponded to these seasons after a few centuries. The Haab' is equivalent to the wandering 365-day year of the ancient Egyptians. Some argue that the Maya knew about and compensated for the quarter day error, even though their calendar did not include anything comparable to a leap year, a method first implemented by the Romans.

*Wayeb'*

The five nameless days at the end of the calendar, called Wayeb', were thought to be a dangerous time. Foster (2002) writes "During Wayeb, portals between the mortal realm and the Underworld dissolved. No boundaries prevented the ill-intending deities from causing disasters." To ward off these evil spirits, the Maya had customs and rituals they practiced during Wayeb'. For example, people avoided leaving their houses or washing or combing their hair.

*Calendar Round*

Neither the Tzolk'in nor the Haab' system numbered the years. The combination of a Tzolk'in date and a Haab' date was enough to identify a date to most people's satisfaction, as such a combination did not occur again for another 52 years, above general life expectancy.

Because the two calendars were based on 260 days and 365 days respectively, the whole cycle would repeat itself every 52 Haab' years exactly. This period was known as a Calendar Round. The end of the Calendar Round was a period of unrest and bad luck among the Maya, as they waited in expectation to see if the gods would grant them another cycle of 52 years.

*Long Count*

Since Calendar Round dates can only distinguish in 18,980 days, equivalent to around 52 solar years, the cycle repeats roughly once each lifetime, and thus, a more refined method of dating was needed if history was to be recorded accurately. To measure dates, therefore, over periods longer than 52 years, Mesoamericans devised the Long Count calendar.

The Maya name for a day was *k'in*. Twenty of these k'ins are known as a *winal* or *uinal*. Eighteen winals make one *tun*. Twenty tuns are known as a *k'atun*. Twenty k'atuns make a *b'ak'tun*.

The Long Count calendar identifies a date by counting the number of days from August 11, 3114 BCE in the proleptic Gregorian calendar or September 6 in the Julian calendar. But instead of using a base-10 (decimal) scheme like Western numbering, the Long Count days were tallied in a modified base-20 scheme.

Thus 0.0.0.1.5 is equal to 25, and 0.0.0.2.0 is equal to 40. As the winal unit resets after only counting to 18, the Long Count consistently uses base-20 only if the tun is considered the primary unit of measurement, not the k'in; with the k'in and winal units being the number of days in the tun. The Long Count 0.0.1.0.0 represents 360 days, rather than the 400 in a purely base-20 (vigesimal) count.

**Table of Long Count units**

| Days | Long Count period | Long Count period | Approx solar years |
|---|---|---|---|
| 1 | = 1 K'in | | |
| 20 | = 20 K'in | = 1 Winal | 1/18th |
| 360 | = 18 Winal | = 1 Tun | 1 |
| 7,200 | = 20 Tun | = 1 K'atun | 20 |
| 144,000 | = 20 K'atun | = 1 B'ak'tun | 395 |

There are also four rarely-used higher-order cycles: *piktun, kalabtun, k'inchiltun,* and *alautun.*

Since the Long Count dates are unambiguous, the Long Count was particularly well suited to use on monuments. The monumental inscriptions would not only include the 5 digits of the Long Count, but would also include the two tzolk'in characters followed by the two haab' characters.

The Mesoamerican Long Count calendar forms the basis for a New Age belief, first forecast by Jose Argüelles, that a cataclysm will take place on or about December 21, 2012, a forecast that mainstream Mayanist scholars consider a misinterpretation, yet is commonly referenced in pop-culture media as the 2012 problem.

"For the ancient Maya, it was a huge celebration to make it to the end of a whole cycle," says Sandra Noble, executive director of the Foundation for the Advancement of Mesoamerican Studies, Inc. in Crystal River, Florida. To render December 21, 2012, as a doomsday or moment of cosmic shifting, she says, is "a complete fabrication and a chance for a lot of people to cash in."

*Venus Cycle*

Another important calendar for the Maya was the Venus cycle. The Maya were skilled astronomers, and could calculate the Venus cycle with extreme accuracy. There are six pages in the Dresden Codex (one of the Maya codices) devoted to the accurate calculation of the location of Venus. The Maya were able to achieve such accuracy by careful observation over many years. There are various theories as to why Venus cycle was especially important for the Maya, including the belief that it was associated with war and used it to divine good times (called electional astrology) for coronations and war. Maya rulers planned for wars to begin when Venus rose. The Maya also possibly tracked other planets' movements, including those of Mars, Mercury, and Jupiter.

## MESOAMERICAN LONG COUNT CALENDAR

"Long Count" redirects here. For the famous 1927 boxing match, see The Long Count Fight.

The Mesoamerican Long Count calendar is a non-repeating, vigesimal (base-20) calendar used by several Mesoamerican cultures, most notably the Maya. For this reason, it is sometimes known as the Maya (or Mayan) Long Count calendar. Using a modified vigesimal tally, the Long Count calendar identifies a day by counting the number of days passed since August 11, 3114 BCE in the proleptic Gregorian or September 6th in the Julian calendar, ("3113) Astronomical dating. Because the Long Count calendar is non-repeating, it was widely used on monuments.

*Background*

Among other calendars devised in pre-Hispanic Mesoamerica, two of the most widely used were the 365-day solar calendar (Haab' in Mayan) and the 260-day ceremonial calendar, which had 20 periods of 13 days. This 260-day calendar was known as the Tzolk'in to the Maya and tonalpohualli to the Aztecs.

The Haab' and the Tzolk'in calendars identified and named the days, but not the years. The combination of a Haab' date and a Tzolk'in date was enough to identify a specific date to most people's satisfaction, as such a combination did not occur again for another 52 years, above general life expectancy. Because the two calendars were based on 365 days and 260 days respectively, the whole cycle would repeat itself every 52 Haab' years exactly. This period is generally known as the Calendar Round.

To measure dates over periods longer than 52 years, the Mesoamericans devised the Long Count calendar.

### *Long Count Periods*

The Long Count calendar identifies a date by counting the number of days from August 11, 3114 BCE in the proleptic Gregorian calendar or September 6 in the Julian calendar, ("3113 astronomical dating). Rather than using a base-10 scheme, like Western numbering, the Long Count days were tallied in a base-20 scheme. Thus 0.0.0.1.5 is equal to 25, and 0.0.0.2.0 is equal to 40.

The Long Count is not consistently base-20, however, since the second digit rolls over to zero when it reaches 18. Thus 0.0.1.0.0 does not represent 400 days, but rather only 360 days.

The following table shows the period equivalents as well as Maya names for these periods:

| Representation | Long Count subdivisions | Days | ~ solar years |
|---|---|---|---|
| 0.0.0.0.1 | 1 K'in | 1 | 1/365 |
| 0.0.0.1.0 | 1 Winal = 20 K'in | 20 | 1/18 |
| 0.0.1.0.0 | 1 Tun = 18 Winal | 360 | 1· |
| 0.1.0.0.0 | 1 K'atun = 20 Tun | 7,200 | 19.7 |
| 1.0.0.0.0 | 1 B'ak'tun = 20 K'atun | 144,000 | 394 |

## Calculating Long Count dates

### *Mesoamerican Numerals*

Long Count dates are written with Mesoamerican numerals, as shown on this table. A dot represents one while a bar equals 5. The shell glyph was used to represent the zero concept. The Long Count calendar required the use of zero as a place-holder, and presents one of the earliest uses of the zero concept in history.

### *Syntax*

The Long Count dates are written vertically, with the higher periods (i.e. *b'ak'tun*) on the top and then the number of each successively smaller order periods until the number of days (*k'in*) are listed. As can be seen at left, the Long Count date shown on Stela C at Tres Zapotes is 7.16.6.16.18.

| 7 | × 144000 | = 1,008,000 days (*k'in*) |
|---|---|---|
| 16 | × 7200 | = 115,200 days (*k'in*) |
| 6 | × 360 | = 2,160 days (*k'in*) |
| 16 | × 20 | = 320 days (*k'in*) |
| 18 | × 1 | = 18 days (*k'in*) |
| | Total days | = 1,125,698 days (*k'in*) |

The date on Stela C, then, is 1,125,698 days from August 11, 3114 BCE, or September 1, 32 BCE.

On Maya monuments, the Long Count syntax is more complex. The date sequence is given once, at the beginning of the inscription, and opens with the so-called ISIG (Introductory Series Initial Glyph) which reads *tzik-a(h) hab' [patron of Haab' month]* ("revered was the year-count with the patron [of the month]"). Next come the 5 digits of the Long Count, followed by the tzolk'in date written as single glyph, and then by supplementary information. Most of this supplementary series is optional and has been shown to be related to lunar data, for example, the age of the moon on the day and the calculated length of current lunation. The date is concluded by a glyph stating the day and month of the Haab year. The text then continues with whatever activity occurred on that date. A drawing of a full Maya Long Count inscription is shown below (click here).

## *Origin of the Long Count Calendar*

The earliest Long Count inscription yet discovered is on Stela 2 at Chiapa de Corzo, Chiapas, Mexico, showing a date of 36 BCE. This table lists the 6 artifacts with the 8 oldest Long Count dates.

| **Archaeological site** | **Name** | **Gregorian Date (based on August 11)** | **Long Count digits** | **Location** |
|---|---|---|---|---|
| Chiapa de Corzo | Stela 2 | December 10, 36 BCE | 7.16.3.2.13 | Chiapas, Mexico |
| Tres Zapotes | Stela C | September 3, 32 BCE | 7.16.6.16.18 | Veracruz, Mexico |
| El Baúl | Stela 1 | March 6, 37 CE | 7.19.15.7.12 | Guatemala |
| Abaj Takalik | Stela 5 | May 20, 103 CE | 8.3.2.10.15 | Guatemala |
| '' | '' | June 6, 126 CE | 8.4.5.17.11 | '' |
| La Mojarra | Stela 1 | July 14, 156 CE | 8.5.16.9.7 | Veracruz, Mexico |
| '' | '' | May 22, 143 CE | 8.5.3.3.5 | '' |
| Near La Mojarra | Tuxtla Statuette | March 15, 162 CE | 8.6.2.4.17 | Veracruz, Mexico |

Of the 6 sites, three are on the western edge of the Maya homeland and three are several hundred kilometers further west, leading most researchers to believe that the Long Count calendar predates the Maya. La Mojarra Stela 1, the Tuxtla Statuette, Tres Zapotes Stela C, and Chiapa Stela 2 are all inscribed in an Epi-Olmec, not Maya, style. El Baúl Stela 2, on the other hand, was created in the Izapan style. The first unequivocally Maya artifact is Stela 29 from Tikal, with the Long Count date of 292 CE (8.12.14.8.15), more than 300 years after Stela 2 from Chiapa de Corzo.

*Correlations between Western Calendars and the Long Count Calendar*

JDN correlationsto the Maya creation date(after Thompson 1971, et al.)

| Name | Correlation |
|---|---|
| Willson | 438,906 |
| Smiley | 482,699 |
| Makemson | 489,138 |
| Spinden | 489,384 |
| Teeple | 492,662 |
| Dinsmoor | 497,879 |
| -4CR | 508,363 |
| -2CR | 546,323 |
| Stock | 556,408 |
| Goodman | 584,280 |
| Martinez-Hernandez | 584,281 |
| GMT | 584,283 |
| Thompson (Lounsbury) | 584,285 |
| Pogo | 588,626 |
| +2CR | 622,243 |
| Kreichgauer | 626,927 |

| | |
|---|---|
| +4CR | 660,203 |
| Hochleitner | 674,265 |
| Schultz | 677,723 |
| Ramos | 679,108 |
| Valliant | 679,183 |
| Weitzel | 774,078 |

***A list of the start dates for 14 Baktuns***

| Long Count | Gregorian Calendar Date(including proleptic) |
|---|---|
| 0.0.0.0.0 | August 11, 3114 BCE |
| 1.0.0.0.0 | November 13, 2720 BCE |
| 2.0.0.0.0 | February 16, 2325 BCE |
| 3.0.0.0.0 | May 21, 1931 BCE |
| 4.0.0.0.0 | August 23, 1537 BCE |
| 5.0.0.0.0 | November 26, 1143 BCE |
| 6.0.0.0.0 | February 28, 748 BCE |
| 7.0.0.0.0 | June 3, 354 BCE |
| 8.0.0.0.0 | September 5, 41 CE |
| 9.0.0.0.0 | December 9, 435 |
| 10.0.0.0.0 | March 13, 830 |
| 11.0.0.0.0 | June 15, 1224 |
| 12.0.0.0.0 | September 18, 1618 |
| 13.0.0.0.0 | December 21, 2012 |

There have been various methods proposed to allow us to convert from a Long Count date to a Western calendar date. These methods, or correlations, are generally based on dates from the Spanish conquest, where both Long Count and Western dates are known with some accuracy.

The commonly-established way of expressing the correlation between the Maya calendar and the Gregorian or Julian calendars is to provide number of days from the start of the Julian Period

(Monday, January 1, 4713 BCE) to the start of creation on 0.0.0.0.0 (4 Ajaw, 8 Kumk'u).

The most commonly accepted correlation is the "Goodman, Martinez, Thompson" correlation (GMT correlation). The GMT correlation establishes that the 0.0.0.0.0 creation date occurred on September 6, 3114 BCE (Julian) or August 11, 3114 BCE (Gregorian), Julian day number (JDN) 584283. This correlation fits the astronomical, ethnographic, carbon dating, and historical sources. However, there have been other correlations that have been proposed at various times, most of which are merely of historical interest, except that by Floyd Lounsbury, two days after the GMT correlation, which is in use by some Maya scholars, such as Linda Schele.

Today, 15:26, Thursday November 6 2008 (UTC), in the Long Count is 12.19.15.14.14 (GMT correlation).

## 2012 and the Long Count

According to the *Popol Vuh*, a book compiling details of creation accounts known to the K'iche' Maya of the Colonial-era highlands, we are living in the fourth world. The *Popol Vuh* describes the first three creations that the gods failed in making and the creation of the successful fourth world where men were placed. In the Maya Long Count, the previous creation ended at the start of a 13th b'ak'tun.

The previous creation ended on a long count of 12.19.19.17.19. Another 12.19.19.17.19 will occur on December 20, 2012, followed by the start of the fourteenth b'ak'tun, 13.0.0.0.0, on December 21, 2012].

### *Significance within the New Age Movement*

Three figures within the New Age, the artist and theorist Jose Argüelles, John Major Jenkins, Daniel Pinchbeck and the late ethnobotanist and psychonaut Terence McKenna, have publicized theories concerning the significance of the end of the cycle. (They arrived at their conclusions separately from one another). They have jointly inspired a number of articles and books that this will be the end of this creation, the next pole shift or, as McKenna speculated in his theories, the end of history and events as "novel" as the origin of life on Earth, which we could not possibly imagine. Jenkins has focused on the occurance of a Galactic Alignment in the "era of 2012". Other, more mundane speculations involve a worldwide catastrophe, such as a pole shift. The idea of the significance of the date has also increasingly passed into popular culture.

### *Inscriptions beyond 2012*

Maya stelae occasionally show dates beyond 2012. Most of these are in the form of "distance dates", where a Long Count date is given with a distance date to be added. For example, on the Tablet of Inscriptions from Palenque the following Long Count date was found: 9.8.9.13.0 8 Ahau 13 Pop (March 24, 603 Gregorian) with a distance date of 10.11.10.5.8. The resulting date is given as 1.0.0.0.0.8 5 Lamat 1 Mol, or October 21, 4772 – almost 3,000 years into the future. The king Pacal of Palenque predicted that on this date the eightieth Calendar Round anniversary of his accession will be celebrated, suggesting he did not believe the world would end in 2012.

### *Summary*

Despite the publicity generated by the 2012 date, Susan Milbrath, curator of Latin American Art and Archaeology at the Florida Museum of Natural History, stated that "We [the archaeological community] have no record or knowledge that [the Maya] would think the world would come to an end" in 2012.

"For the ancient Maya, it was a huge celebration to make it to the end of a whole cycle," says Sandra Noble, executive director of the Foundation for the Advancement of Mesoamerican Studies, Inc. in Crystal River, Florida.

To render December 21, 2012, as a doomsday or moment of cosmic shifting, she says, is "a complete fabrication and a chance for a lot of people to cash in."

"There will be another cycle," says E. Wyllys Andrews V, director of the Tulane University Middle American Research Institute (MARI). "We know the Maya thought there was one before this, and that implies they were comfortable with the idea of another one after this."

## *Calculating a Full Long Count Date*

As stated, a full Long Count date not only includes the 5 digits of the Long Count, but the 2-character Tzolk'in and the 2-character Haab' dates as well. The 5 digit Long Count can therefore be confirmed with the other 4 characters (the "calendar round date").

Taking as an example a Calendar Round date of 9.12.2.0.16 (Long Count) 5 Kib' (Tzolk'in) 14 Yaxk'in (Haab'). One can check whether this date is correct by the following calculation.

It is perhaps easier to find out how many days there are since 4 Ajaw 8 Kumk'u, and show how the date 5 Kib' 14 Yaxk'in is derived.

| | | |
|---|---|---|
| 9 | × 144000 | = 1296000 |
| 12 | × 7200 | = 86400 |
| 2 | × 360 | = 720 |
| 0 | × 20 | = 0 |
| 16 | × 1 | = 16 |
| | Total days | = 1383136 k'in |

## *Calculating the Tzolk'in Date Portion*

The Tzolk'in date is counted forward from 4 Ajaw. To calculate the numerical portion of the Tzolk'in date, we must add 4 to the total number of days given by the date, and then divide total number of days by 13.

(4 + 1383136) / 13 = 106395 and 5/13

This means that 106395 whole 13 day cycles have been completed, and the numerical portion of the Tzolk'in date is 5.

To calculate the day, we divide the total number of days in the long count by 20 since there are twenty day names.

1383136 / 20 = 69156 and (16/20)

This means 16 day names must be counted from Ajaw. This gives Kib'. Therefore, the Tzolk'in date is 5 Kib'.

## *Calculating the Haab' Date Portion*

The Haab' date 8 Kumk'u is the ninth day of the eighteenth month. Since there are twenty days per month, there are eleven days remaining in Kumk'u. The nineteenth and last month of the Haab' year contains only five days, thus, there are sixteen days until the end of the Haab' year.

If we subtract 16 days from the total, we can then find how many complete Haab' years are contained.

1383136 - 16 = 1383120

Dividing by 365, we have

1383120 / 365 = 3789 and (135/365)

Therefore, 3789 complete Haab' have passed, with 135 days into the new Haab'.

We then find which month the day is in. Dividing the remainder 135 days by 20, we have six complete months, plus 15 remainder days. So, the date in the Haab' lies in the seventh month, which is Yaxk'in. The fifteenth day of Yaxk'in is 14, thus the Haab' date is 14 Yaxk'in.

So the date of the long count date 9.12.2.0.16 5 Kib' 14 Yaxk'in is confirmed.

### *Piktuns and Higher Orders*

As mentioned in the Syntax section, there are also four rarely-used higher-order periods above the b'ak'tun: *piktun*, *kalabtun*, *k'inchiltun*, and *alautun*.

It is a matter of dispute whether the first *piktun* occurs after 13 or after 20 b'ak'tun. Most Mayanists think that in the majority of inscriptions, where only the last five Long Count positions are used, the count recycles at 13 b'ak'tuns, whereas, if longer cycles are used, the count continues to the end of the 20th b'ak'tun (b'ak'tun 19) before a piktun is registered. In the same way, the fact that a 13-katun cycle was used, didn't negate the fact that there are 20 katuns in a b'ak'tun.

The inscription on Quirigua stela F, or 6, shows a Long Count date of 9.16.10.0.0 1 Ahau 3 Zip (March 15, 761 Gregorian). The huge distance date of 1.8.13.0.9.16.10.0.0 is subtracted and the resulting date is given as (18.)13.0.0.0.0.0.0.0 1 Ahau 13 Yaxkin, which is equivalent to a day over 90 million years in the past.

However, there is another distance date on Quirigua Stela D or 4, that gives a date of 9.16.15.0.0 7 Ahau 18 Pop (February 17, 766 Gregorian), to which is added 6.8.13.0.9.16.15.0.0, to give a date of (13.)13.0.0.0.0.0.0.0. This is over 400 million years after the date the stela was erected! It was by calculating a number of these distance dates that Eric Thompson was able to determine that the date of creation in 3114 BCE – 13.0.0.0.0 was actually 0.1.13.0.0.0.0.0.0 in the extended version.

At Yaxchilan, on a temple stairway, there is an inscription that includes four levels above the alautuns. The inscription reads: 13.13.13.13.13.13.13.13.9.15.13.6.9 3 Muluc 17 Mac. This is equivalent to October 19, 744, but the higher cycles do not conform to Thompson's calculation. The same applies to a Late Classic monument from Coba, Stela 1. The date of creation is expressed as 13.13.13.13.13.13.13.13.13.13.13.13.13.13.13.13.13.13.13.0.0.0.0.0, where the units are 13s in the nineteen places larger than the b'ak'tun.

# 9

# 2012 - Transition of the Ages

## 2012 - THE TRANSITION OF THE AGES ONGOING UPDATE AND ANALYSIS

Over the last few years increasingly more people have heard about "2012" in some context.

Sadly, the whole "2012" scenario has, as with many others, become the objective of massive confusion, speculation and opportunism, which has and continues to very seriously undermine the very real implications of this great transition of the ages that all life on Earth as well as humans is facing and indeed increasingly experiencing now.

## 2012 IN PERSPECTIVE

You may discuss all 2012, transformational and Earth change related matters in the dedicated forum - please do participate.

## LATEST 2012 UPDATE

Current probability estimates for known potential factors influencing the final outcome of transition, 2012 and Earth changes events :

1. Galactic alignment: Current probability of influence estimate - 75%
2. Solar emissions: Current probability of influence estimate - 20%
3. Near Earth Object: Current probability of influence estimate - 5%

*Definitions*

**Galactic Alignment:** The alignment of the December solstice sun with the Galactic equator as a result of the precession of the equinoxes. This definition also includes the more general alignment of the solar system, including Earth, with Galactic Centre. Of particular interest are the Energy and forces associatesd with this even, and in particular those associated with the super-massive black hole at the centre of the Galaxy, the spiral arms, and associated forces. The black hole is probably also associated with the "nuclear bulge" at the Galactic Centre at 6 degrees Sagittarius.

**Solar Emissions:** All types of emissions eminating from the Sun, including but not limited to coronal mass ejections and solar flares

**Near Earth Object:** All types of extra-terrestrial body of sugnificant size and mass, including but not limited to asteroids, comets and planetoids.

As many readers of this book will no doubt be aware, either by first hand experience, or by hearing or reading about them from other sources, at the time of writing of this book, major events and changes are occurring at all levels, and increasingly so. These events are not only occurring throughout the world but also beyond, extending deep into our solar system. These events, which are wide-ranging, often profound, and both physical and non-physical in nature, herald the continuance of a great transition of the ages, and one with potentially profound consequences for humanity, life on Earth and Earth Herself.

This great transition, which I have long been aware of, is no doubt a primary factor for the inspiration behind the writing of this book, the principle purpose of which is to reveal to readers your own true Divine nature, purpose and ultimate destiny and above all how to realize it, while there is still time remaining on Earth to do so.

I sincerely believe, know and indeed expect that the understanding, assimilation and application of what you learn in this book will prepare you for these approaching events and associated long term consequences as we travel together as One through this great transition of the ages.

I would like to make it absolutely clear from the outset that these events are in no way "random" or "chaotic" in nature, but rather an aspect of the Divine, immutable order and perfection of the Universe, of our Prime Creator, God, and natural cycles of the Universe. I would also like to make it absolutely clear that these events are not part of some "retribution" to "punish" a "wicked" or "sinful" mankind—these are simply superstitions having absolutely no basis in fact whatsoever.

From the outset I would also like to make the following absolutely clear such is its great importance to all humanity:

We must not, under any circumstances, allow ourselves to be influenced in any way whatsoever by external events, "prophecies", sensationalism, purveyors of doomsday scenarios or conspiracies of any type, or by those claiming any special knowledge, powers or connections of any sort in relation to "2012", "the end of the age" or any associated scenarios, or to be influenced in any way by the hidden agendas of governments, those seeking power and control on a global scale or by the popular media and their covert controllers.

The next few years are absolutely crucial for humanity. We are experiencing a great transition of life representing the culmination of millions of years of evolution of human Beings and all life on Earth as well as Earth, Gaia Herself. The outcome of this transition will not be predetermined in any way, shape or form by "chance" or other superstitious notions.

Only one factor at this stage, at the time of writing can be considered as absolute certainty. Whatsoever the collective Consciousness of humanity and of all life on Earth expects to happen over the next few years and beyond, will happen. We are facing the ultimate proof that we really do create our own reality at all levels, both as individual aspects of God, and as the collective Mind and Consciousness of the human race.

We are now experiencing, and will increasingly experience the culmination and transition of a great cycle or "age", an integral aspect of even greater such cycles in the Universe, all of which ultimately originate from The Source, The First Cause, God. These are completely natural cycles of life which exert their presence and influence with immutable precision and perfection, as fundamental aspects of the greater workings of the Universe in all glorious spheres of life and reality.

Cycles are always present in our lives at every level. Some cycles are so tiny they cannot even be measured with scientific instruments, and others so vast that they are far beyond the current perception of humans. However, the truth of the very existence of such cycles is everywhere—we only have to look at nature for example and the cycles of the seasons. Energy, radio waves, sound frequencies can all be measured in terms of distinct "cycles per second". Without such cycles events in the Universe would be chaotic, but this is clearly not the case because the Universe would not be sustainable in such a state of chaos—only Divine order and perfection can exert its immutable influence in maintaining the harmonious equilibrium of the Universe in all spheres of life and reality.

However, herein is the paradox. As with all Energy, this natural cycle is influenced by Mind, aspects of which include thoughts, imagination, expectations, intent and emotions. This cycle of Energy has always existed and will always exist, and, like all Energy, will exert its influence in accordance with the Consciousness of its participants¬—in this case life on Earth.

We will proceed in this chapter therefore by objectively examining the range of possible scenarios that might exert an influence during the next few years, both in the interests of knowledge, and to form a basis through which we can form a balanced perspective, expectations and state of Consciousness, which may prove to be so crucial in shaping the coming events.

For many people, the first awareness that "something is happening" or will happen, arrived by way of hearing about the now iconic date, December 21, 2012 which, over the last three decades has quite literally assumed a life of its own as a very powerful and pervasive Thought Form. Therein is one of the important issues we face—like any Thought Form it must, in accordance with immutable Universal principles, and the of Energy focused upon it, manifest, and thereby become self-fulfilling in accordance the nature of the thoughts that the majority of people associate with the "2012 Thought Form".

Since this now iconic date of December 21, 2012 first emerged into the Consciousness of humanity there have been countless interpretations spanning the entire spectrum of implications for mankind, ranging from catastrophic to ecstatic and almost all scenarios in between. Let us first then take a closer look at the facts surrounding this date, which has become such a point of focus, trepidation and even fear for so many people, often very worried for the well-being of themselves and families. This is not surprising considering the large and increasing array of "products" appearing on the market about "how to survive 2012", and sensationalism, as well as the widely held but erroneous belief that 2012 means "the end of the world".

As previously mentioned, many people are now focusing thought Energy on "2012", "December 21, 2012", "the end of the world" and other similar thought processes, which in turn, with the thought power of tens of thousands or even millions of people collectively focussing on these concepts, have become very powerful "Thought Forms"—Energy configurations in their own right, which have now literally assumed a life of their own. The more people focusing on these 2012 related thoughts, the more powerful, pervasive and resilient these Thought Forms will become and the less transient they will be in nature.

When in altered states of Consciousness, for example during meditation, in a trance state, or even just before, during and after sleep, we can "connect" with these powerful 2012 related Thought Forms which can present themselves as an "important message from within", with the receiver of the message as the focal point. The Ego of the receiver then takes over and convinces the conscious Mind of the person that they have been the recipient of important "privileged information", or even that they have received a "premonition". Sometimes even the Ego leads the person so far as to believe that they are even a "chosen one" in some way. Such a person then tells family and friends, or even the media, as well as writing about it on the Internet, until soon, in the Minds of many it becomes a fact.

Because by now there might well be thousands of people focussing on this single original "message", the original "Thought Form" that gave rise to it in the Mind of the person gains even more strength, resilience and pervasiveness, and therefore in turn becomes even more "real" to those focussing on it, who in turn then relate it to others as if it were a fact.

This then I believe is a phenomena we are increasingly seeing at the time of writing, specifically, a collection of 2012 related Thought Forms manifesting under the umbrella of a much more pervasive "2012" Thought Form" now reaching a critical mass in the Consciousness of people throughout the world.

Let us continue by putting this Thought Form aside, and investigate some of the fundamental facts surrounding "2012".

It is most notable that before the 1970's, almost no one had ever heard of "the end of the Mayan calendar" or therefore of "2012" and related matters, indeed many had not heard of the Maya themselves. It is only since the Mayan long-count calendar was deciphered in the last 20 years or so that 2012 with its "end of the Mayan calendar" or "end of the world" connotations have entered into the human Consciousness.

Summarizing in a page or so in the context of this chapter the entire 30 or more year history of how the "2012" phenomena came about is most assuredly impractical due to the now vast array of people, factors and theories of all types involved, often supported and motivated by individual agendas and interests. Following however is an overview of the most significant factors for consideration, which will be sufficient to provide the basis for further analysis of these factors in the context of the Transition of the Ages to which this chapter is dedicated.

The Mayan long-count calendar is just one of a larger set of calendars created by the classic Maya people of Mesoamerica around 2000 years ago. The classic Maya were highly advanced in many cosmological, astronomical, astrological, astrophysical and mathematical abilities—considerably more so in fact for the most part, than most of science today.

To the Maya, their calendars were much more than simply measurements of the passage of time for their own convenience in the same way that contemporary calendars, clocks and other measurements of "time" are. They were and still are "books of life", into which are encoded countless levels, collectively charting and predicting cycles of the Universe itself, as well as serving as a reference point for all matters involving the daily lives and Spiritual evolution of the Maya people at all levels of the Mayan culture and society. So important were these calendars that the Mayan people structured their lives and constituted their entire society and infrastructure around them. The Mayan elders and shaman would teach the populous through visual means in the form of ball games and other public performances, conceptually similar to those of the ancient Hindu traditions for example, as well as many cultures that made use of plays, song, dance and other audio-visual methods which serves both as entertainment and education.

The most important calendar of the Maya is known as the "Tzolkin". The Tzolkin measures a year over the course of 260 days as opposed to the 365-day cycle of the Gregorian calendar used today in so called "modern society". The descendants of the classic Maya, of which there are still several million residing in Mesoamerica, still use the Tzolkin today.

The calendar upon which most people are focussing in the context of "2012" is known as the "Long Count". The Mayan long-count calendar is divided into these units:

1 kin = 1 day

20 kins = 1 uinal = 20 days

18 uinals = 1 tun = 360 days

20 tuns = 1 katun = 7,200 days

20 katuns = 1 baktun = 144,000 days

A complete long count great cycle has 13 baktuns in total and so the last great cycle, the end of which we will reach on December 21, 2012, started on August 13, 3114 BCE.

Great cycles measure the "ages" or "suns" of mankind, marking the transformation of mankind to the next level of evolution. These "ages" were not only measured by the Maya, but also by other great civilizations of the past such as the Aztecs in Mesoamerica, the Chinese in the Far East and many other ancient cultures over the preceding three millennia or so.

The end of previous great cycles and the beginning of the next have often been associated with major events that have influenced the destiny of mankind such as the great flood, the destruction of Atlantis, Lemuria and other "lost" civilizations, as well as major ancient cataclysmic events throughout history. In many ancient cultures these cataclysms, as in the great flood, have also regarded as "cleansing" or "purgative", after which only a small percentage of the original populations survive.

Of course, much of the Mayan long-count calendar, and in particular these historical cataclysmic events precedes modern recorded history, so we know little about most of these ancient events that might have coincided with the end of these cycles or "ages", "eras" or "suns" going back over millions of years. It is very possible that the huge asteroid or comet that struck the Yucatan Peninsula around 65 million years ago resulting in the end of the age of the dinosaurs, also coincided with the end of one of these "ages", as did several other known "extinction events", each one of which heralded a new era and new evolutionary direction for life on Earth, without which humans might not be here today, at least as the "dominant species".

The Maya are a shamanic culture who made extensive use of Mind-expanding substances known as "entheogens" in order to attain altered states of Consciousness, enabling access to the inner realms of life. Although many entheogens are hallucinatory in nature, there are classes of entheogens that can apparently bring about genuine inner experiences, and which were known to and used by the Maya and many other ancient civilisations. One such class of entheogens belongs to a group of chemical compounds known as the "Dimethyltryptamines", of which there are various derivatives and chemical variations including N,N-dimethyltryptamine (DMT), 5-Methoxy-N,N-Dimethyltryptamine (5-MeO-DMT) and 5-Hydroxy-N,N-Dimethyltryptamine (5-OH-DMT) known as "bufotenine" due, being extracted from the skin of toads of genus "Bufo".

Dimethyltryptamines, usually abbreviated to "DMT", appear to have specific qualities for producing genuine Spiritual experiences. Dr. Rick Strassman conducted extensive research into the effects of DMT on numerous volunteers over a period of years. Subjects frequently reported contacts with all manner of Beings and situations. So conclusive were these findings that Dr. Strassman named DMT "The Spirit Molecule".

Without going too deeply into the way DMT is metabolized and influences Consciousness, the most important effect seems to be related to its interaction with the "pineal gland" of the brain, corresponding to the so-called "3rd eye" or "brow chakra". We already know that the brow chakra is associated with "inner visions" in this way, and especially with clairvoyance. I am of the view that DMT-influenced inner journeys were very likely a major source of the inner knowledge of the Maya.

In addition to the Maya, there have been, and still are, many people using DMT and similar entheogens, returning from inner journeys with information that precisely relates to December 21, 2012 as being a time of transformation for all mankind. Many of these people had previously never heard of the Mayan calendar or of the significance of 2012, but the message is always remarkably similar, an impressive independent confirmation of the significance of a 2012 event.

In addition to advanced, non-terrestrial knowledge acquired by the Mayan shamans in this way, they also engaged in devoted observation of the night sky from their dedicated observatories. The resultant observations, messages and records were recorded in stone structures called "stelae" at their many sacred sites, and on thousands of written records known as "codices", together containing a vast array of information. All but a very few of these valuable codices were later totally destroyed by the Roman Catholic church in their zealous efforts to forcibly convert the Maya and all Mesoamerican races to Christianity, and in particular Roman Catholicism.

The Maya therefore had a great depth of knowledge regarding the cosmos and cosmic cycles, particularly as they relate to the "galactic centre" and above all the pivotal event which is estimated to occur on December 21, 2012, and the basis therefore of the entire 2012 phenomena. This cosmic event is the "galactic alignment" which is alignment of the December solstice sun with the Galactic Equator, an event only occurring every 25,800 years or so, and is a result of the precession of the equinoxes. The galactic alignment coincides with the end of each cycle of the Mayan long count calendar, and is therefore the fundamental basis for the 2012 "end date" phenomena.

The important fact to keep in mind, however, is this - The "end of the Mayan calendar" does not, in and of itself, imply "the end of the world". The "end of the world" is an erroneous interpretation placed upon these events by people, due either to a genuine lack of understanding, or in support of some other motive. The end of one cycle or "age" of the Mayan long count calendar simply marks the beginning of the next calendrical cycle, or "age".

It should be made absolutely clear that the flow of the Universe, The Source, The Prime Creator, The First Cause, God, is, always has been and always will be in the direction of Life and expansion, the only factors to consider being the mode in which these Universal, Divine processes manifest. Contrary to the doctrines of religions, God is not "vengeful", "jealous" or "angry", and does not therefore exact "punishments", "revenge" or "Divine retribution". God knows only Unconditional Love for all creation, and accordingly all Universal processes extending from the infinite Mind of God are for the ultimate benefit of all creation, including humanity.

It is believed in some cultures that these great cycles of Energy, or "ages" alternate between "dark" and "light", and that we are currently nearing the end of a "dark age" after which will begin an age of light. Hindu teachings define these eras in terms of the "Yuga's". We are currently nearing the end of Kali Yuga.

So, the big question is this—what does the end of this current great cycle mean to us experientially both as a race of human Beings, and for each of us as individuals?

In the interests of a balanced approach to these extremely important questions we must consider all possibilities, which, in the very broadest terms consist of the following categories:

1. Catastrophic: A globally destructive cataclysm.
2. Eschatological: A Spiritual transformation
3. Progressive: The continuation of an ongoing process.

## Catastrophic

The classic Maya, who, as discussed, are at the root of the events life on Earth is facing fundamentally tracked "ages", or "cycles", not individual events, and nowhere in the records left by the Maya, to the extent they have been yet discovered, is it suggested that Earth is to experience a cataclysmic event.

As previously noted, it is a fact nevertheless that there is growing evidence in support of such events in the distant past, which may very well have coincided with the end of previous ages. It is entirely possible that a global cataclysm is necessary as a purgative prelude to, and catalyst for a major transformation or change in direction for humans, in order to clear away the millennia of dross that now subsumes the Consciousness of humanity, buried under which humanity has become substantially blind to its own true Spiritual nature. Humanity could on the other hand move towards the high path of enlightenment and evolution by conscious freewill.

From an observational perspective, there are currently few known factors that the Maya could have tracked with the potential to result in a catastrophic outcome in the near future, although numerous theories and unsubstantiated claims have emerged in recent years. There are however most certainly known factors that the ancient Maya would have known about, and which could well form the basis of any predictive aspect of their long count calendar which ends on 21 December 2012.

One compelling and very real factor with the potential to precipitate profound changes on Earth and solar system generally is increasing solar activity, i.e. from the Sun, the cycles of which the Maya could certainly have tracked. Solar activity has at the time of writing, been at an unusually high level, and at a time when such activity is historically indicated to be at a minimum. Also at the time of writing, Earth has been subjected to an unusually high level of activity from the Sun including but not limited to powerful X class solar flares and the much more powerful "coronal mass ejection" or "CME", in the form of super-heated radioactive plasma. These events were most certainly not in isolation, and are very highly likely to increase as we move towards the next solar maxima, expected most significantly to occur around the year 2012. Current indications are that this coming solar maxima could be unprecedented in recorded history in its sheer magnitude. We cannot determine at this stage just how high this level of solar activity will attain, but, if it is as seems possible, the effects upon Earth due to solar storms in the form of CME's and other powerful solar emissions could be profound in many ways. Such a possibility most certainly includes Earth receiving a "broadside" from a single massive coronal mass ejection, the effects of which could well be catastrophic for most life on Earth. It is entirely possible therefore that around 2012 life could face the cataclysmic consequences of one or more powerful solar events with highly unpredictable consequences for humans, all life, and all life-sustaining infrastructure.

It should be mentioned that current climatic extremes are being blamed on so called "climate change", erroneously associated with so called "greenhouse gasses", the use of "fossil fuels" and other environmentally polluting by-products of human activity. While no form of environment polluting activity should ever be condoned, to solely blame such agents for "climate change" is to be dangerously and naively oblivious to the real causes, notably solar activity and other wider ranging Energy influences originating from beyond Earth, which, for the most part are at frequencies of Energy beyond those measurable by current scientific instruments. This can be demonstrated by virtue of similar changes occurring on other planets in our solar system, thus conclusively eliminating human so called "greenhouse gases" or "fossil fuels" as a cause. While scientists, governments, industry and others would seek to commercialise "climate change" or "global warming", the true and most important origin of the changes Earth is increasingly being subjected to are being largely and dangerously overlooked with potentially catastrophic results.

Another major "wild card" associated with these and other possible events seems to be the precipitation of a "pole shift" which can either be geomagnetic in nature where the north and south poles exchange places, an event that is known to happen over long periods of time, or geophysical whereby the current position of the physical poles, in relation to the Sun, suddenly move by several degrees, or even by twenty degrees or more. Such an event could imply profound consequences for Earth and all life on Earth, in ways which we cannot fully predict.

There is increasing evidence being discovered by sea divers of the extensive remains of major ancient civilisations, now lying 2000 feet or more under the sea. How did they get there? Many have heard of the fabled lost civilisations of Atlantis and Lemuria as well as others. Most people have heard of the biblical "Great Flood". Further evidence suggests that the north and south poles have not always been cold, and indeed in the quite recent past Antarctica may have been abundant with life. We can only speculate in the context of 2012, but clearly strong evidence most certainly exists for profound and very sudden geophysical events occurring in the past, which seem to happen with immutable frequency, often coinciding with the catastrophic submerging and subsequent destruction and consequential loss of once great and advanced civilisations.

The classic Maya based much or their long count calendar and in particular the 2012 end date around observations of our Galaxy, and in particular the Galactic Centre where the super-massive black hole almost certainly exists. It is very possible in my view that as we transition through the galactic alignment that was being tracked by the Maya, which is likely occurring now, the effects of this alignment, the mechanism for which has been previously described, and in particular the massive Energy influence of the super-massive black hole could well pull the solar system, including the Sun, all planets and Earth into alignment with it, resulting in a geophysical pole shift of perhaps 20 degrees or more. As previously mentioned, this could well be catastrophic, resulting in massive geophysical effects including earthquakes, massive volcanic eruptions, huge tsunamis and much more. Most life on Earth would be very seriously compromised as has likely happened many times in Earth history. Again, the Maya would most definitely know about these galactic cycles and would also be aware of their consequential transformative potential in many possible ways, including the potential for evolution or destruction, being dependent on the Mind state and consciousness of human beings and all life on Earth before and during these events.

### Eschatological

In this scenario, the outcome of the transition of the ages may manifest as a potential Spiritual transformation or enlightenment of mankind, being, as previously emphasised, ultimately depend on the thoughts, expectations and Spiritual status, i.e. Consciousness of both the collective Mind of the human race and of each individual. It should also be made absolutely clear that in no way will religious devotion be a factor. The only factor relevant to each individual will be true Spiritual evolution—an immutable Universal Principle.

Mankind is currently in the grips of an escalating downward social spiral precipitated by many factors, including but not limited to rampant materialism and often greed fuelled by the demands of the Ego. This cannot and will not be sustained. The root causes of this situation is that most humans perceive everyone and everything as being separate from themselves, and view the gaining of money as the basis for happiness. Existence therefore becomes competitive, adversarial and aggressive, with people fighting for material supremacy while protecting themselves against perceived threats from "others". In reality there is no such separation. The illusion of separation is perpetuated only by the five physical senses. Everything in the entire Universe is an equal, integral and Divine aspect of everything else in the Universe and of The Source, The First Cause, God. We all exist as individuated Energy fields within the Great Universal Mind of conscious, intelligent, vibrating Energy in which we live and move and have our Being.

Should we experience an eschatological event associated with the transition of the ages, in my view one of the most likely outcomes of such an event would be the veil of the illusion of separation that has blinded humans of their true Spiritual nature for so long would dissipate, along with the related illusions of "time" and "space", thereby leaving people "Spiritually naked" in a true multi-dimensional state of awareness, with the twin illusions of "space" and "time" no longer exerting an influence over Consciousness, and where our thoughts manifest instantly as opposed to the currently perceived time delays. This will enable those who are Spiritually prepared to view life, reality and people in a different way, with an emphasis on Oneness, service and

Unconditional Love, with materialism, lack and competitiveness no longer being meaningful. The effects of The Law of Attraction would be experienced instantly. So by what mechanism could these events possibly manifest?

As previously discussed, the classic Maya almost certainly fixed the end of their long count calendar to coincide with the galactic alignment and were also certainly aware of the super massive "black hole" that exists at the very centre of our galaxy, and which could well exert its influence at the time of the galactic alignment. In addition to the physical implications of this galactic event, there are also Energetic and therefore Spiritual implications. Again, and this is most important: How humanity and all life on Earth experiences this event will be entirely determined by one primary factor – Consciousness.

Einstein's Law of Relativity describes, among other things, the rate of time, and scale of space. For example a clock may be observed to run slower at lower altitudes, where the gravitational potential exerted on the clock is higher. The gravitational potential of a black hole, in this case the galactic centre is so massive that "time" itself is suspended and the dimensions of "space" reduced to zero. In other words "space" and "time" as experienced on Earth cease to exist altogether.

We, along with all life on Earth, are currently bound together in the same shared quantum reality by virtue of the fact that we are all at the extremity of, and thereby subjected to, the same extreme gravitational potential, and have been since before recorded history. As we approach 2012 and beyond we may well be travelling through the spiral arms of the black hole at the galactic centre, associated with greatly modified gravitational potential to which we will all become progressively subjected as this process progresses, as will every planet in our solar system and beyond. Without going into the extensive and complex quantum mechanics behind this process, the ultimate outcome of this scenario will be that the twin illusions of "space" and "time" would cease to exert their influence. When this finally takes place, and this process is accelerating even now, as mentioned previously, humans will be left "Spiritually naked" in an environment where everything is perceived for what it really is, and where our thoughts, feelings emotions and other powers of the Mind will manifest into our experience instantly. This will be a pivotal juncture for all humanity. Each of us and all life will be freed to realise our true Spiritual potential based upon our individual state of Spiritual evolution knowledge, wisdom and other factors. Those who are thus ready will transition to a quantum reality, a plane of vibration that most closely matches their individual vibration. Although this would happen in due course anyway, this could be a "mass evolution" event. Those not Spiritually prepared will gravitate to another "time-space" bound reality. It should also be mentioned that the galactic alignment could also result in other unknown consciousness influencing effects including magnetic, radiation and other Energy influences.

Although this is largely conjecture, my dedicated involvement in these important matters has enabled me to observe an ongoing awakening of Consciousness of humanity on many levels that leads me to believe that this process could already be taking place and exponentially accelerating. This also leads me to feel that humanity is experiencing the potential for a glorious opportunity in its Spiritual evolution, towards realising our ultimate reality. It is however still for each individual to realise and accept this, and to prepare themselves accordingly. Humanity is facing events that could result in almost total catastrophe, or enlightenment and evolution, and again the eventual outcome will be decided by humanity and life itself.

### Progressive

This final scenario is based upon the observation that natural Spiritual transformation and transition processes are already very much in progress and appear to be exponentially increasing at this time. This leads me to consider the possibility that December 21, 2012 simply represents a symbolic date in recognition of this ongoing event, as opposed to representing the final date of any causation in absolute terms. In other words, this iconic date simply represents a convenient marker in time as measured by the Gregorian calendar, in recognition of a series of ongoing cosmic events that will continue to progress through 21 December, 2012 and on into the "future". As discussed previously, it is thought that the Maya derived the basis of their "long count calendar" upon cosmic observation conducted over a long period of time, extrapolating these observations to form the basis of a calendrical system representing galactic cycles of around 25,800 years, the end of which is marked or symbolised by the so called "galactic alignment"—an event resulting from the "precession of the equinoxes".

In brief, this "precession" arises from the fact that Earth wobbles very slowly about its axis, which in turn causes the relative position of the equinox to move backwards, i.e. to "precess" at the rate of around 1 degree every 71.5 years. The entire precessional cycle takes around 25,800 years to complete, culminating in the end of a Maya "long count" calendrical cycle, and the beginning of the next cycle. Thus it may be seen that the end of the calendar, or cycle is not the "end of the world" as has been erroneously widely supposed, but rather the end of the current single Mayan long count cycle. The question therefore is this - is the "galactic alignment" a symbolic or a causal event in and of itself as previously discussed in the previous scenarios.

It might be that the actual date of December 21, 2012 could simply be a convenient symbolic representation, based upon the galactic alignment, of a much greater cosmic event the Maya were tracking, and which they expected to exert its influence during this period, but with a different origin of causation that humanity may well not be yet aware of. There is very strong evidence at many levels, both physical and non-physical to suggest that we are indeed in the throes of such an ongoing process. At a physical level we are seeing and experiencing increasing extremes of weather and associated anomalies, increased volcanic and seismic activity, and of course an exponentially increasing climatic warming trend. These types of changes appear to be occurring throughout the entire solar system, not only on Earth, and cannot therefore be the result of any localised pollution and other such influences.

From my own perspective, as a person who receives messages from, and communicates with numerous people around the world, I am observing a very real "Spiritual awakening" taking place, with increasing numbers of people becoming progressively aware of their true infinite, unlimited, immortal, Spiritual, Divine, nature, needing to know what it all means, and how they should make changes in their lives accordingly.

In addition, we are seeing various factions, many negative or dark in nature, often with very selfish motives, which, realising there is not much time left before the Minds and lives of people can no longer be controlled as they are currently, are doing everything they can to bring forward and execute their agendas of domination and control, regardless of the wider consequences for humanity and life on Earth. We will not discuss these factions lest we give them more power, but suffice it to say, by comparison with the Universal forces of change currently exerting themselves, the efforts of these dark agencies are completely futile, and can be likened to someone standing on a beach with view to holding back the tides. Giving serious attention to these factions is therefore neither useful, productive or appropriate—they are best completely ignored.

Planet Earth Herself, a great planetary Spirit, often known as "Gaia", with Whom we are inexorably connected, is currently in the process of making Her own joyous evolutionary transition to the next vibrational level of the Universe on the path of Her own glorious return to our Divine Creator, in exactly the same way that humans, all life, and everything in creation will inevitably do sooner or later.

There is compelling evidence that this process is underway right now. The Schumann Cavity Resonance, often referred to as the "heartbeat" of Earth, has always in the past maintained a steady frequency or resonance of 7.8Hz. In the last few of years, however, the resonance has recently increased to around 12Hz with 13Hz being pivotal. Gaia is increasing the frequency of Her own Spiritual body as She prepares to make Her own evolutionary transition, something we should all celebrate.

In conclusion, we can see that regardless of the theories and agendas of the various groups interested in this process for whatever reason, there is indeed very real and important changes occurring that must ultimately affect all mankind, life on Earth and the solar system, and planet Earth, Gaia herself.

Due to the multitude of such theories, factions and agendas exerting themselves during this natural process, many people are understandably becoming very confused, bewildered and concerned for the future of themselves and families, particularly in view of the increasing number of "survive 2012" type agendas appearing, implying a pending global catastrophe. We must recognise the many unsubstantiated ideas, theories and agendas for what they are, choosing instead to focus within, and on what we know to be incontrovertible true, based upon what we personally experience, know and intuitively feel.

My own message is clear and unequivocal. We are all, both as individuals and equal aspects of the human race and of all life on Earth and of the Universe, experiencing a completely natural cycle of transition, orchestrated by Divine intelligence, Who Unconditionally Loves us all. How we experience and emerge from this transition, both individually and collectively as the human race will, as always, be determined by one factor and one factor only – individual and collective Consciousness, and our own unique state of Spiritual attainment and evolution.

What we have discussed in this chapter and are witnessing and experiencing at all levels is the confluence of an infinite number of quantum probabilities, quantum potential, any or all of which can exert themselves in precise alignment with the influence of Mind and therefore individual and collective Consciousness over the next few years. What we ultimately experience as the transition progresses therefore is already taking shape in our own Mind and therefore Universal Mind in Which we all experience our collective Consciousness.

We each create our own reality, and never has there been a greater opportunity to realise this great truth than the age in which we are living now. Nothing is to be gained by focussing on material, outer events, however dramatic they may seem – they are an illusion and a distraction. Nothing is to be gained and everything is to be lost by listening to the voices of doom, or those who claim to represent your "best interests" as events unfold. They are pursuing their own agendas that are very often biased towards power, fear and control, rather than evolution.

If you really wish to know the outcome of the transition of the ages, or of December 21, 2012, or of any related event, then rejoice, because you have the power to determine and experience that outcome, both individually and as a member of the human race. Humanity can have and achieve anything it desires during the coming age, so choose Peace, Harmony, Love, Service and true Spiritual Evolution, and they shall be yours with everyone else sharing the same glorious new reality.

We must therefore focus within in order to realise our own true reality, in the absolute knowledge that once the transition of the ages is complete, only those who have turned to focus within, and rediscovered their own true, infinite, immortal, Self, and are ready and prepared to progress beyond the material illusion of the physical world, will emerge to become the first members of the next Divine evolution of human beings – Homo Spiritus.

## GALACTIC ALIGNMENT 2012

As many of you will know I write from time to time about the subject collectively known as "2012", in order to dispel many of the myths and false claims associated with it, and to shed Light on what is really a very serious subject indeed if fully understood and approached in the right way, and one which will increasingly affect us all over the next few years as we will see.

This page will be updated as more knowledge is made available to me, and my own understanding of these crucial and pivotal events, iconically represented by the date December 21 2012 increases. So please do bookmark this page and check back from time to time. This entire 2012 scenario is very much an unfolding event, and exponentially so.

You may read my earlier previous 2012 related articles here: Previous 2012 related articles

As already mentioned, we are already beginning to see and experience the effects of the "2012 phenomena" in many ways, some very subtle, based in consciousness, others much more obvious and dramatic such as climatic extremes and disasters caused by weather extremes, in particular hurricanes, typhoons and foldings.

At the same time it is increasingly important for humanity generally as well as all life on Earth and Earth, Gaia herself, that as many people as possible discover and fully understand the truth about the event collectively known as "2012" and what it means in practical terms.

It has been, and still is my ongoing mission in fact to discover and reveal the absolute truth regarding 2012, and what it means to each of us and life on Earth generally. Knowledge is power, but only if it is the right knowledge based in fact, and for this reason I have been very careful about what I have said on this subject, restricting myself to only writing about those factors that I know and believe to be true based upon my own research inspired from and by within.

Many of you will know from my website that I have rated the possible sources of causality during these transitional times in terms of percentages, and that I have ranked the Galactic Alignment as by far the biggest causal factor.

I now believe the other possible causal factors, including the Sun and "near Earth objects" are actually secondary factors of causation to the primary source of causation - the Galactic Alignment.

We have to keep in Mind that the classic Maya were an extremely advanced race, and not ones given to fantasy or the promulgation of "prophecies", better known as "fortune telling". Central to the classic Mayan culture was an observation of the cosmos, which in turn gave rise to their central philosophies and calendrical systems, of which "2012" is just one small part, forming the basis of just one of their calendars - the Long Count, which takes into account the event that has since come to be known as the "Galactic Alignment". Although this event is central to the issues under discussion, hitherto no one has really explained it in practical and verifiable terms, a situation this article seeks to rectify with the expectation that al of the hype and misinformation out there will fade into the background.

Many people have asked why the "Galactic Alignment" is such an important event in the context of life on Earth, and therefore today we will examine this complex but extremely important issue in greater depth. The first question we must ask ourselves is "what exactly is the Galactic Alignment" or at least how may we best define it?

In the broadest terms, the Galactic Alignment has been defined as the alignment of the December solstice sun with the Galactic equator due to the precession of the equinoxes.

Precession is caused by the earth wobbling very slowly on its axis shifting the position of the equinoxes and solstices one degree every 71.5 years. Because the sun is one-half of a degree wide, it will take the December solstice sun 36 years to precess through the Galactic equator. As we will see however, this event in and of itself is symbolic of, and a metaphor of a much greater but related event.

It is this event, which is cyclical, that is to say occurs with immutable frequency, that the Maya were measuring in the context of their "Long Count" calendar that famously "ends" on the now iconic date if 21 December 2012.

However, I am now of the firm belief that this is a convenient but highly appropriate and accurate symbolic marker for a much greater and more important event that is taking place over a number of years before, during and after 21 December 2012.

The Maya used the Sun to reference the central point of our solar system, and one that can be used in conjunction with Earth and the plane of the Galactic Centre to describe the "Galactic Alignment", which, according to the Maya, will take place on 21 December 2012, and used as the focal point for both their Long Count Calendar representing the transition from one great "age" to the next".

In fact the Sun, in and of itself is somewhat superfluous to this metaphor as we will see later. That said, it is clear that the Sun will actually participate in this process as will all planets in our solar system, and will likely participate, as it is indeed doing right now, on any resultant causation experienced by Earth and all life on Earth.

Another important feature of Mayan philosophy is that time, rather than being linear in nature as currently believed by science, is rather spherical, and therefore time, like the Universe itself has a beginning and an end. At the end of a cycle of time however, there is a renewal or evolutionary event. Again this forms the basis of the Mayan Long Count Calendar which has proven to be extremely accurate. This cycle of time ends, according to the Mayan Long Count Calendar on 21 December 2012.

I have said this before and I will say it again - the Maya were one of the most brilliant and truly advanced races ever to have walked the planet, if not the greatest. Their abilities in Astronomy, Cosmology, Physics, Astrophysics and Math were far in advances of anything seem today, notwithstanding all of the technology being deployed. The Maya have been right all along, and for good reason.

In view of all of the myth, speculation and sensationalism surrounding 2012, and the ongoing and escalating observable events that are increasingly taking place, I believe the time has come to take a very close look at what is actually going on that we may understand and prepare better for what may be to come, while dispelling all of the myths, mis-information and sensationalism that currently and dangerously abound.

2012 is not a "prophecy" and never was a "prophecy" it is rather a prediction deeply based in fact, one that can be measured and indeed was measured by the Mayans, verified and equated to past significant events in Earth's history.

Please note that I say "may be to come". The truth is no one, including myself knows for sure what will happen over the next few years, if anything at all, but we can look at the facts and the precedents at least in order to become properly informed and thereby prepared, and also dispel all that which is not true but could become true as self fulfilling events under the influence of Mind and Consciousness.

I am not almost certain that there will be no single event ocurring on 21 December 2012, which, as mentioned above, is simply a convenient symbolic representation of a much greater event that is already taking place. So, assuming we are still here, I suggest that you do not cancel your appointments for 22 December 2012, because if all goes as it should do you will be attending those appointments. With those caveats duly stated, let us then look now at the facts relating to the "Galactic Alignment", what it really is and means, and how it can affect us at every level, Mind, Soul and body, as well as all life on Earth and planetary Spirit Gaia, to Whom we are inexorably connected, Herself.

At the very centre of our Galaxy there is what astrophysicists call a "super-massive black hole". The Energy and density of this super-massive black hole is so great that not even light itself can escape, photons of light being sucked into the black hole along with everything else that approaches it including stars and planets.

This is why it is called a "black hole", because light itself no longer exists in that region having been subsumed by the massive Energy vortex of the super-massive black hole.

Now this super-massive black hole is absolutely fundamental to the entire issue of 2012 and what we are and will increasingly continue to experience, and here are reasons why.

The gravitational Energy and therefore spin rate of the super-massive black hole is so immense that it actually flattens out to form a "super-massive black hole plane", like a massive, intensely dense disk, characterised by an immense outwardly radiating Energy vortex. It is this planar characteristic of the black hole due to the gravitational Energy being radiated out from the super-massive black hole that gives rise to the very "flat" appearance of galaxies generally, all of which I believe have a super-massive black hole at their centre. I am personally of the view that a black hole and associated dark matter may be the precursor of a galaxy. There are probably countless other younger black holes with associated dark matter in the Universe that have not yet began to form its own constellation of stars and later planets and moons, each with the so called "dark matter" forming the fabric of the galaxy, which, together with the gravitational Energy of the super-massive black hole and associated cosmic material, forms and then binds the galaxy together.

In absolute terms a galaxy, including our own galaxy, the Milky Way, is extremely, amazingly in fact thin. When viewed edge on it could be likened comparatively to viewing the blade of an extremely thin and sharp blade. In practice of course this plane of the galaxy is still a huge distance across, but still comparatively speaking, taking into account the vast scales involved, the Galactic Plane is extremely thin.

So we have our galaxy, at the centre of which is a super-massive black hole manifesting an inconceivably massive gravitational Energy vortex that, together with dark matter, holds together as well as influences the fabric of our galaxy, of which we, on Earth are on the outer edge of a spiral arm.

As this black hole gravitational super-Energy extends to the very edges of the galaxy - it must do to hold the form of the galaxy together including our solar system on the outer edge, just as the gravitational pull of the Sun extends far enough to hold the planets of our solar system in orbit or planets in turn hold their moons in orbit - it is all relative to scale, range and the gravitational Energy potential being manifested.

So this Energetic influence of the super-massive black hole over the galaxy, our Sun, the Solar system and of course Earth always exists - there was never a time when it did not exist. The only factor that varies is the degree of Energy being exerted over the solar system and therefore Earth at any one time - and therein is the crux of the matter, and the very key that unlocks the mystery of 2012 as we will see later in this article.

The Maya may or may not have known of the super-massive black hole, or of the physics relating to it, but they would have definitely known about Galactic Centre and the dark rift, or "nuclear bulge" at the centre of the Galaxy which they symbolised through a mythical entity known as "Xilbalba", also mythically representing the "underworld" and the process of death and re-birth which of course is directly relevant to everything related to 2012 and the transition process. The Maya also certainly knew about the Energy and other forces originating from Galactic Center, which featured prominently in their creation myths and deities, including their chief deity, Hunab Ku, believing these forces at Galactic Centre to be the origin of time and therefore the controller of time.

The Maya are a shamanic culture who made extensive use of Mind-expanding substances known as "entheogens" in order to attain altered states of Consciousness, enabling access to the inner realms of life. Although many entheogens are hallucinatory in nature, there are classes of entheogens that can apparently bring about genuine inner experiences, and which were known to and used by the Maya and many other ancient civilisations. One such class of entheogens belongs to a group of chemical compounds known as the "Dimethyltryptamines", of which there are various derivatives and chemical variations including N,N-dimethyltryptamine (DMT), 5-Methoxy-N,N-Dimethyltryptamine (5-MeO-DMT) and 5-Hydroxy-N,N-Dimethyltryptamine (5-OH-DMT) known as "bufotenine" due, being extracted from the skin of toads of genus "Bufo". Through these shamanic practices, the Maya Shamans would have unquestionably been able to gain access to the central Sources of the collective knowledge and events of the Universe, in all spheres of life and reality, existing as Energy mysticaly known as "The Akashic Record". There is no information relative to the "past", present" or probable "future" of the earth, as existing as quantum potential, that the Maya would not have has access to.

In addition, through a projection of consciousness known in occult terms as "Mental Projection", the Maya Smana would have been able to instantly project him/herself to the physical centre of the Galaxy in order to observe the events there. As Mental projection takes place beyond the Energy of the physical Universe, and is not therefore subject to physical factors such as the massive gravitational potential of the super-massive black hole, the Maya Shaman could easily observe the events manifesting there. Although I am speculating with this next suggestion, I believe it possible that the Maya Shaman would use the nuclear bulge, or Xilbalba as the necessary point of reference to project to these distant events with precision.

The Maya also knew about the Precession of the Equinoxes and therefore the relative position of Earth relative to other cosmological and astrological entities, including Galactic Centre, and which gives rise to what the Maya, and numerous other cultures know as "ages".

In the west we know these "ages" in terms of the signs of the zodiac. We are currently in the age of Pisces, the fish, and are entering the Age of Aquarius, the water bearer. In astro-theological terms this is why Jesus is always associated with "fish", and indeed why the mitre of the Pope is a metaphor for the head of a fish.

We should also note that in the Bible, Jesus, represented by fish,

says:

"Teaching them to observe all things whatsoever I have commanded you: and, lo, I am with you alway, even unto the end of the age". —Matthew 28:20.

The "age" being referred to is the age of Pisces the fish.

Jesus also said:

"And he said unto them, Behold, when ye are entered into the city, there shall a man meet you, bearing a pitcher of water; follow him into the house where he entereth in". — Luke 22:10

This is a metaphor for the sign of Aquarius the water bearer. Jesus is saying that when we enter the "city" a metaphor for the next age, we will be "meeting" the new age of Aquarius", represented by the water bearer.

So back to Galactic Centre and the end of the age.

Over the course of 25,800 years or so the trajectory of Earth takes us above and then below the plane of Galactic Centre and therefore the gravitational Energy influence of the super-massive black hole at its centre, in a long but precise oscillation that can be observed and measured as the Maya indeed did. This was also described by Plato and is therefore known as the "Platonic year".

The Earth goes through one complete precessional cycle over a period of approximately 25,800 years, Plato's "Great Year" during which the positions of stars as measured relative to the equator slowly changes. During the course of this cycle the north axial pole of Earth transitions from where it is now, around 1° of Polaris, in a circle around the ecliptic pole, with an angular radius of around 23.5 degrees. This shift moves 1 degree in around 180 years, where the angle is taken from the perspective of the observer, not from the center of the position of the observer.

As we will see later, this angular radius of 23.5 degrees is very significant to some of the possible causal events.

During a complete cycle of oscillation the trajectory of Earth, relative to Galactic Centre, oscillates up through and back down through the plane of the super-massive black hole at Galactic Centre as observed, measured and recorded by the Maya, forming the basis of their Long Count Calendar, subjecting all in its path, including Earth to the massive Energy forces radiating from the super-massive black hole at Galactic Centre.

Now, there is absolutely no doubt in my Mind that all previous major events throughout history have coincided with the transition of Earth through the super-massive black hole Energy plane of Galactic Centre and therefore the immense Energy influence of the super-massive black hole radiating from there. The further Earth is way from the plane of Galactic Centre the less will be the effect of the Energetic forces radiating from there, and conversely the nearer Earth gets to the plane of Galactic centre the greater will be the Energetic influences exerted. Of course this event, the transition of Earth through the plane of Galactic Centre has never before happened in recorded history, with the possible exception of the Great Flood as mentioned in Genesis, and in 27 other independent cultures throughout the world that I have so far identified. We can therefore reasonably assume that this event actually happened.

So this then is what we are experiencing now as, over the next few years, Earth once again transitions through the plane of the super-Energy radiating from the super-massive black hole at Galactic Centre the Energy of which both maintains our position in the Galaxy, but while varying in direct proportion to natural, but precise and immutable cycles of oscillation and associated influence.

The next question is "how can these events tangibly affect us"?

This event has the potential to affect us in many ways, both physically and Spiritually.

At a physical level as this event unfolds, and the super-massive Energy of the black hole at Galactic Centre exerts its influence, we can expect a wide variety of direct and indirect consequences. Indirect consequences could be the effect on the Sun which will increase its activity in response to the Energy radiating from the super-massive black hole. We are already increasingly seeing this manifest in the form of increasing solar activity, and in particular sun spots, solar flares and most dangerous of all coronal mass ejections. If Earth were to receive a broadside from a coronal mass ejection, the outcome would be absolutely devastating.

Locally, as Earth transitions into alignment with Galactic Centre and the super-massive black hole Energy radiating from there, the axis of rotation of Earth could well be "pulled" into alignment with the plane of the Energy, resulting in a geophysical pole shift of the 23.5 degrees mentioned previously. Again, the outcome of such an event could well be catastrophic giving rise to, including but not limited to massive land movements, volcanic activity, massive tsunamis hundreds or even thousands of feet high and much more. I believe that this geophysical pole shift has already started, and accounts for many of the abnormal weather conditions increasingly being experienced. Whether this will be an accelerating process or whether any final shift will be sudden, as seems to be the case in the past, we cannot be certain.

It is for example entirely possible that the initial shift will be almost imperceptible, but as the alignment progresses the gravitational potential exerted becomes sufficient to very suddenly cause Earth to succumb, and shift 23 or more degrees on its axis in a moment - the truth is we simply do not know. We can say that previous such events, must have happened so quickly that the civilisations of the time did not see it coming and were largely unprepared.

We know this has happened in the past by virtue of the remains of ancient, clearly advanced civilisations that are being discovered 2000 feet of more under the sea. And of course most will know that this fate also befell Atlantis and Lemuria as well as other major antediluvian cultures as well as the diluvian Great Flood.

The Atlantean hierarchy, the Magicians and others almost certainly knew something was coming, some escaping, but the majority, the general populous, who, like now are always the last to know, likely did not.

Additional compelling evidence may be found in Siberia, where recently large numbers of frozen Mammoth carcasses, complete with tusks that are being taken for ivory are being exposed as the current warming cycle progresses resulting in a thawing of the permafrost allowing these remains to be exposed and retrieved.

The most significant discovery however is the fact that the flesh on many of these carcasses is as fresh as the day the animal would have died, with little or no evidence of decomposition. So fresh in fact is the flesh on many of these animals that dogs are able to eat it without ill effects. Observers report that the flesh looks very similar to beef.

In addition, so fresh were man of these Mammoth remains that they still held fresh, undigested food in their mouths and stomachs as if they were grazing perfectly normally before their extremely sudden and unexpected demise.

The only possible explanation, and one which would account for the actual extinction of the Siberian Mammoth is that they were literally deep-frozen in situ where they stood, and subsequently became buried deep within the ice. The most likely explanation for this, especially in the context of the other factors discussed earlier, is that the Earth very suddenly shifted about its polar axis, effectively shifting the area where the Mammoth were grazing much further north - and event that probably took place within hours, accounting for the perfect preservation of the Mammoth remains.

It is highly likely that this "pulling" of the Earth plus and minus 23.5 degrees on its axis, as it oscillates above and below the Galactic Plane of the super-massive black hole has happened countless times in the past, and will continue to happen in the future with immutable frequency. It is clear from all the evidence that these events happen extremely suddenly and without warning, in the past resulting in catastrophic loss of life and entire civilisations, the evidence and remains of which are only recently being discovered.

These pole shifts might also account for the "ice ages" North America and much of Europe periodically shift 23.5 degrees towards and away from the polar regions, thus being subjected to polar climates until the pole shift reverses allowing the ice to thaw once again.

An additional possibility is the Galactic Alignment acting as the catalyst for a geomagnetic pole shift. In this case instead of, or in addition to the polar axis of the Earth being pulled 23.5 degrees, the magnetic north and south poles might invert, so magnetic north would become magnetic south and vice versa. Again there is abundant evidence in the geological record supporting the fact that this magnetic reversal has happened many times before diring the history of the planet. If this were to happen then it is most likely that Earth would stop rotating for perhaps two or three days, before reversing and rotating the other way. Again this has been recorded in history by ancient records that describe the three days of darkness, after which the Sun rose from the opposite side od of the sky, for example in the east instead of the west as it might have been then.

Such a reversal might profoundly affect the tectonic plates upon which the land masses "float", giving rise to massive earthquakes, volcanic eruptions, tsunamis, and other serious disasters.

Now that said I believe this to unlikely for one very good reason - in the past this event has not been predictable, and therefore ocurred at very specific timescales, in fact several hundreds of thousands of years seems to be the "margin for error" of this type of event.

As the events we are facing are totally predictable, and unambiguously associated with cyclical events, in this case the Galactic Alignment, I would personally rule out a geomagnetic pole shift as a probability, except possibly as a secondary manifestation of the primary event.

In conclusion therefore, all factors considered, a geophysical poleshift is a much more plausible event associated with the Galactic Alignment, with possible secondary factors including abnormally high solar activity in the form of coronal mass ejections, solar flares and other solar activity due to the influence on the Sun of the super-Energy originating from the super-massive black hole at Galactic Centre.

Another possibility is a type of pole shift that is geomagnetic in nature where the north and south poles invert, so magnetic north becomes magnetic south and magnetic south becomes magnetic north. We already know that this event has happened many times throughout history, and is recorded in the geological record.

We also know that the magnetic field of the Earth is rapidly weakening, as indeed it is on the Sun, possible accounting for the increase in sun spot activity as well as solar flares and coronal mass ejections. It is almost inevitable that the geomagnetic pole reversal of Sun and Earth will occur in the not too distant future. The difficulty is however in calculating precisely when. It would seem that previous geomagnetic pole shifts have ocurred at plus or minus tens or even hundreds of thousands of years apart, and therefore do not appear to be the result of any measurable or observable factors that can be calculated or extrapolated from known existing data. All we can say is that we are heading for such a geomagnetic pole shift which could take place at any time in the next few thousand years.

I am of the view that, unlike the galactic alignment which can be precisely predicted, possibly resulting in a geophysical pole shift, a geomagnetic pole shift is considerably more unpredictable and not subject to any known factors that we are currently aware of, or the Maya could have measured.

It is extremely unlikely therefore that the Maya would have been able to fix their Long Count Calendar, and in particular 21 December 2012, precisely to a predicted geomagnetic pole shift, with its resultant consequences which could indeed be profound if ocurring. Such a magnetic event could and almost certainly would affect consciousness and may well have many wide range of geophysical consequences, but it is unlikely to have the potential to affect the very fabric of space-time itself, unlike the gravitational potential of the galactic alignment as previously discussed. We must always keep in Mind that none of these events mystical events, or chaotic events, or events arising from "prophecies", these events are rather absolutely immutable, measureable and predictable due to know, observable cosmic events, that the Maya knew about, recorded and used as the basis for their Long Count Calendar that "resets" on 21 December 2012.

Now what of the Spiritual consequences, and the ones we should all be focusing on?

As previously discussed, the classic Maya almost certainly fixed the end of their Long Count calendar to coincide with the Galactic Alignment and were also probably aware of the super massive "black hole" that exists at the very centre of our galaxy, although they might not have understood the astrophysics, instead representing it mythically, and which could well exert its influence at the time of the Galactic Alignment. In addition to the physical implications of this galactic event, there are also Energetic and therefore Spiritual implications. Again, and this is most important:

How humanity and all life on Earth experiences this event will be entirely determined by one primary factor - Mind and Consciousness.

Einstein's Law of Relativity describes, among other things, the rate of time, and scale of space. For example a clock may be observed to run slower at lower altitudes, where the gravitational potential exerted on the clock is higher. The gravitational potential of a black hole, in this case the galactic centre is so massive that "time" itself is suspended and the dimensions of "space" reduced to zero. In other words "space" and "time" as experienced on Earth cease to exist altogether.

We, along with all life on Earth, are currently bound together in the same shared quantum reality by virtue of the fact that we are all at the extremity of, and thereby subjected to, the same extreme gravitational potential, and have been since before recorded history. As we approach 2012 and beyond we may well be travelling through the plane of the super-massive black hole at Galactic Centre, associated with greatly modified gravitational potential to which we will all become progressively subjected as this process progresses, as will every planet in our solar system and beyond.

Without going into the extensive and complex quantum mechanics behind this process, the ultimate outcome of this scenario might be that the twin illusions of "space" and "time" would cease to exert their influence. If this finally takes place, and this process is accelerating even now, as mentioned previously, humans will be left "Spiritually naked" in an environment where everything is perceived for what it really is, and where our thoughts, feelings emotions and other powers of the Mind will manifest into our experience instantly no longer being subjected to the twin forces of space-time.

This would be a pivotal juncture for all humanity. Each of us and all life would be freed to realise our true Spiritual potential based upon our individual state of Spiritual evolution knowledge, wisdom and other factors. Those who are thus ready will transition to a quantum reality, a plane of vibration that most closely matches their individual vibration. Although this would happen in due course anyway, this could be a "mass evolution" event that appears to occur from time to time. An opportunity to take the "fast-track" of evolution if the opportunity is recognised and acted upon.

Those not Spiritually prepared will gravitate to another "time-space" bound reality similar to Earth, if Earth is no longer habitable. No one is "destroyed" to oblivion. As immortal, infinite, Spiritual Beings we all continue, but as two varieties of human - those who took the opportunity and those who did not. The latter, as mentioned, will live on somewhere, to prepare themselves for evolution, which can take place at any time, when ready, but in any case when the next great evolutional event comes around with immutable certainty.

So again we can clearly see that the super-massive black hole and the equally super-massive Energy that it radiates outwards from its plane can potentially have a dramatic effect on Earth, humanity and all life on Earth in many different ways.

In the unlikely event that the event is based around a geomagnetic pole shift, there are certainly considerable possible implications for consciousness, becaye we already know that even small changes in a localised magnetic field can influence consciousness, trigger out of body experiences and much more.

So a wide ranging geomagnetic pole shift would certainly have the potential to transform consciousness should it take place, possibly resulting in a new phase of evolution for humanity based upon Spiritual rather than material factors as has hitherto been the case, resulting in mankind being in the tentative position it finds itself in today.

One question that may arise is what, if any consequences were there for humanity at previous transitions of the great 25,800 year cycle?

We are restricted by the fact that there are no records dating back that far, and so the only record available is the fossil record. According to the paleoanthropological fossil record our immediate and most recent ancestor, Cro Magnon man appeared as the next evolution of our species, succeeding Neanderthal man which subsequently became extinct. It is most likely therefore that the transition of the current great cycle, "year" or age, symbolically represented by the iconic December 21 2012, will result in the next evolution of humanity that I refer to as "Homo Sprirítus" but the shamans of Mesoamerica, who know this evolutionary transition is imminent refer to as "Homo Luminous".

Does this mean that every human will be transformed under these circumstances? No not at all. Only those sufficiently Spiritually evolved and prepared can metamorphose, everyone else returning to their inner origins where their Higher Self will continue the process either on Earth, if inhabitable, or on some other suitable planet somewhere in the Universe.

Of course Spiritually we are all infinite and immortal, so no one "ceases to exist" - everyone continues the great adventure on their unique path and quest for perfection on the path of return to Source, the Divine, The First Cause from Whence we came in the beginning.

I am now absolutely certain that the Maya and their use of the Galactic Alignment through their Long Count Calendar as a metaphor, symbolically marking the end and beginning of "ages" were absolutely correct, and that the associated planar super-Energy radiating from the super-massive black hole at Galactic Centre, which the Maya may or may not have been aware of, is the focal point of any causal effects and associated events that we might experience over the next 15 years or so, probably peaking around the end of 2012.

The final, and probably ultimate question therefore is how we, as humans on Earth, at the mercy of these incomprehensibly massive cosmic events can emerge in the best possible Light.

The answer in a word is Consciousness and ultimately the most fundamental Universal Principle of all - Mind.

Even faced with the enormity of these cosmic events we still, as always create our own reality. There is never a single moment where we are at the "mercy" of circumstances "beyond our control", and this is probably the ultimate verification of this truth at every level. Even facing events of this magnitude we still, every single one of us have absolute control over our own destiny - a sobering thought while emphasising the truth that as Source Energy, God, we can still determine our reality, even in the face of massive, natural, cosmic forces.

I have said this before and I will say it again - whatever the collective consciousness of humanity expects to happen will happen - without question. An additional factor is the overall state of Spiritual consciousness of mankind viz a viz Spiritual evolution as opposed to an obsessive focus on material things driven by the Ego.

The next few years are, for humanity, an Divinely orchestrated opportunity, the nature of which only takes place every few thousand years to evolve or to regress, or even to start again after almost total destruction. In previous prediluvian epochs the Lemurians, Atlanteans, humanity at the time of the Great Flood event chose the latter at some level of consciousness, and paid the price, probably setting humanity as a whole back millennia. We must learn from their mistakes and not allow history to repeat itself - yet again.

The person known as "Jesus" came here 2000 years ago for one major reason - to ensure that humanity does not make the same mistake again. As it is however humanity is making the same mistake again and worse - much worse. The teachings of Jesus were seized by the Romans and turned into a theology based religion, which has contributed in no small way to setting humanity even further back in its Divine quest for perfection in the interests of power and control.

Since then other factions have emerged with the intent, at all costs, to take control over the entire world and everyone on it, and due to the ever increasing egotistical, material focus of humanity, they are, even now achieving their dark side objectives.

The situation of Earth today outwardly, in some respects has never looked bleaker, but I, myself, from what I see and know, believe at the same time that it has never looked better.

I now believe that this time the forces of Light will prevail and that humanity, if motivated to do so, will experience a glorious transition. I believe this to be true because, for the first time in history, we have a global medium of information that we call the Internet, with the power to reach billions of people. This is no accident - nothing happens by chance. Before it was a few powerful, often corrupt people that controlled the masses, as indeed is the case today through certain factions, but today we have the Internet which is hugely more powerful as a global instrument of information, and one that will help in no small measure in the battle between Light and Dark, and ultimately the hearts, Minds and consciousness of all humanity, Earth, Gaia and all life on Earth.

However, the high vibration forces of Light under the influence of Mind is many, many orders of magnitude greater than the low vibration forces of darkness as mentioned above, to such an extent in fact that even now time remains to turn around the situation of humanity in order to claim the glory that rightfully belongs to humanity in the form of an eschatological outcome, resulting in the evolution from Home Sapien to the next generation of mankind, as has happened several times in the history of Earth, to Homo Spiritus, or as some are now describing us - "Homo Luminous".

This is one reason I was inspired by Source to write my book Our Ultimate Reality: http://www.ourultimatereality.com/our-ultimate-reality-the-book.html

And the reason I am here in dedicating my life to the education of humanity in order to secure the best possible outcome in the events we are facing. Of course I am only one of a number of people on the same mission, all approaching the propagation of knowledge through different resources approaches.

Ultimately it is for every single person fortunate to understand these crucial issues to teach family, friends and others, thus raising awareness and expanding consciousness over the next few years in preparation for what almost certainly to come, and indeed is already happening as any conscious person can clearly see.

So what does this mean in practical terms starting from this moment?

It means that everyone must only focus on Spiritual evolution, turning your back on material things, the cravings of the Ego - one factor that literally "sunk" the Atlanteans - and towards service to others before service to self, and above all Unconditional Love for all creation.

We must also realise Source, Universal Mind, God within, and become conscious channels of expression, experience and thereby expansion of Source - a reason Source created us in the beginning, and blessed us with freewill with the great responsibility that brings.

If each and every one of us enlighten just one other person over the next few years our time on Earth will have been worth it and make no mistake everyone accomplishing this will be blessed. Of course the more people we can reach, the more will be the exponential effect on the collective consciousness, and the greater the likelihood of a glorious outcome to these immutable events.

Everyone must stop taking notice of and preferably even reading the popular media who are owned and managed by the instruments of the forces of darkness, who would seek to physically control the world and the Minds of all humanity.

Everyone must be aware of the covert actions of governments and other entities designed to progressively assume control over the populous, and to resist and reject it.

The forces of darkness know very well that their "window of opportunity" is closing and they must capture the Minds of humanity now, before it is too late and they are annihilated.

The stakes for humanity and Light are high and never been higher. Many ancient writings, including the Maya and other Mesoamerican and global cultures have described a "great battle in the heavens between the forces of darkness and the forces of Light". This drama is symbolised and metaphorically depicted throughout these cultures - they all knew, beyond doubt, that this moment in our history would arrive. The book of Revelation is almost exclusively about these events if only people understood it.

We are in the midst of that battle right now, today, and it is getting more and more intense by the moment - literally.

I must add, for the sake of completeness, that nothing at all might happen over the next few years, and that we will look back on these times as the event that never was.

That was the mistake however the Atlanteans and many other cultures made - one of complacency and "it will never happen to us". Famous last words. The Atlanteans never knew what hit them, as with the other now long lost civilisations that we know about and indeed have recently been discovered thousands of feet under the sea.

It is not a gamble that humanity can afford to take - the stakes are high and never been higher in the history of the planet, and a glorious victory is ours for the taking providing we do not repeat the mistakes of the past epochs and Galactic transitions.

On the one side we have the forces of Light, the Source, God, the First Cause, and on the other the forces of darkness - the ancient factions of power and control that would seek to imprison the Mind and Soul of humanity, and deny us of our ultimate glorious destiny - at least for the next few thousand years until the next window of opportunity opens as once again we reach the end of another age and its transition to the next, where all of these factors once again will play out in the "Heavens" and on Earth.

I would suggest that humanity does not wish to endure several thousand years of imprisonment, after which it will be even harder to ascend towards our true destiny.

The time is Now!

Everyone must therefore focus exclusively on inner growth, know only the glorious truth of who we are and where we are going, and do our best to ensure that as many others as possible do the same through education, never through coercion.

Of course there are those who will not be ready this time around, Their time will come but in the meantime it is incumbent on us to make their lives better, and to finally give rise to the biblical prophecy of "Kingdom of Heaven on Earth" for our children and future generations in readiness for the next great transition when their time will surely come, and we will be ready to help them, just as those evolved Spirits before us have, and still do help us.

Only those who are ready for these events and can prepare themselves will become consciously aware of them, and that means every single person reading this newsletter without exception. As always however the choice is yours and yours alone by virtue of the freewill vested in, and entrusted to us by our Divine Creator.

Finally - I do not put this forward as the definitive definition of the events collectively known as "2012", because at the final analysis no one really knows and probably will never know until after the event. I do believe however that this article does represent the most comprehensive and justifiable diagnosis and prognosis, deeply based in fact and knowledge, and one which will at least serve as a basis of what we might expect, what it all means and above all how we might prepare over the next few years at both an individual and collective level.

This then is by belief and truth, if it were not the case I would not have written about it here. As always though I will conclude with this caveat:

This is my truth and which truth I believe to be true at every level according to my own research, knowledge and in particular information made available to me. It is however your life, your future and your Spiritual path, and accordingly it is for you and you alone to accept or reject what I have written here, in whole or in part, and to plan your own life accordingly - especially over the next few years. You are here, as are we all for a reason, and to experience and potentially benefit greatly from this opportunity. Whatever we can say about the possible causal effects of Galactic Alignment, we can definitely say, without question, that it only happens every few thousands years, and once this event is missed, there will be no further such Divinely orchestrated opportunity for to come. As the well known sayings goes, "it is better to be safe than sorry" and "hindsight is a wonderful thing".

Whether any of these events happen or not, in whole or in part, absolutely nothing is certain except life itself and our infinite, eternal and Divine Spiritual nature as inseparable channels of expression, experience and thereby expansion of Source Energy, who some know as "God, and I know as Universal Mind, everyone should be striving to fulfil their own unique and collective reasons for incarnating here on spaceship, planet Earth at these pivotal times, and should be turning their back on material, ephemeral, transient things, in favour of ongoing perfection and Spiritual Evolution.

As mentioned at the beginning of this article, the transition around which 2012 is iconically revolves is very much an evolutionary situation, and accordingly this page will be constantly updated in the Light of new information and analysis. My previous 2012 related articles may be viewed here: You can read my initial 2012 related articles here:

## THE "GLOBAL WARMING" MYTH

I receive many messages on the subject of "global warming". I assume that this is due to the fact that hardly a week, or often a day goes by without some extreme weather condition, most recently severe flooding in many parts of the world.

Yesterday it even snowed and settled in Baghdad which is unprecedented. All the residents left there homes in wonder to marvel at this amazing spectacle.

I think it is fair to say that wherever you live you will have experienced extraordinary weather conditions over the last few months, and most probably increasingly so.

The official position on the part of the major government of the world is that "global warming" or "climate change" due to "carbon emissions", "fossil fuels" etc is the cause. In fact this is a complete and utter myth whether the major governments of the World believe it or not. There is not one serious scientist involved in these areas that believes this official line with regards to global warming.

In fact the term "global warming" is very misleading in and of itself, because what we are seeing goes far beyond simply warming - we are rather seeing rapidly altering weather patterns of increasing extremity.

Here is a typical quote from a scientist who knows the truth:

*"It is the greatest scam in history. I am amazed, appalled and highly offended by it. Global Warming; It is a SCAM. Some dastardly scientists with environmental and political motives manipulated long term scientific data to create in [sic] allusion of rapid global warming."* — John Coleman, Founder of Weather Channel

From my own extensive research I would definitely agree with this view, although this is only part of the entire equation.

There are then two major aspects to the "climate change" issue:

1. What is the real meaning and cause behind it?
2. What is the real agenda of the World governments?

In future newsletters we will look much more closely at these issues, but for now I will summarise as follows:

*1. What we are really experiencing are immutable, natural cycles of Energy and weather patterns that have occurred throughout history.*

Scientists have proved this conclusively by drilling deep core samples, in other words by sinking very long, narrow tubes deep into the ground at Antarctica, lake beds and other suitable undisturbed areas al around the planet.

The deeper samples contain an abundance of evidence that enables scientists to determine the weather conditions prevailing at any particular juncture in Earths history, at least for tens of thousands of years. The results conclusively prove the fact that climate changes occur with immutable frequency with cold spells, or "ice ages" and warm spells, both of which accelerate as they reach a peak. Earth is currently reaching such a natural weather cycle peak.

In addition however we have the "2012 effect" which, as we know from previous newsletters, is ultimately due to the influence of great galactic Energy cycles originating from Galactic Centre, and are reaching a peak of causality over the next few years.

Many people have heard of the "Great Flood" of biblical times. I have been conducting considerable research into the Great Flood as the only recorded global cataclysmic event, and have so far found independant references to the Great Flood in 28 different cultures of the time throughout the planet - cultures that had no connection with each other. This event seems to have destroyed perhaps 80% of life, including human life at the time - perhaps much more.

Thus we can conclude with reasonable certainty that this event did indeed take place, and almost certainly coincided with a Galactic Energy Cycle and transition of great or lesser age, this time manifesting as a great flood, but in other such transitions or transitional quarters manifesting as other catastrophic events. The end of the age of the dinosaurs as well as previous and post extinction events almost certainly coincided with these Galactic transitional Energy cycles.

However, this time there is a third influence - the Sun. During 2012 the sun will achieve a maximum period of activity, greater than anything ever witnessed and recorded in human history, likely resulting in massive Energy emissions known as "coronal mass ejections" and solar flares, probably of the highest magnitude "X Class" type, which could approach or even hit Earth directly.

So we can conclude, with reasonable certainty, that the next few years will be pivotal for humanity in terms of "climate change" alone, notwithstanding the numerous other "2012" factors that I have written about previously as we inexorable progress together throughthe transition of this great age and into the next.

Again though, and this is crucially important - the final outcome of these events or more specifically our experience of these events, at both an collective and individual level, will be determined by just one factor - human consciousness. Plain and simple - whatever humanity expects to happen over the next few years will happen. It is for this reason I am keeping you fully updated in this newsletter with the facts and only the facts.

*2. The major governments of the world are turning "climate change" into yet another cabal like the drugs industry, banking industry, and more. A cabal generally seeks to take the money off consumers while the consumer feels grateful for it at the same time.*

In this case you will see increasingly more "eco friendly" products sold on the basis that if you buy them you will be "helping climate change". You have probably seen advertising like this already - expect much more. These businesses will endeavour to cause people to purchase their "eco friendly" products in the context of "saving the world from the effect of climate change" while feeling good about it.

This has been a basic overview of a much larger and very important subject. In future newsletters we will look at these factors as well as 2012 related factors in much more detail.

In the meantime it is extremely important to keep this, very real and experienced aspect of the transition of the ages that we are all experiencing together in perspective.

We cannot escape the apparent reality of the ever increasing extremes of weather conditions, but as we know, "thoughts are things", and the more people focus on these situations, the more they will manifest into our experience.

We must also understand that we no longer live in a democracy, we live in a mediocracy where the power of the popular press, in turned owned and controlled by those on the the path of darkness, seeks to control the Mind of the populous at every level in order to prevail over the next few years.

My advice to you is to never read, watch or listen to the so called "news". Much of the time it is not "news" at all, it is Mind control plain and simple.

Similarly I advise that you pay no heed to advertising that promotes products in the context of doing your part to combat "climate change".

That said, and this is most important notwithstanding the above, absolutely anything and everything we can do to help the planet, the environment and each other we must of course do first and foremost, but, most importantly, for all the right reasons.

For example, changing to a powder that washes your clothes at 30 degrees instead of 40 degrees will not help, but being diligent with what chemicals you use around the house most certainly will help the environment generally. Also, and most importantly, endeavour to transition to a natural, harvestable whole food diet and away from animal based products which are, in any case, toxic to human physiology and can reduce life expectancy by 7 to 15 years as well as causing chronic, debilitating diseases.

Finally, above all please keep in Mind that as humans we have but one task to perform over the next few years, and that is to be prepared Spiritually, Mentally and Consciously for what is to come over the next few years - a main reason I was inspired to write my book Our Ultimate Reality. Every Human Beings has a choice, just as with the transition of other great cycles or ages.

## 2012 IN PERSPECTIVE

As we progress inexorably towards the now iconic date of 21 December 2012, the rumour, speculation and fantasy machine is moving into overdrive resulting in ever more confusion, concern and fantasy.

Speculation about what it all means for humanity ranges from the sublime to the ridiculous and every eventuality in between, with an equally wide range of hidden agendas.

My observations have led me to believe that the vast majority of these ideas presented as fact originate from a wide array intangible evidence, and misinterpretation of the facts, or even fiction, with proponents often cobbling together fragments of stories from a wide range of sources in order to create a new idea, often presented as fact, but with no supporting evidence.

Many such ideas point towards monuments and artefact's that might be loosely related to 2012 and the transition in some way, and declare them to be evidential.

Another potentially dangerous trend is the increasing number of people claiming to "channel" a wide variety of exalted Beings, including, but not limited to Jesus, Archangels, Ascended Masters, Pleaidians, and Planetary Spirit Gaia Herself.

I will not spend too much time on this subject, but suffice it to say that, as with so called "prophecies", I do not regard any information from a channeled source to be evidential in any way. It is virtually impossible to known who the non-physical communicators really are, what their motives are and how they know what they claim to convey.

I can say that probably 99.9% of such communicators are Astral entities, who will claim to be anyone the channeler believes them to be - keeping in Mind these entities know the thoughts of the channeler - in order to be taken seriously, and they have no hesitation in outright lying about it.

Of course some such entities genuinely wish to assist humanity, and simply see such deception as necessary and justified; but others seek to deceive humanity in order to drag humanity down with them.

I could not say which variety of entity form the majority, but I do know that the consequences of making a wrong choice are so serious as to not to take the risk in the first place.

That said, I also believe there are a very few genuine channels for genuinely advanced Beings, who are certainly interested in guiding humanity through the transition that we are facing in the next few years. These advanced Beings are usually recognisable for Who they are due to the mode of communication and the messages conveyed.

Such evolved Beings, often evolved human beings in fact, reside at much higher level of Energy vibration than the physical Earth. It would therefore be virtually impossible for such an evolved being communicating from that level of vibration, to directly communicate with a person residing in a mortal body on the Earth level of vibration - such an situation might well physically "kill" the channeler, or at the very least drive them insane. There are however various mechanisms that can be and are employed in order to mediate the difference in these Energy levels, effectively acting as a "step-down transformer" as is familiar in electrical circuits, and acting in much the same way for much the same reasons - everything is Energy.

This is usually managed from the Spirit side of the channel, aware as they are of the importance of these Energy differences, and hos best to reconcile them for the purposes of communication, without harming the channeler.

Turning to other forms of "evidence" often presented, often pointing to the Maya themselves - even the records in stone left by the Maya called "stelae" cannot be regarded as evidential per se, because although they most certainly indicate the "end times" we are currently experiencing, absolutely nowhere do these records indicate how these end times will be experienced.

In addition to the records left in stone, the Maya also created thousands of documents recording their culture known as "codices" which would have surely revealed considerably more about the Maya and their culture and calendrical systems. However, when the Europeans arrived, the Roman Catholic church ordered the total destruction by burning of these codices, as part of their policy of forcibly converting the Mayan people to the Roman Catholic church, the consequences of which can only be imagined.

A further example of symbolic evidence, and one that has become increasingly popular in recent years is the "Cross of Hendaye" located in South West France. This artifact consists of a cross upon a large stone bases, upon which are carved various alchemical symbols, which some have interpreted to be indicative of some forthcoming catastrophe and the end times.

Whilst I fully understand the Hermetic and alchemical symbolism depicted on this monument, and would agree that it is almost certainly related to the transition of the ages that we are now experiencing, the question still arises as to who constructed this monument, why, what did they use as the basis of their message, and did they know something that we as yet do not?

The point is this - it is easy to become captivated by the monument and its symbolism, which is after all most interesting, but without knowing its history it remains yet another interesting artifact with no proven basis in fact or firm evidence of what we are facing. Accordingly, to me at least, they simply represent yet another piece in a large and complex jigsaw puzzle, all the pieces to which we may or may not discover and interpret.

Now before I proceed, I would once again like to make one fact absolutely clear, and I simply cannot stress this enough:

Whatever the consensus Mind and Consciousness of the human race and of all life on Earth believes will happen over the next few years, will indeed happen - of that you can be absolutely sure.

If the majority believe in a cataclysm then the Universe will oblige, and perhaps 95% of all life on Earth could be destroyed.

If on the other hand the majority believe in awakening, enlightenment and Spiritual evolution, then this will be the result, and humanity will have progressed to the next evolution, of human that I refer to as "Homo Spiritus".

These are not random processes.

In the past there have been numerous examples of both including but not limited to the evolution of humans from for example Neanderthal to Cro Magnon, the first recognisable "modern" humans that led to where we are today, and also massive purgative or "mass extinction" events as with the "great flood" and of course Atlantis and Lemuria as well as numerous other great civilisations, the evidence for which has actually been discovered 200 feet under the sea in various parts of the world. How did these large, sophisticated and robust civilisations suddenly transition from normality to 2000 feet beneath the sea, possibly in a very short space of time?

I also believe it likely that other mass extinction events such as those that wiped out the dinosaurs, also coincided with the transition of these ages, which relate to life on Earth, not just humanity. It should be clear to anyone as to how the end of the "age of the dinosaurs", eventually facilitated the evolution of human beings. These events are not random either in terms of periodicity or consequences. They are rather completely normal aspects of greater Universal cycles of Energy. I am of the view therefore that all of these great, pivotal events that shaped the future of life on Earth, ultimately leading to where we are today, coincided with the end of one great age, and the beginning of the next.

It is also likely that these ages were divided into lesser and greater ages, the lesser occuring every 6000 years or so at the precessional quarters of the equinox, resulting in the different ages of "modern" man for example, and the end of a great age every 25800 years or so after one complete cycle of the precession of the equinox, resulting in a potentially much greater evolutionary leap.

This alone would appear to provide some tangible indication that we are indeed approaching an era of great change, the precise nature of which will be finally decided by the consciousness of humanity.

I am however, due to the importance and consequences of what humanity is facing over the next few years, only concerned with the facts. There simply is not time to pursue fantasies and speculation at a time when humanity must prepare itself for what is to come.

Humanity, accompanied by all life on Earth is rapidly approaching a "speed bump" on our collective path. How we approach and negotiate this speed bump will determine whether humanity and life on Earth will crash and burn - or evolve - it really is that simple. The key, as I have mentioned before and will continue to so so is human Consciousness together with the Consciousness of all life on Earth, and of course Earth, great Planetary Spirit Gaia herself.

I therefore turn to the Mayans for tangible clues to what awaits us. The classic Maya were one of the most advanced races ever to have walked the Earth - keeping in Mind that we must not make the error of equating "advancement" with "technology", in fact the reverse is true in absolute terms.

The Mayans were many things including but not limited to Astronomers, Cosmologists, Astrophysics ts, Mathematicians and Astrologers. For all that however they had two main tools at their disposal for their work, which made it all the more impressive and they were these:

1. Observation of the cosmos
2. Shamanic exploration

At this stage I will refrain from discussing the shamanic aspect for reasons I will make clear later.

From an observational perspective the Maya were dedicated observers of the night sky, which became central to Mayan mythology and the Mayan culture generally. They would also have been observers of the Sun and therefore solar activity.

What were the Maya fundamentally looking for?

The answer is almost certainly predictable "cycles" which would then in turn form the basis of their entire culture at all levels, as well as the future of humanity, all life on Earth and Gaia Herself.

The entire Universe operates in cycles, some so minute or so massive that we cannot detect them from our temporal respecified scientific instruments, but others in between which are much more obvious such as the cycles of the year we known as the four "seasons".

The Maya were interested in cycles of every magnitude, knowing them to fundamentally influence reality as a whole, with which of course we are all intimately connected. The resultant Mayan calendrical systems functioned in many ways like modern astrology, but many orders of magnitude more advanced and accurate, and which were clearly capable of operating accurately from time scales of seconds, to probably millions of years, or even the entire lifespan of the planet.

So what was it in the night sky the Maya were particularly interested in which led to the creation of their Long Count Calendar, and consequently the iconic 21 December 2012 end date for their calendar?

The answer is the Galaxy, or more specifically Galactic Centre relative to Earth, also to include the Solar System. The Maya also observed and measured the precession of the Equinoxes as previously mentioned.

In addition to tangible observation, the Maya were also acutely aware of non-physical cycles of Energy and the potential causal effects upon life on Earth, and in particular human beings.

The Maya supported their physical observations with Shamanic observations which were facilitated by the use of a very specific group of chemical compounds extracted from natural sources, Mind-expanding substances known as "entheogens" of which there are various derivatives and chemical variations including N,N-dimethyltryptamine (DMT), 5-Methoxy-N,N-Dimethyltryptamine (5-MeO-DMT) and 5-Hydroxy-N,N-Dimethyltryptamine (5-OH-DMT) known as "bufotenine" due, being extracted from the skin of toads of genus "Bufo".

So the Maya were not only able to observe physical cosmic cycles, they were also able to observe non-physical cycles of Energy, as well as to access the vast and information stored as Energy, often conceptualised as the "Akashic Record", which contains all the information in the entire Universe, including physical parallel Universe and inner Energy Levels, throughout what people know as the "past", present" and the quantum probabilities that we may regard as the probable future. Shamanic exploration would also have enabled the Maya to project their conscious awareness to the Galactic Centre itself, for closer observation and therefore understanding of the Energy and cycles emanating from there.

These then I am certain formed the basis of the knowledge of the Maya, and their legacy today, as well as the immediate destiny of the human race and all life on Earth.

Now at this point I must stress that the Maya never, ever put forward "prophecies". A "prophecy" is the supposed prediction of future events. I would like to make it absolutely clear that it is absolutely impossible to contrive such a prophecy, and anyone who purports to do so, or to "tell the future" might be regarded in that context.

"Time" does not exist except as an illusion of the corporeal senses and the conscious sphere of operation of the Mind as it operates within the sphere of the space-time continuum. Accordingly the "future", like "time", does not exist except as a human concept.

What people erroneously refer to as the "future" only exists as an infinite number of probabilities, one or more of which can eventually exert their influence under the influence of Mind in the present moment of Now - the "future" only becomes true in the actual moment it is observed and experienced in the present moment of Now.

In the context of the transition we are facing, there are a very wide range of quantum probabilities that have the Energy potential to exert an influence over the next few years. These include but are not limited to physical factors such as the Sun, Galactic Centre and extra-terrestrial objects, and non-physical potential in the form of Energy including cycles of Energy.

And again Universal Principle will hold true - the potential factors that will finally exert their influence will be directly proportional to Mind and Consciousness in that moment of Now.

So the Maya new about these factors based upon their observations, and factored them into their predictions. Note I use the word "prediction"" because the legacy of the Maya is predicated in fact and not in some form of mystical speculation based upon the Conscious Mind and/or the Ego otherwise known as "prophecy".

So 21 December 2012 is not a "prophecy" it is a scientifically derived prediction that the classic Maya were able to formulate based upon their physical observation of the cosmos, and non-physical shamanic explorations, together with their vast understanding of these Universal forces which were uncontaminated by individual interest, agenda or motive, influence of the Ego, or some other ulterior motive in the interests of power and control.

This then forms the firm basis of my own research into 2012.

Turning to the Mayan Long Count Calendar, what were the Maya concerned with?

I absolutely believe, by virtue of extensive research by Mayan researchers of whom I have the utmost respect, that the Maya were concerned with events related to the centre of our Galaxy, i.e.

Galactic Centre, as it relates to Earth and in particular the precession of the equinoxes a confluence and significance of which the Maya were unquestionably aware of by virtue of their cosmic and shamanic observations and astounding ability to make sense of it all. It is indeed this "sense" that we must replicate as our source of understanding of information relating to the transition that we are now facing.

It is clear from the ancient artifacts, notably in the form of the stone "stelae" remaining at classic Mayan sites, and their culture which included strategically positioned "ball parks", that the Maya, in this context were primarily concerned with events at the centre of our Galaxy, in other words Galactic Centre which they clearly deemed to be instrumental in shaping the future direction of humanity and life on Earth.

What then lies at Galactic Centre that could be of so much interest and significance to the Maya, and which could possibly be implicated in any future evolutional direction for our small planet?

The solution, I believe rests in an aspect of the Galactic Centre that we cannot actually see, but yet many scientists now believe exists, and the Maya absolutely knew existed - specifically a super-massive Energy structure known as a "black hole".

It is beyond the scope of this short newsletter to discuss the science of black holes generally, but in any event we are only concerned with its characteristics as pertains to the transition of the ages and of any related 2012 event.

A black hole has associated with it massive Energy, and it is this Energy that we are concerned with and the Maya were almost certainly concerned with when formulating the potential causation as a result of the events predicted by their long count calendar.

Energy is everything - literally - Energy shaped by Mind - either Universal Mind in the context of all creation, the Macrocosm, or individual Mind in the context of our own individual experiential reality - our own individual Universe - the Microcosm.

It is almost certain that this massive Energy vortex at Galactic Centre - the same Energy that probably holds the very fabric of the Galaxy together - will form the primary influence over the range of events that could manifest over the next few years, in turn under the influence of the collective Mind or Consciousness of the human race, which will in turn contribute towards the shaping of the next phase of existence, evolution or otherwise of the human race and of all life on Earth.

Like all Energy, this particular Energy will ultimately respond to only one primary influence - Mind at both an indivudual and consensual level. Of course ultimately all Universal events and the Divine operation and order of the Universe are all under the influence of Universal Mind, of which we and all in creation are integral, inseparable aspects - everything is ultimately connected.

Of course this Galactic Centre Super Energy Field is not the only possible influence by any means. In accordance with the range of potential events and challenges facing life on Earth over the next few years, many other factors external to our planet will or could exert an influence, including, but not limited to Solar activity and extra-terrestrial bodies, often known as "Near Earth Objects".

Of one factor I am absolutely certain at this juncture. The primary source of infiuence over the immediate destiny of humanity, life on Earth and Earth herself will be Energy, the only real questions being these:

1. What will be the origin of the causal Energy?
2. In what form will the Energy manifest?
3. What will be the causal effects of that Energy?
4. What influences will determine the causation?
5. Over what time period will the causation extert its influence?

These then are the questions I will be seeking to answer as events unfold.

But again, and I will keep repeating this statement due to its extreme importance:

All of the factors listed above will ultimately be determined by one primary factor - Mind - of which consciousness is a fundamental aspect. Whatsoever the consensus of humanity, life on Earth and Earth Herself Expects to happen, Believe will happen, and has Faith in happening, will happen - of this truth I have not the slightest doubt.

Most of the so called "modern countries" on Earth are no longer governed by a democracy but rather by a mediocracy, in ottherwords through the power of the press and other popular media. These in turn are largely controlled by those who seek to deny humanity of its true destiny in the interests of power and control. It is crucal therefore not to look towards external factors for guidance, but rather always start by looking within and asking the right questions, as well as seeking those who wish only to see humanity evolve to its next glorious evolution, but at the same time accepting only that which you know intuitively to be true.

It is however beyond the scope of this short introduction in this newsletter to expand upon these factors further, and we will indeed surely do so in a future newsletter, but for those interested I have also prepared a short overview, to expand upon this brief introduction, and which will also form the basis of my ongoing analysis of 2012 and the transition of the ages as events progress.

## 2012 AND THE CYCLES OF LIFE

As the days, weeks and months roll by I know from the messages I receive that more and more people are becoming aware of the changes occurring at all levels, wishing to know why. Others are anxious about "2012" and what it will mean for themselves and their families.

These changes are manifesting in terms of awareness, consciousness and in the outer physical world where dramatic changes, the details for many of which have been withheld from people generally are taking place. Who could fail to notice these changes with the worlds glaciers melting at a dramatic rate, mass extinctions, and unusual behaviour in the animal kingdom who are highly tuned to change unlike humans who have a predominantly material focus.

It is important to understand however that what we are experiencing is not the end of the world in terms of life but the end of a great age, a great cycle of Energy.

Everything in creation moves in cycles, some of which are vast, and others which occur of much shorter, sometimes imperceptible frequencies, some of which are obvious, others which are not.

For thousands of years our ancient ancestors, free from the material focus of "modern civilisation" were tuned in to these cycles, and by observing the cosmos and many other natural factors were able to chart these peaks and troughs as well as the manifestations associated with them.

Many of these were deeply encoded as for example in the I-Ching, the Chinese "Book of Changes" which rather than being for mantic purposes was in fact measuring Energy and cycles at all levels, including forecasting the forthcoming events of 2012.

The Maya, in their now famous Long Count Calendar which also transitions to a new cycle on 21 December 2012, measured and predicted these great events.

According to my current research I believe it is very possible that the person known in Greek as Jesus came here 2000 years ago to prepare mankind for these events, by teaching the teachers who would teach other teachers and so on until finally, by now, everyone should have been prepared:

> "Again, the kingdom of heaven is like a net that was thrown into the sea and caught fish of every kind; when it was full, they drew it ashore, sat down, and put the good into baskets but threw out the bad. So it will be at the end of the age. The angels will come out and separate the evil from the righteous and throw them into the furnace of fire, where there will be weeping and gnashing of teeth.
>
> 'Have you understood all this?' They answered, 'Yes.' And he said to them, 'Therefore every scribe who has been trained for the kingdom of heaven is like the master of a household who brings out of his treasure what is new and what is old.'" — Matthew 13:47-52.

Here Jesus is saying that the end of an age is coming at which point there will be a "dragnet" which will harvest those who are ready, and only those who are ready will "be saved" and transition to the Kingdom of Heaven", while everyone else will be cast back in to the "furnace of fire".

Alas, as in the entire bible, the true meaning of these words were lost when men, who were not ready to understand, and also sought control for their own purposes, interpreted these ancient words in theological terms, thus setting mankind on a course that was never intended, and the true meaning was lost until now.

Much of the original meaning was lost, either by accident or design, when it was translated from the original ancient Greek, to Latin and later other languages as well as being creatively interpreted by orthodox religion in such a way as to create conditions for control over people through fear and guilt.

The "furnace" referred to is not some notional fiery existence "down below" as the guest of "the devil", but rather the furnace of initiation, Spiritual progression, where our Spirit is refined as we progress to the higher levels of vibration of the inner worlds of reality, worlds of glory and splendour far beyond the comprehension of carnate humans, a place that may be conceived as "heaven".

This is also the true meaning of alchemy, the transmutation of base human characteristics symbolised by the heaviness of lead, to the Gold of the refined, higher vibration Spirit.

The biblical account of turning "water in to wine" means the same.

So 21 December 2012 represents the turning point in just such a cycle where humans and indeed all life have the potential to take the next evolutionary leap, leaving the "furnace" of Earth well behind.

The word to emphasise however is "potential". When the time comes only those who have realised that potential will be "harvested" and move on to the next phase of evolution; this is why great teachers allowed two thousand or more years for this process to take place.

"Harvested" is of course a metaphor for Spiritual evolution based upon consciousness and therefore vibration.

What we are experiencing now is the end game where a culmination of numerous factors that can influence humans, all life and Earth herself is taking place, the results of which, will be determined by one factor only; consciousness at all levels.

There will be no "chosen" ones; each person has the opportunity to determine their own destiny, the only choice being whether to accept it or not, and if so to consciously pursue that destiny.

There has never been a better time to be human on Earth, but opportunities on this scale only coincide with these massive cycles of Energy, so everyone should be at least aware of this that they may shape their own immediate destiny, whether they will be caught in the "dragnet" or be weeping and "gnashing teeth" out of frustration of a missed opportunity this time around.

It has taken millions of years to reach this stage, and we are living on Earth at the time of the birth of a new type of human; Homo Spiritus".

Again though, individual and collective consciousness is crucial to the outcome for humans collectively, whether it be catastrophe or Ecstasy; the potential instruments of both are amassing now.

At the peak or troughs of previous cycles there has been cataclysm such as the great flood, the destructions of Atlantis and Lemuria and many others that we are not aware of.

There have also been ages of great, abundance, happiness and progress akin to "kingdoms of Heaven on Earth".

The Hindu tradition tracks these ages of darkness and light by means of their "Yugas".

The Satya Yuga is a Yuga of a golden age where people experience true Spiritual nature with the high vibration that brings, resulting in a Utopian existence of joy, health and connection with our Source.

Then comes the Treya Yuga and the Dvapara Yuga and finally the Kali Yuga, the trough of existence where humans focus almost entirely on the physical aspect of existence, where materialism and survival rules, and power is the driving force and the craving of many. So what does all this mean in practical terms? It means quite simply that we are nearing the end of an age, the turning point of a great cycle of Energy, and an opportunity to determine what happens next at both a collective and individual level.

Each and every person therefore should seize this opportunity for progression to the step on the path back to our Creator and therefore perfection. Some people ask whether the Astral worlds are "heaven". The fact is they might seem like heaven to those living there, but they only have life on Earth, after which the Astral is fashioned by the Minds of humans, as a benchmark.

The lower to mid levels of the Astral are therefore a reflection of the current age of desire and materialism, and is therefore transient in conjunction with and part of these great Energy cycles.

When life on Earth changes so too will the Astral worlds, until one day the Astral worlds will simply dissipate back into its original substance, no longer required to support human desires.

I would like to conclude with these important points:

1. We do not know at this stage, and will probably never know until the time comes, whether 21 December 2012 will bring a sudden climatic event or whether it will simply mark a turning point.
2. We must be prepared for a climatic event otherwise complacency will cause most people not to be ready for what happens next.
3. Such preparation is of the Mind not in physical terms. If everyone prepares themselves mentally and in terms of consciousness for a great event at all levels, then that is what the outcome will be; there is nothing to fear; the Universe flows only in the direction of evolution, expansion and well-being, and we must flow in the same direction in order to be aligned with The Source and prepared for what happens next.

## MORE ON THE YEAR 2012

It was not my intention to continue this topic this week, important though it is, but the wei ht of messages received has been such that I felt it better to deal with some of these today.

During 2007 I will be extending my 2012 news and information services as we move within 6 years of this pivotal event.

Perhaps the best way of addressing this is to address some of the main questions arising from last week.

*1. End date. Several people sent me a message, for which I thank you, pointing out the fact that a prominent 2012 researcher and Mayanist, Carl Calleman, identifies the end-date of the Mayan calendar as October 28, 2011.*

I am fully aware of this and have previously researched his ideas. In view of the questions raised I decided to do so again.

First we must recognise the fact that we do not know for sure; no one does. The end-dates put forward are the results of a lifetime of work by several extremely dedicated, scholarly and intelligent people, who fully stand by and justify their findings.

I have utmost respect for Carl Calleman and his contributions to the entire 2012 and Mayan area which are of the utmost importance.

However, I am of view that the October 2012 end-date might well be the result of applying incomplete information or principles in its derivation. Although the underlying basis appears to be solid enough, it does however appear to selectively omit factors which are crucial in the context of the derivation as a whole; it is somewhat like baking a cake without one of the basic ingredients to make it rise.

A discussion of the fundamental assumption that caused this end-date would take several newsletters to explain, but the crux of the 14 month or so deviation from the widely accepted end-date is this:

With reference to the Mayan measure of time as it pertains to the long-count calendar, Carl Calleman appears to make the assumption that 1 Imix to be the beginning of the Tzolkin. A situation that could never occur. The result of this is that the end-date is erroneously transposed forward by just over a year.

This appears to be a fundamental misunderstanding of the interpretation of the Mayan glyphs, and enough, in and of itself to erroneously transpose the end-date.

One hopes that in the interest of clarity, Carl Calleman will address this issue again before too long.

*2. Auric Time Scale: This relates to my brief overview of the Auric Time Scale last week during which I mentioned the "implosion of time", a concept that appears to have worried some people.*

In recent years there have been various mathematical models proposed, purporting to represent the eschatological processes we are currently experiencing.

Of these The Auric Time Scale and Timewave Zero whci lots "fractals of novelty" over several thousand years. There is now evidence that the I-Ching, which many of you may will have heard of, also points to an end-date of 2012.

The Auric Timescale is the work of a highly respected and brilliant Russian scientist, Dr. Sergey Smelyakov. Dr. Smelyakov holds an MA level degree in applied mathematics as well as doctorates in numerical methods and mathematical modelling and cybernetics; his credentials are beyond reproach.

Auric Time Scale is an extremely complex mathematical derivation, consisting of many pages of computations. I intend to make these available to you as soon as possible.

In extremely broad terms The Auric Time Scale is a series based upon the "Golden Mean" and Phi, ultimately describing cosmic and terrestrial events occurring throughout history; events known as "bifurcation points", which have the potential to influence the course of mankind.

Dr. Smelyakov has formulated his equation in conjunction with the Mayan long-count calendar, and produced a series of correlations between bifurcation points and bifurcation eras, and major events of the past, that had the potential to influence the direction and therefore the evolution of mankind, up to and including the final evolutionary bifurcation point, fixed, in accordance with this model, to 21 December 2012.

If we examine these correlations closely we see that they may well be true, the main caveat being that the timescales involved are so large in the beginning, we cannot precisely correlate dates with events.

Here however are just a few such correlations; to list them all is far beyond the scope of this newsletter:

Bifurcation Era 0:

The last geomagnetic inversion (3.2 - 2.9 millenniums BC)

Total Solar eclipse at vernal equinox (3306 BC)

Beginning of the Kali Yuga (about 3100 BC)

Beginning of the Mayan Calendar (3113 BC)

Bifurcation Era 1.

Emergence of Sumerian civilization and Babylon (about 3000 BC): in those times they were provided with the star ascending tables and (at least, since 2500 BC) they used the Solar-Moon calendar

Significant intensification of the tectonic activity coincides with growth of concentration of precipitated uranium (about 1200 BC)

The Golden section of the Mayan Calendar (from the end to the beginning),

1155 BC Fall of Troy (1194 BC)

End of the age of creating of the Mahabharata (1500 - 1200 BC)

Discovering of Tibet and China by the Europeans

Beginning of the Iron Age (1200 - 1180 BC)

Gautama Buddha (621 -544 BC)

Historical Maitreya (V-th century BC), Mahatma, successor of Gautama Buddha

Zoroaster (VI-th century BC)

Pythagoras (570 - 496, or 582 - 507 BC),

Initiate, the most known of the mystic philosophersPlaton (427 - 347 BC)

Bifurcation Era 5:

The most terrible earthquake on record in the world, China,

1556 Dreadful epidemic of plague in Europe (1563) at great conjunction of Mars, Jupiter and Saturn Flashes of Supernovas: in 1572 (Tycho Brahe) and in 1604 (Kepler)Europe:

Beginning of Renaissance, development of capitalism, Reformation and dissemination of Christianity over the world,

Establishing of world-wide empires, great geographical discoveries of 15 - 16 centuries

And this is just a small sampling of the correlations resulting from the work of Dr. Smelyakov

In the past, bifurcation points have occurred at very large time intervals, but as we approach the final bifurcation point of 21 December 2012, we become more focused on bifurcation points as opposed to eras. A bifurcation point should, in accordance with the Auric Time Scale, correspond to a major influential even that can be either terrestrial or cosmic in nature.

It is these bifurcation points that will be the "sign posts" we follow pointing to the 2012 end-date.

The detonation of the first nuclear weapon at the Bikini Atoll corresponded to a bifurcation point.

More recently bifurcation era 10 is correlated with the rise of a "new world order" which seeks to take advantage of world chaos to enforce a single world order, or dictatorship. I must stress "seeks", because without the cooperation of the collective consciousness of mankind, it cannot prevail; and it is there that the battle-lines are currently drawn.

We recently experienced a bifurcation point that commenced on November 22, that appears to have coincided with an extreme series of Solar events an X9 flare, followed by an X6 on Dec. 6th, an X3 on Dec. 13th and an X1 on Dec. 14th. This resulted in fantastic auroral displays, but more importantly resulted in a proton flux bombardment from the Sun.

I should point out that all this has occurred during a solar minimum!

2012 also coincides with the greatest solar maximum known to man, the potential consequences of which we are still endeavouring to comprehend, but are nevertheless inexorably related to whatever awaits us during that time.

There are no single factors involved in the 2012 scenario.

As ever; the "future" will be determined by the collective consciousness of mankind our therefore our influence over reality at a quantum level.

I view all of these events therefore as quantum probabilities; any or all of which come come into effect based upon the consciousness of mankind, and which could well mean the difference between a catastrophic or eschatological outcome.

So what does this mean to us as we approach the 2012 end-date?

The nature of the Auric Time Scale is such that as we approach the end-date the interval between bifurcation points becomes progressively smaller. This means that these bifurcation events will occur with increasing frequency, and instead of occurring years apart will start to occur months, then weeks, then days apart, until finally, on 21 December 2012, they will start to occur minutes apart, then seconds apart and finally milli-seconds apart until the end of the bifurcation cycle is reached, and the mystery of the next phase of mankind and indeed all life would be revealed.

Again though; I really must stress, in no uncertain terms, that this is simply one of a number of mathematical models pointing to 21 December 2012, a model that I personally believe has substance, but which I do not present as fact to the extent this is the way events will definitely unfold.

Again, and this is crucial to understand, the ultimate outcome can and will be decided by the collective consciousness of Mankind.

So what does this mean experientially?

What will we feel? What will we become?

To answer that we need to look at how we would experience these events in the context of time.

What is time?

To many people "time" is measured by the hands or numbers of a clock, or perhaps the position of the Sun in the sky.

These however are simply mechanical and convenient methods of measuring this thing called "time".

In reality time is experiential, not mechanical. We experience time in accordance with our Mind and our relationship with time at any particular moment.

We can experience time as something that seems to take forever, or something that passes in an instant.

For example here is an observation regarding time made by Albert Einstein in the context of his special theory of relativity:

"Put your hand on a hot stove for a minute, and it seems like an hour. Sit with a pretty girl for an hour, and it seems like a minute. That is relativity." - Albert Einstein.

According to the Auric Time Scale we are experiencing an implosion of time and therefore of space as the space-time continuum is inter-dependant.

Even now we experience 24 hours as 16 hours although to many it might not yet be apparent. I have heard many people comment however on how "time" seems to be "speeding up"; it really is.

As we approach the final bifurcation marking the transition of mankind, assuming this scenario is the correct one, which is yet to be proven, at the point time implodes we will transition from experiencing "time" to a state of experiencing "non-time".

This is a very natural state that everyone will experience after a transition to the non-physical worlds at the change known as "death". The people in the Astral worlds, often known as "the afterlife", and beyond have no concept of "time" or of "space".

Let me stress that this final event is nothing to do with "death", I simply use it as an illustration. At that final bifurcation point everyone would experience the transition to "non-time and space" in a different way.

Some would experience their entire life in a moment; some many or even all lives.

Many would know the encumbrance of the physical body, the "clay" that binds us to the physical planet and will wish to be free of it. Many would finally realise the truth of the illusion that they have been living and will wish to leave Earth and travel directly to a "real" existence, beyond the illusion of form, to the 5th density of the Spiritual worlds.

Others, in that moment, will know our Supreme Creator.

The illusion of time and space would be torn away forever along with the facade of egotism, materialism and greed that has dominated, blighted and retarded mankind for so long.

Those choosing to stay would create the "kingdom of Heaven on Earth", and continue to incarnate on other Earth-like planets in the course of individual evolution.

Above all it would be a great event marking the evolution of mankind to the next level, from Homo Sapien to Homo Spiritus.

There is nothing to fear but fear itself. Only the collective consciousness of mankind can truly determine the outcome, and fear would bring about a fearful outcome.

And again, this is the scenario according to the Auric Time Scale. We do not know whether this is accurate or true at this stage. We do know however that as we progress inexorably towards the end-date Auric Time Scale will be tested time and again.

These are great events to be embraced and to look forward to.

There has never, ever been a better time to be a human being on Earth.

**QUESTIONS ON 2012**

Since my first newsletter on the subject of 2012 and my creation of a dedicated forum to these important matters at the Astral Pulse, I have received numerous messages about 2012.

The majority of these are of a concerned nature, and even of fear for the future of themselves and families.

First of all we need to be absolutely clear on one important fact:

21 December 2012 is not the end of "time" or even the "end of the Mayan calendar". The Mayans; an extremely advanced

race, had many calendars and other instruments of phenomenal accuracy, and the long-count, to which 2012 relates, is only one of them.

The long Count itself is does not stand in isolation; it is simply the end of a Long Count in an infinite series of such Long Counts.

The big question is; what does it represent?

Some believe it represents a very rare cosmological event known as a "Galactic Alignment".

The Galactic Alignment is the alignment of the December solstice sun with the Galactic equator. This alignment occurs as a result of the precession of the equinoxes.

Precession is caused by the earth wobbling very slowly on its axis and shifts the position of the equinoxes and solstices one degree every 71.5 years. Because the sun is one-half of a degree wide, it will take the December solstice sun 36 years to precess through the Galactic equator.

The precise alignment of the solstice point, the precise center-point of the body of the sun as viewed from earth, with the Galactic equator was calculated to occur in 1998.

Thus, the Galactic Alignment "zone" is 1998 +/- 18 years = 1980 - 2016. This is "era-2012."

This Galactic Alignment occurs only once every 26,000 years, and was what the ancient Maya were pointing to with the 2012 end-date of their Long Count calendar.

The end of the Long Count also coincides with the end of a Mayan "Sun" or "age".

The fundamental questions therefore are these:

1. Is the galactic alignment capable of effecting Earth in and of itself?
2. Or is it simply symbolic of a much deeper meaning?

Whilst many believe the Energy of the galactic alignment has the potential to cause the magnetic poles of the Earth to reverse, so north becomes south and south becomes north, the effects of which could be catastrophic, I personally do not believe this to be the case.

I say this because the galactic alignment is not something that will simply happen on 21 December 2012. As the peak of this event could occur or has already occured anywhere between 1980 and 2016, there is a better than average chance that it has already occurred and we are clearly still here.

Notwithstanding that, as this is a 36 year event, one day will does not have the potential to cause a catastrophe in and of itself.

I am of the view that the Galactic Alignment is therefore symbolic of a much deeper and greater meaning, a meaning we have still yet to fully determine.

The classic Maya were very involved with symbolism, as were many ancient races such as the Egyptians, Sumerian's and other great races. Many large, now ruined Mayan cities for example contain massive "ball game courts" which are designed and aligned cosmologically.

It seems likely that, as with the Hindu Vedas for example, these games were actually dramas and plays designed and performed in order to teach the populous in terms they could understand.

Before looking further at the most likely 2012 scenarios, let us take a look at a scenario that could potentially have a catastrophic outcome, and which the Maya would certainly have known about. We must always do this in the interests of completeness and knowledge; regardless of the potential implications.

During 2012 Earth is to experience the largest maximum of Solar activity; i.e. of the Sun, ever experienced. The resultant energies, particularly if directed towards earth, have the potential for considerable and dramatic physical effects including but not limited to a magnetic pole shift, a reversing of the direction of the movement of the tectonic plates of the Earth, resulting in massive earthquakes, tsunamis and volcanic activity, and a blotting out of the Sun resulting in another ice age.

Let me stress however I personally, at this stage, regard this as highly unlikely. We will see and feel the effects, but large-scale displays of Aurorae are the most likely outcome. That said the Maya knew much more than we do and 21 December 2012 is not the end of a "Sun" or "age" for no reason. The Maya were a shamanic race who made use of entheogenic substances, mostly based upon DMT, which has several variants the most relevant of which is Dimethyltryptamine and N,N-dimethyltryptamine. Another variant is 5-MeO-DMT which is more of a psychedelic variant.

DMT has been extensively researched in considerable detail with numerous subjects by Rick Strassman, a scientist. Dr. Strassman discovered profound capabilities of DMT for Spiritual experiences deep into the inner Energy levels of the Universe. His findings were so profound that he named DMT "The Spirit Molecule".

In my view it is very possible that by highly expert use of DMT, developed over the course of centuries, that the Mayan Shamans were able to access information from Inner Energy levels, the Causal sphere of the Universe, from probably the "Akashic record", Energy that the average person could not possibly directly access without a Spiritual or entheogenic process such as that exerienced with DMT.

I am of the view therefore that the Maya absolutely do know what December 21 2012 will bring, and of its significance for mankind.

I therefore currently feel that 21 December 2012 could well be an eschatological event, which takes mankind to the next level of evolution, from Homo Sapiens to "Homo Spiritus".

This being the case for some, or many, depending on how this scenario progresses, will find the illusion of space and time stripped away, and the material, physical world exposed for the illusion it truly is. Some humans would leave Earth, travel straight through the 4th density, the Astral planes, straight to the 5th density where the next phase of life will be revealed.

Those not Spiritually advanced enough might remain on Earth but with multi-dimensional awareness. Ego, greed and materialism would give way to love, service and compassion on the way to further evolution. If this is the way these events proceed, there is nothing to fear; those remaining will finally enjoy conditions that we are always intended to enjoy before religion, materialism and selfishness temporarily destroyed it; the "Kingdom of Heaven on Earth".

I would like to add that there is no evidence to suggest that on 21 December 2012 a "switch will be flicked" and everything will change. That could happen, but it could also be a process that, having started around 1987, could take as long as several hundreds of years to reach a final conclusion. The truth is we just do not know at this stage, and, with only 6 years to go, we have to accept the fact that we might never know for sure until it happens; always assuming it will happen; nothing at all is a certainty; only The Source, The First Cause, God knows All.

There is plenty of evidence for both scenarios however.

In a future newsletter I will discuss one such scenario that would indicate a sudden eschatological event on 21 December 2012, known as the "Auric Times Scale" which is based upon a series of events known as "bifurcation points" accelerating in frequency in accordance with a system known as "The Golden Mean" based upon the "Phi". Bifurcation points tend to coincide, in theory, which major events that have direct influence over humanity, such as for example the detonation of the first nuclear warhead in the Bikini Atoll.

The Auric Timecale shows us that bifucation points occur at an exponetially increasing frequency until, on 21 December 2012, they occur firstly minutes apart, then seconds, then milliseconds until finally time itself implodes.

However; there is a potential twist.

We know, from previous newsletters that there is no such thing as the the "future" except as a human concept; there is only the present moment of "Now". So absolutely nothing is certain. Although the stage is set, in my view, for events to unfold as discussed above, as ever, the ultimate outcome is dependant on mankind and therein lies the twist, the danger.

I cannot stress what I am about to say enough:

The ultimate outcome of 2012 will not be decided by some outside "force", "prophecy" or "prediction", mathematical equation or conspiracy; it will be determined, as always, by the collective consciousness of mankind, of all life, all Spirit and of course the consciousness of Gaia, the Earth Herself, Who is in any case in the process of transitioning to the next density.

Everything you see on Earth is an illusion created by the collective consciousness; particularly of mankind. The thoughts of mankind perpetuate that illusion constantly to create an illusory state perceived by the mediation of the 5 physical senses, causeing it to appear "real".

Therefore; whatever the majority of the 6.5 billion members of the human race believes will be the outcome of 2012 will be the outcome; there can be no other possible conclusion.

Make no mistake; Earth and the consciousness of mankind are inexorably linked; they are inseperable and canot function indpendendantly.

There are many insidious agencies among the human race who wish to progressively imprison mankind in single world dictatorship for their own selfish purposes; a process that has been continuing for centuries and is becoming dangerously close to realisation.

When mankind evolves these low vibration humans and other entities will lose all of their power instantly. They know it and they are desperate and will do anything within their powers to capture and imprison the consciousness of mankind.

The main weapon they have for this is the media including newspapers, television and movies among others; to which they know the human race is addicted and follows without question.

There are countless examples of this process occurring at all levels and they are increasing all the time.

A very recent example is a movie called "Apocalypto" which has Mel Gibson and others portraying the ancient Maya as little more than a bunch of savages, thereby discrediting their massively important legacy and of course events of 2012.

This film is an absolute disgrace from that perspective. The Maya were massively more advanced in most ways than "modern society"; technology is not "advancement". Advancement is understanding the true nature of reality and what we must do as human beings in order to fulfil our true destiny, a destiny that dark agencies are seeking to deny us.

The cosmological, astronomical, astrophysical, astrological and mathematics abilities of the classic Maya were far in advance of anything taught in Universities today. They were highly organised, and like the ancient Egyptians, performed truly remarkable feats of urban planning and architecture with no techology and no machinery to speak of. Spiritually the Maya were far in advance of the average human and materialism was a concept that they would not have had any concept of.

We must, at all costs resist the future media attacks however subtle they might seem. This is a window of opportunity for mankind that must be ceased at all costs or it will be set back for tens of millennia thereby plunging mankind into a new "dark ages", a dark ages that would make the last dark ages seem like a non-event.

I will discuss these aspects more fully in future newsletters. But until then please remember:

The ultimate outcome of 2012 will not be decided by mathematical equations or "prophecies" or "predictions" or any external force, known or unknown, it will rather be decided by the collective consciousness of the human race which is unfortunately hugely influenced by the media.

## INTRODUCTION TO THE YEAR 2012

One question that frequently arises is that of the year 2012.

Many people will have heard that December 21 2012 is a day of great significance, mostly in the context of that date being the very end of the Mayan calendar and everything that implies.

The big question on the minds of most people is "what is the significance of this date"? What will happen to Earth? What will happen to all of us?

This is a huge subject, and one that goes way beyond the scope of this newsletter. However, it is also an extremely important subject, and one that I will be focusing on through various resources in the future. Today however we will take a look at some of the basics surrounding 2012. What is the real significance of December 21 2012? The reason this date has become so well-known is because it is the date that represents the "end of the Mayan calendar".

Why is this so important?

It is important because the Mayan's, like many of the ancient races of millennia ago, were in fact extremely advanced in many areas. By "advanced" we do not necessarily mean in terms of "technology", which in itself does not mean advancement at all, but as astronomers, mathematicians and builders; among other things. Like the ancient Egyptians, to whom they were almost certainly related at some time, probably linked through the legendary continent of Atlantis, which is not actually a legend, the Mayans built the most amazing structures that defy explanation; being beyond beyond the capabilities of so called "modern man.

The Mayans were also incredible observers, mathematicians, and keepers of ancient and sacred knowledge. Using these abilities they were able to construct calendars which not only chart time, but also charted the cosmos, and forthcoming great world events. We know that such an event, perhaps even the final event, is to take place on December 21 2012. The big question is what? This is a question that will be addressed in the future both here and through other resources which will be announced in due course. Only by endeavouring to fully understand the year 2012 and putting it into the right context can we be fully prepared for this event. In fact; there are three major issues that we need to consider and to face in the next few years. These are:

1. December 21 2012
2. Earth planetary changes
3. The agenda of terrestrial and extra-terrestrial factions

Although at first glance these might seem separate, they are in fact linked in various ways.

But today let us take a look at some of the very basics of 2012.

The ancient Mayans had many advanced abilities and most importantly ancient knowledge, probably originating from sources that are not immediately apparent at this time. Among these abilities were mathematics, astronomy, and prophecy based upon past world and astronomical events.

The Mayans knew that nothing ever happens by "chance" in the Universe, even though it often seems like it from a narrow human, temporal experiential perspective. The Mayans knew that everything happens in cycles of varying lengths, cycles that correspond precisely to past and future cosmic and world events.

Many of these events are the result of the one factor common to everything in the Universe without exception; Energy, which can manifest at any level from the Universal to the individual.

This is why Astrology, and I do not mean the "horoscopes" of the tabloids, I mean genuine astrology, is so significant, charting as it does the effects of a confluence of Energy being prevalent at the time of arrival on Earth, and which has so much influence over our physical life. Energy is everything! The ancient Maya knew this, and were able to observe the effects of these confluences and events, and thus, with their seemingly amazing mathematical abilities, track future events.

The Maya had several calendars of varying lengths, the most significant of which were the "Short Count" and the "Long Count".

The Short Count is compiled by combining the "tzolkin cycle" with the solar year and the Venus cycle of 584 days, thus generating short periods of 13, 52 and 104 years. It is however the "Long Count" cycle that is of the most interest, the end of which is also the end of all Mayan calendars.

The Long Count is derived from nested cycles of days multiplied at each level by the key Mayan number, 20, resulting in the following periods:

1 Kin which is a day

20 Uinal

360 Tun

7200 Katun

144000 Baktun

The only deviation to multiplying by 20 is the tun level where the uinal period is instead multiplied by 18 for the 360 day tun.

The Maya used this counting system to track an unbroken sequence of days from the time it was inaugurated.

Long Count dates are separated by dots. For example: 6.19.19.0.0 equals 6 baktuns, 19 katuns, 19 tuns, 0 uinals and 0 days. Each baktun has 144000 days, each katun has 7200 days, and so on.

If we add up all the values, 6.19.19.0.0 indicates a total of 1007640 days have elapsed since the Zero Date of 0.0.0.0.0. The much discussed 13-baktun cycle is completed 1872000 days, 13 baktuns, after 0.0.0.0.0. This period of time is the Mayan "Great Cycle" of the Long Count.

Each Baktun has corresponded with a major cycle on Earth, which are too extensive and complex to go into here. Suffice it to say that The 13 baktuns and 20 katuns collectively represent a perfect fractal of the 260 unit 4th dimensional timing matrix spread out as a chronotopology that we simply call "history". Each katun represents one of 260 kin. The baktuns represent a set of morphogenetic fields, each with 20 lesser waves rising in a pitch of climax during the 13th and final baktun 1620 CE to 2012 CE.

This final baktun represents the time where, driven my the ego, materialism and money, "history" and therefore mankind has reached a saturation point, where "history" simply has nowhere else to go. And it is this event that was always charted precisely by the Mayan Long Count calendar to coincide with the end of this great cycle of Energy.

Historically it can be demonstrated that every quarter of the long cycle, approximately every 6400 years, there has been a major catastrophic Earth event for the last three such quarters. These include great floods, earthquakes, and other global events. Such events are documented as the "great flood", the destruction of Atlantis, etc.. The final quarter is December 21 in the year of 2012.

It should also be mentioned that other mathematical systems, notably the Chinese I-Ching, which was also once used as a calendrical system, also point to the year 2012, as do other lesser known systems it seems.

So these are the calendrical and mathematical considerations, but there are other considerations. On December 21, 2012 there will be a galactic alignment of the "galactic equator", and what the Mayans refer to as "The Sacred Tree", with our star, the Sun, at the very centre of this alignment.

This in itself is no coincidence. This alignment has on our solar system astrological, astronomical and Universal considerations, and in particular the corresponding Energy effects both on Earth and indeed the entire solar system.

So that, in extremely basic terms in the interest of keeping it simple for now is the basics of the math and associated events from a historical and chronological perspective relative to the Earth space-time continuum.

The question is; what does it all really mean for us?

The honest answer is we do not really know at this stage at least in the process, although I and others are very much tracking it.

There is however too much data and historical evidence to conclude that nothing will happen. The only question is in what form will it take; the possibilities including physical, Energy or Spiritual, or indeed a combination of of all of these.

If we look at solid evidence we can observe the following factors:

**Schumann Cavity Resonance:** The Schumann Resonance can be likened to the "heartbeat" of Earth. Scientifically it is due to the space between the surface of the Earth and the conductive ionosphere acting as a waveguide. The limited dimensions of the earth cause this waveguide to act as a resonant cavity for electromagnetic waves in the extra low frequency ELF band.

Historically the Schumann Resonance has held steady at a frequeny of around 7.83Hz, however in recent years Schumann Resonance has increased to as high as 12Hz, the highest possible believed to be 13Hz.

**Earth Magnetic Field:** The magnetic field of the earth gives rise to the magnetic poles as used for navigation purposes. This magnetic effect is caused by Earth behaving like a giant elecro-magnet caused by the molten iron core and the rotation of the Earth.

The magnetic field of Earth has been progressively reducing over the years, and in fact appear to be doing so proportional to Schumann Resonance although they may not be directly connected.

Evidence of this can be seen by the fact that some sea mammals such as dolphins, porpoises an whales use the magnetic poles for navigation purposes, and there has been a large increase in these creatures going off-course and beaching themselves.

Finally, extinctions of species on Earth is 100 to 1000 times higher than the historical average, being greater than at any time in fact since the last dinosaur extinction 65 million years ago.

So what does the future hold for us between ?

The truth is we still do not know. Everything I have summarised today could be a series of coincidences or they could all converge to point to some major world event. We just do not know and there is certainly no value in speculation.

It would be totally inappropriate to state for example, as some are, that "the world will end in the year 2012". The entire scenario is far too complex to make sweeping, dogmatic statements of that nature. Although some event seems likely, we do not know the scale of such an event, how it will manifest or how it will affect the planet, humans and all life, or how long the entire process will take.

One thing we do know beyond all doubt is that everyone will survive and be the better for the experience; the only question is in what form, physical, Astral or Spiritual.

One thing is clear however, everyone has a window of opportunity to change for the better. The next few years could be spent evaluating your life, your relationship with fellow man, animals and the planet, and then taking the appropriate steps to become as aligned and prepared as possible for any coming events.

Earth has been a major learning opportunity, an opportunity to evolve. if, and I do say if the physical planet is to come to an end, then what happens next on an individual level will depend entirely on where you are Spiritually at that precise time. Consequently there has never been a better time to place yourself in the best possible light in preparation for whatever is to come.

This is one of the major reason I wrote Our Ultimate Reality, which sets out these vital steps.

Again though, and this is most important,every single person will survive. We are all immortal, Divine Beings, aspects of the Supreme Being, and our true destiny is faı greater than the temporal learning experience of this planet we call "Earth", our lives upon which are as the blink of an eye in comparison to all eternity.

Everyone, sooner or later, regardless of this Earth event we call "the year 2012" will move on to sphere of life and reality that are glorious beyond the remotest comprehension of Earthly man, and that is the true destiny and objective of everyone on the sacred path back to The Source, The Prime Creator, some simply call "God".

Above all approach the future with joy, faith and sincere gratitude for our Earth experiences.

And always know that there is nothing to fear but fear itself; so as we approac the year 2012 be fearless; all will be well.

**CONSPIRACIES IN PERSPECTIVE**

Not a day goes by it seems without extreme and often unprecedented weather or Earth event striking some part of the world. Most recently these have been in the form of severe flooding and earthquakes.

I also receive numerous messages from people asking about so called "conspiracies", mostly involving government, but also the "new world order" and "extra terrestrials", asking what we should be doing and how to protect themselves and families from these perceived threats.

The answer is simple - do absolutely nothing.

The more Energy directed in the direction of these perceived threats, whether real or not, the more life they assume, and the more of a threat they become. In other words it is self-fulfilling in exactly the same way as "prophecies" can be self-fulfilling.

At the final analysis, whether these "threats" exist or not there is only one point of true focus in order to ensure the best possible future, and that place is Within.

The Universe only flows in the direction of expansion, well-being and Unconditional Love, these being the natural states we should all enjoy. At the same time The Source, The First Cause, God has blessed us with the ability of freewill, and thereby the means by which we can create our own experiential reality in accordance with our perceived needs and Spiritual evolution.

Although ultimately the Universe will always prevail, humans can still, on both a personal and collective level influence the "future" as it relates to the temporal confines of Earth, and therefore immediate temporal experience, which to people on Earth can seem to last for a lifetime. This might produce what seems to humans to be an almost desperate or hopeless situation, for example as in the "dark ages" in past Earth history, but which to the Universe the merest blip in the grand scheme of things.

In short - there is an easy and a hard way of doing things.

Historically, due to a lack of understanding and other very human traits such as the quest for power and material gain, humans have invariably taken the hardest way, and many continue to do so.

What we are seeing and experiencing today during this great transition of the ages is a confluence of factors, as yet remaining quantum probabilities, any or all of which can finally exert their influence in what would become the event or events that would shape the future of humanity, for hundreds or even thousands of years.

Everything we are seeing, feeling and experiencing right now represents the pieces on the cosmic chess board, all of which are maneuvering for position, waiting for checkmate in this particular game. As in a game of chess there is the white side and the black side, the Light side and the dark side - we must ensure that the Light side wins the game. As in the game of chess, the Light side made the first move and in the final end-game will make the final and decisive move, but we still need to ensure that humanity wins this round for the forces of Light.

In short - what humanity expects, feels and believes will happen over the next few years will happen. Focus on cataclysm and that will be the experience. Focus on a single global fascist dictatorship controlling powerless humans, and that will be the outcome. Focus on some other external influence such as extra-terrestrials and that will be the outcome. Or all of these could happen at the same time.

The truth is the coming transition of the ages is potentially the beginning of a golden age for humanity and all life on Earth, if only we would focus on that one outcome. Everywhere I look, and from the countless messages I receive it is very clear to me that humanity is awakening to their true infinite and Spiritual nature, just waiting to be realised.

The way forward is simple but profoundly important - focus within and on Spiritual growth, service to others and Unconditional Love for all life, and the outcome for mankind will be glorious as we externalise the Kingdom of Heaven within to the Kingdom of Heaven on Earth.

In practical terms this means totally disregarding all so called conspiracies and external events of all types as if they do not exist at all. Do not read publications that promote or even report these things, all they serve to do is make them more real. Ideally do not read or watch the news in papers, on the TV or the Internet.

They are simply reinforcing all of these negative factors and thereby making them more real, notwithstanding any hidden agendas of the factions controlling the media. The media exerts a strong influence over the Minds of people, and this is one of the very greatest dangers facing everyone in the future.

There is no "past" as such or "future", these are simply temporal illusions perpetuated only by the five physical senses within the space-time continuum of the physical three dimensional Universe, so why be concerned with such illusions?

There is, in reality, only "Now" and it is in the present moment of Now that we create our own reality based upon our thoughts, feelings, emotions,desires, expectations and many other factors. If all mankind focuses only within, with Unconditional Love and trust in The Universe, The source, God, of Whom we are all inseparable aspects, then the natural flow of the Universe will inexorably exert Divine influence, resulting in a new golden age for humans and all life on Earth, everything else simply fading way in to the background as unrealised quantum probabilities.

## BEHIND THE "CONSPIRACIES"

I receive many messages about so called "conspiracies" and asking what I think about everything from "ET's" and "UFO's" though the so called "new world order" and "incidents" such as "9/11".

First of all, as I mentioned in a recent newsletter, the very best course of action is to totally disregard all such media "reporting" and do absolutely nothing whatsoever. The more people think about and focus on these incidents, real or otherwise, the more Energy they are given and the more powerful they will become.

People have since commented on how difficult it is to simply ignore these events considering the extensive "media" reporting of them in the newspapers, on television, Internet news sites etc.

Again my advice is very simple and in my view crucial:

Never read the newspapers, and never watch or listen to media reports on television or radio or on Internet news sites.

We have absolutely no need whatsoever to read about what has already "happened", or what might "happen" in the future. We all create our own reality in the present moment of Now, and reading about what "happened" yesterday, causes those events to be impressed upon the Subconscious Mind, in turn causing them to become part of the Now, eventually manifesting in to three dimsnsional experience and therefore finally becoming self perpetuating and self-fulfilling. The more people focussing on wars, famine and terrorism for example, the more real they become.

Again, for the avoidance of any doubt - reading, watching or listening to the "news" as broadcast by the popular media, is totally counterproductive to our own individual reality, and the consensus reality of the human race. I should point out that I am not referring to genuine information in all its forms, which can often be valuable or even necessary, but rather the independant reporting of external events, much of which focusses on the negative.

It is particularly important not to discuss or worry about the specific "conspiracies" that seem to be appearing everywhere these days, again for the reasons mentioned before, and particularly in the context of the transition of the ages we are currently experiencing.

I have stated many times within these newsletters, in my book and on my website that there is one over-riding factor and one factor only that will determine the outcome of the next few years - the Mind and consciousness of humanity and indeed of all lifeon Earth and Earth herself. Collectively Earth is one single organism of which we are all a part, and therefore we all influence the consciousness and therefore manifested reality of that organism to some extent. That consensus reality is instrumental in what happens next.

Plain and simple, whatever the collective consciousness of humanity, all life and Gaia herfself predominantly expects to happen, will happen.

We have all of the choices already at our disposal ranging from catastrophic through ecstatic and everything in between as we can observe from the increasingly extreme conditions manifesting on Earth and in the solar system generally on the one hand, and the exponentially increasing Spiritual "awakening" that is currently occurring on the other. In between there are the "power and control" factions who desire neither a catastrophic or ecstatic outcome, but to rather maintain the current status quo where the vast majority of people are unwittingly being taken in by manipulation at all levels, and unless this changes can eventually be controlled as part of a single world facsist government.

The so called "war on terror" has been, and continually is being contrived towards this end, by events and manipulations including, but not limited to the now infamous "false flag" event that preceded the invasions of Afghanistan and Iraq, and which are being used to threaten various other countries as a prelude to similar actions under the general heading "the war on terrorism" which the American, British, Israeli people as well as other counties in the world are expected to at least subscribe to if not support.

Very often when we hear politicians speaking, they often use one word as a sound byte above all others, and that word is "terror" - a word that is often very precisely and extensively woven into speeches, interviews and propaganda of all types. The people constructing these speeches know that by repeating a word often enough on TV or in any media the word is impressed upon the Subconscious Mind of the viewers or readers until it becomes an absolute reality to those people. The objective therefore is to cause as many people as possible people to become so fearful of "terror" that they will accept anything from their "benevolent" government without question, out of desperation, for protecting themselves and families against a perceived "threat" that is in reality completely contrived.

The most powerful weapon that these factions have aside from instilling fear and terror, is to continue to perpetuate the illusion of "separateness", thereby causing people to erroneously believe that they are alone, powerless and in need of "protection" from so called "acts of terror" and other fictitious events and situations. By perpetuating the illusion of separateness these factions believe that they can divide and conquer humanity.

On the other hand these factions know that if and when people awaken to the truth of their own glorious, Spiritual nature as integral and equal aspects of The Source, our Divine Creator, God, with unlimited powers and Whom nothing can possible harm, then these global power factions become powerless. Everyone will know, beyond all doubt that we all create our own reality, and can choose what thoughts we allow or disallow into our Mind and consciousness, only allowing those thoughts that are consistent with health, abundance and freedom as well as Spiritual evolution, and rejecting all thoughts that are contrary to these.

The puny physical efforts of these global power factions seeking control are totally, and utterly powerless against the one fundamental principle of the Universe correctly directed - Mind, Spiritual Awakening and Unconditional Love.

Knowing this and knowing time is short, these factions know they need to act quickly.

Our course of action then is simple:

1. Never watch read or listen to "news reports" in any media. Focus only on those things you most desire to experience.
2. Know, beyond doubts that we are infinite, immortal aspects of God and that nothing can possible harm us except our own thoughts.
3. Know that we create our own reality - no other person can create our reality for us in absolute terms.
4. Focus on service to others before service to self.
5. Embrace the most powerful force in the Universe - Unconditional Love.

In the words of a well known musician, now passed on:

*When the Power of Love overcomes the love of power, the World will know Peace* — Jimi Hendrix.

These words are almost prophetic in the context of the world today and in particular during the next few crucial years as we make the transition from one great age to the next, and where humanity is choosing between an age of darkness or a glorious age of Light.

Together we can ensure that the next age is an age of Love, Light and "Kingdom of Heaven on Earth" as our legacy for our Children.

# Bibliography


*Aurobindo, Sri: Vyasa and Valmiki, Acharya Press, Pondicherry, 1956.*

*Avalon, Arthur and Ellen: Hymns to the Goddess, Ganesh and Co., Madras, 1964.*

*Bhattacharji, Sukumari: Literature in the Vedic Age, Kali Ram Press, Calcutta, 1984.*

*Bose, D. N.: Dharmashastra: Their Philosophy and Occult Secrets, Kali Press, Calcutta, 1965.*

*Chaturvedi, M.D.,: Hinduism, The Eternal Religion, Bharatiya Vidya Bhavan, Bombay, 1992.*

*Coomaraswamy, Ananda K.: Contemporary Indian Philosophy, Geroge Allen & Unwin, London, 1936.*

*Datta, M. R.: The Secret Serpent, Kali Ram Press, Calcutta, 1913.*

*Dhar, Niranjan: Vedanta and Bengal Renaissance, Minerva Associates, Calcutta, 1977.*

*Eliot Deutsch: Advaita Vedanta: a Philosophical Reconstruction, East-West Center Press, Honolulu, 1969*

*Farquhar, J.N.: Modern Religious Movements in India, Munshiram, New Delhi, 1967.*

*Garbe, R.: The Philosophy of Ancient India, Chicago University Press, Chicago, 1899.*

*Grant, G. P.: Philosophy in the Mass Age, Copp Clark, Toronto, 1959.*

*Grisenold, H.D.: Insights into Modern Hinduism, Oxford, New York, 1934.*

*Harding, Elizabeth: Kali: The Black Goddess of Dakshineshwar, Nicolas-Hays, York Beach, 1993.*

*Heimann, Betty: Facets of Indian Thought, Geroge Allen & Unwin, London, 1964.*

*Jain, J.C.: Life in Ancient India as Depicted in the Jain Canons, Akarshan Press, Bombay, 1947.*

*Jain, Jyoti Prasad: Jain Sources of the History of India, Bhagawati Press, Delhi, 1964.*

*Keith, Arthur Berriedale: The Religion and Philosophy of the Veda and Upanishads, MacMillan, Delhi, 1925.*

*Kottackal, Jacob: Religion and Ethics in Advaita, C.M.S. Press, Kottayam, 1982.*

*Levy, John: The Nature of Man According to Vedanta, Routledge & Kegan Paul, London, 1956.*

*Mathew, Arnold: Culture and Anarchy, The University Press, Cambridge, 1935.*

*Munshi, K M.: Glory that was Gurjaradesa, Rawat Press, Bombay, 1955.*

*Narla, V.R.: The Truth about the Gita, Narla Institute, Hyderabad, 1988.*

*Ramakrishnananda, Swami: Life of Sri Ramanuja, Sai Kalyani Press, Madras, 1959.*

*Samsookha, Puranchand: Lord Mahavira, Kali Ram Press, Calcutta, 1957.*

*Sengaku Mayeda: A Thousand Teachings: the Upadesasahasri of Sankara, University of Tokyo Press, 1979.*

*Sivaramamurti, C.: Sri Lakshmi in Indian Art and Thought, Kanak, New Delhi, 1982.*

*Subramaniam, Kamala: Mahabharata, Rawat Press, Bombay, 1971.*

*Thomas, P.: Kama Kalpa or the Hindu Ritual of Love, D. B. Taraporevala Sons, Bombay, 1965.*

*Vable, D.: The Arya Samaj. Hindu without Hinduism. Vikas Publ., Delhi, 1983.*

*Wendy Doniger: Siva: The Erotic Ascetic, Oxford University Press, Delhi, 1998.*

# Index